11/10/91

What Went Wrong with Perestroika

By Marshall I. Goldman

Soviet Marketing: Distribution in a Controlled Economy

Comparative Economic Systems

Soviet Foreign Aid

The Soviet Economy: Myth and Reality

Ecology and Economics: Controlling Pollution in the 70's

The Spoils of Progress: Environmental Pollution in the Soviet Union

Détente and Dollars: Doing Business with the Russians

The Enigma of Soviet Petroleum: Half Empty or Half Full?

U.S.S.R. in Crisis: The Failure of an Economic System

Gorbachev's Challenge: Economic Reform in the Age of High Technology

What Went Wrong with Perestroika

MARSHALL I. GOLDMAN

W · W · NORTON & COMPANY
New York · London

To

Jessica Ann, Samuel Todd, and Jacob Charles

First Edition.

The text of this book is composed in Times Roman, with display set in Benguiat Medium. Composition and manufacturing by the Haddon Craftsmen, Inc.

Library of Congress Cataloging-in-Publicaton Data
Goldman, Marshall I.
  What went wrong with Perestroika / Marshall I. Goldman.
    p.   cm.
  Includes index.
    1. Soviet Union-Politics and government—1985– 2. Gorbachev, Mikhail
Sergeevich, 1931– . 3. Perestroika. I. Title.
DK288.G59 1991   91–16281
947.085′4—dc20

ISBN 0-393-03071-7

W.W. Norton & Company, Inc., 500 Fifth Avenue, New York, N.Y. 10110
W.W. Norton & Company, Ltd., 10 Coptic Street, London WC1A 1PU

1 2 3 4 5 6 7 8 9 0

Contents

ACKNOWLEDGMENTS 9
PROLOGUE—AUGUST 19–24, 1991 11

1 A Hero Abroad, A Failure at Home 15

2 The Pre-Gorbachev Era—Trying to Modernize—
An Old Story 31

3 Patch and Procrastination—If It's Broke,
Don't Fix It 52

4 Mikhail Sergeevich Gorbachev Goes to Moscow:
A Learner's Progress 69

5 Mid-Course Correction 94

6 The Effort Collapses 128

7 The Reaction Comes 172

8 Where Does the Soviet Union Go from Here? 203

9 Epilogue 224
August 26, 1991 236

NOTES 239
INDEX 249

Acknowledgments

As always, an author owes much to those around him. First there is Wellesley College. My colleagues there have been tolerant of my foibles beyond anything I should have any right to expect. In addition, the two named chairs I have held there, the Wellesley Class of 1919 Professor of Economics and the Kathryn Wasserman Davis Professor of Soviet Economics, have not only paid my salary but facilitated my research. I am grateful to all the members of the Class of 1919 and Mr. and Mrs. Shelby Cullom Davis, two close friends.

Equally important is the Russian Research Center at Harvard University. I have been the Associate Director there for over fifteen years, and it has been an exciting and gratifying experience. For better or for worse, little of my research and writing would have been possible without its research facilities and comraderie. I am particularly appreciative of Adam Ulam, the Director during much of that period. It is amazing how well we have worked together—in some ways an odd couple, but only because it has been odd that Adam has been so tolerant and patient. I have enormous respect not only for Adam's intelligence and scholarship but for his wisdom. There are not many like him.

Then there are my assistants. To say the least I am not an

easy person to work for, but Cathy Reed, Judy Mehrmann, and Amy Randall have held up admirably and allowed me to write and administer at the same time. I am also grateful to Sue Gardos in the Library and Elizabeth DeBra and Lisa Bader who helped with various research and proofreading chores.

Acknowledgment is also due to a journal and a publishing house. I have included material from two articles I wrote previously, one entitled "Gorbachev the Economist," which is reprinted by permission of *Foreign Affairs* from the Spring 1990 issue © 1990 by the Council on Foreign Relations, Inc., and the other, "Economic Reform in the Soviet Union—Why a Need for Checks and Balances" in *The Impact of Perestroika on Soviet Law,* edited by A. J. Schmidt, © 1990, Kluwer Academic Publishers, printed in the Netherlands and reprinted by permission of Kluwer Academic Publishers.

I must also say a word about Donald Lamm, my editor and friend. Editors are not supposed to be thanked publicly, but it would be a miscarriage of respect and credit if I did not confess how much I have enjoyed working with him during the course of publishing my last three books and how much I have come to depend on his insight and judgment. It would also be unfair if I neglected to mention his assistant, Amy Cherry, who has tolerated my almost weekly phone calls (at least during one of my publishing frenzies).

Last there is my family. I have thanked them before, my mother, my sister and her family, and most of all my wife and children which by extension now includes spouses and grandchildren. My wife and I often wonder why we have had such decent children and why those who are married have found themselves such complementary and well-suited spouses—she may be right, I guess they do take after her. And as for my wife, I value her not just as a wife but as a best friend and intellectual companion.

April 1991
Cambridge, Mass.

Prologue—
August 19–24, 1991

Mikhail Gorbachev's safe return from what he thought would be his usual uneventful vacation in the Crimea this week evoked a worldwide sigh of relief. On August 19 and 20 it looked as though a hardliner coup aimed at Gorbachev's ouster would succeed. Concerned about what they saw as the collapse of the Soviet economy and the disintegration of the Soviet Union as a political entity, eight of Gorbachev's closest advisors sought to usurp his power for themselves.

After all Gorbachev had done in the West, how could Gorbachev's associates turn on him? Those of us outside the Soviet Union saw him as the leader who brought an end to the Cold War and, with it, arms control, the opening of the Berlin Wall, and the end of communism in Eastern Europe. The Soviet people also appeared to be beneficiaries. Gorbachev had brought them perestroika and glasnost.

For the people inside the Soviet Union, however, the perception was different. From their point of view, Gorbachev had indeed made some important changes, but not all of them were for the better. In Soviet eyes Gorbachev was directly responsible for the deepening crisis in the Soviet economy. Gorbachev's indecisiveness and incompetence in economic reform had brought on a new form of economic chaos. The Soviet GNP in the first half of 1991 had already dropped over ten percent, and in April most retail prices had been increased by three hundred percent. Moreover, Gorbachev had fired or failed to support his initial advisors. Those like Eduard Shevardnadze and Alexander Yakovlev had been most committed to the process of liberalization and democratization. To replace them, he turned instead to a band of hardliners.

However misconceived his economic reforms, Gorbachev's political reforms succeeded far more successfully than probably even he had envisaged. In a relatively brief six and a half years, his efforts to break the monopoly of the Communist Party, introduce secret elections, and encourage freedom of expression helped create an atmosphere of political pluralism. Even in protest, orderly crowds of a half million or more would gather to shout their support for democracy or sovereignty. This was something seldom seen in Russian history. Gradually large numbers of Soviet people came to lose their sense of fear and accordingly, their fear of the Party, the police, and the KGB.

It is that newfound sense of humanity and dignity that ultimately prevailed over these last few days. This was precisely the goal that Gorbachev in December 1985 had set for his country just before his election as general secretary. Walking through Moscow's streets the last few days, as I did, and seeing the new pride, discipline, and decency of the people was something I never had experienced before in the Soviet Union and frankly never expected to see. Not surprisingly, after their heroism and willingness to stand up to tanks, censorship, and lies, they not only impressed foreigners, but they impressed themselves and gained a new sense of personal worth and integrity.

But for me, the culmination of this undoing of seventy-four years of communism was standing in front of KGB headquarters on Thursday night, August 22, watching as two giant cranes lifted the statue of Felix Dzerzhinsky, the founder of the KGB, from its pedestal. There was no greater symbol of communist repression. The statue and the crowd the next day blocking the headquarters of the Moscow Communist Party reflected just how deeply Gorbachev's revolution had taken hold. But the tragedy for Gorbachev was that while he had set the process in motion, it was his vexatious rival, Boris Yeltsin, to whom the people of Russia and most of the rest of the Soviet Union had come to look. It was Yeltsin, the popularly elected president of the Russian Republic, they shouted for, not Gorbachev. Gorbachev had survived the coup, but realistically he, along with the perestroika process as he understood it, was no longer acceptable to the Soviet people. Yet as a result of the reforms initiated by Gorbachev, the Soviet people rallied around the idea of democracy and, in one of the few times in their history, fought off an attempt to return to the totalitarian ways of the past. The study that follows attempts to explain why such a result, tragic for Gorbachev but exultant for the Soviet people, was inevitable.

Letter from a Soviet high-school student, February 14, 1991:

Last week I was standing in a terrible line for meat. Do you know how long I was standing there? I am even afraid to tell you, I was standing there for five and a half hours.

We had lines (as you know) but they were not so big and we stood in those lines not for everything. But now we have lines for everything. Beginning with meat and shoes and ending with matches and salt. We stand for rice, for sugar, for butter, for thread, for deodorants, and . . . it is an endless list. You know I've forgotten the taste of "Russian" cheese? It is not a joke. I'm serious, I really don't remember it.

Earlier I never cried. I have a strong character, but now I cry very often. We're becoming like animals. If you'd see our wild, mad, and hungry people, in terrible and not less wild lines, you'd be in shock. Every country helps us. We already openly asked for alms and we accept them very calmly. We forget about one very good word. Pride. I am ashamed for my country.

1

A Hero Abroad, A Failure at Home

Rarely, if ever, in modern history has a national leader captured the admiration, respect, and even adulation of the outside world as has Mikhail S. Gorbachev. Winston Churchill came close. Popular adulation and appreciation for his efforts certainly transcended the borders of the United Kingdom, at least as far as his allies in the war effort were concerned. Not surprisingly, the Germans, Italians, and Japanese were considerably less enthused. By comparison, the Gorbachev phenomenon (Gorby to his fans) was all the more unique. In contrast to Churchill, Gorbachev became most popular among those who were the Soviet Union's antagonists. Where heretofore it was a sign of disloyalty or even political or psychological imbalance for an American or West European to say kind words about or applaud a Soviet leader, during Gorbachev's early years he often had a higher popularity rating than our own national leaders.

The reasons for Gorbachev's worldwide popularity were not hard to find. More than anyone else he was responsible for the easing of international tensions on the arms race. He also allowed the freeing of Eastern Europe, hastening the end of the Cold War. In addition, for several years he not only tolerated, but encouraged, the political and economic liberalization of his own country.

Before Gorbachev, both liberals and conservatives in the West taunted the Soviet Union for its refusal to allow dissent, travel, emigration, a free press, free elections, private businesses, and openness to the outside world. The ultimate argument of conservatives such as Ronald Reagan was that if the Soviet Union really wanted to join the family of nations, it would have to tear down the Berlin Wall. Such a challenge was made in the secure knowledge that no such happening would occur. Typically the Soviets would invariably issue their own complaints (often justified) about immorality, corruption, poverty, homelessness, and unemployment in the West. In addition, they insisted that in any case the Berlin Wall was the concern of the German Democratic Republic, a sovereign country. Hence, the Soviet Union could not order the GDR to tear down the Berlin Wall, even if the Soviet Union thought it was a good idea, which it clearly did not.

Into the midst of this tug of Cold War, there appeared a leader who after a year or two of defending the status quo suddenly began to reverse decades of irreversible dogma. Nothing seemed sacred any more, except perhaps religion, which for almost seventy years was not. Even Soviet religious leaders suddenly discovered that it was again possible to open and welcome people to churches, synagogues, and mosques, and publicly preach their faith. Soviet newspapers became aggressively critical. Such hitherto spineless mouthpieces as *Moscow News, Ogonyek,* and even *Izvestiia* overnight became critics, muckrakers, and iconoclasts. The jails and prison camps were virtually emptied of political prisoners. Reflecting the change in atmosphere, a major general in the KGB suddenly began to speak out against the KGB's abuse of human, civil, and criminal rights. Even notorious apologists for every turn in the Soviet domestic and international political line, such as Georgii Arbatov, the director of the Institute of the United States and Canada, and Vladimir Pozner, the Soviet TV commentator,— began to concede the error of their—and their country's— ways. In repentance, Arbatov acknowledged that past Soviet foreign policy more often than not had been aggressive and frequently at fault. For good measure, at a session of the Supreme Soviet, the Soviet parliament, Arbatov also launched an attack on Soviet military behavior and leadership, implying that it was the military that had caused the Soviet Union's problems.[1] A similar turnabout came from Pozner, who for years had a rationalization for every Soviet policy. Most stunning of all, in November 1989, almost to everyone's amazement, including Gorbachev's, the Berlin Wall came crashing down. And just like holy relics of other eras, parts of the destroyed Wall were sold as mementos of a miracle.

No wonder Gorbachev was so popular. It was more than just his charisma and ability to "work the crowds." There was a sincere appreciation among the majority of Americans, West Europeans, and most of the world for what Gorbachev had done.* In that spirit, President George Bush, suddenly during the last few hours of his June 1990 Washington summit, decided to commit the United States to a trade agreement and the promise of most favored nation status (lower tariffs on Soviet imports equivalent to those of virtually all of America's trading partners) for the Soviet Union, even though it had not fulfilled all the specified preconditions. George Bush did this to express his appreciation for Gorbachev's efforts and demonstrate American support.

Foreigners therefore read of Gorbachev's accelerating decline in popularity inside the Soviet Union with confusion and even disbelief. Whereas Soviet public opinion polls gave him favorable ratings of 80 or 90 percent or more in the early years of his administration, by July 1990 his overall popularity rating had plummeted to 20 percent, and in 1991, because of very negative feelings, to what was described as less than zero. In contrast, according to a poll conducted by the National Center for Sociopolitical Studies in the Soviet Union, Boris Yeltsin, the chairman of the Supreme Soviet of the Russian Republic, (in

---

*In the late 1980s, whenever I would criticize Gorbachev for some policy mistake, inevitably members of the audience would rise to his defense. Even those who agreed with the criticism would argue that whatever his shortcomings, they hoped that somehow Gorbachev would remain in power.

June 1991 he would be elected the president of the Russian Republic) was viewed as the most popular leader by 27 percent of those polled. Another Soviet poll, conducted by *Dialog*, gave Yeltsin a 59 percent overall popularity rating.[2]

As with Churchill, who despite his brilliant record in World War II was unable to hold his party's majority in the House of Commons after the war, Gorbachev's domestic constituency has had a very mixed reaction to his activities. Indeed, some inside the Soviet Union insist that Gorbachev's popularity abroad was due to the fact that he has sold out his own country and the principles of communism. After Gorbachev's 1989 visit to Rome and Malta, for example, Alexander Melinkov, a delegate from Siberia to the Supreme Soviet, sarcastically asked why a Soviet leader needed the "blessings" of the Pope and the applause of the West.[3] As these ideologically orthodox critics saw it, Western businessmen and statesmen were happy because Gorbachev had abandoned Soviet socialism for capitalism. Others complained that Gorbachev surrendered Eastern Europe, disarmed the Soviet Army, and allowed the Soviet Union's most hated and feared adversary, the Germans, to reunite. In their view, in less than a year Gorbachev sold out the 26 million lives the Soviet people lost in World War II.[4] Others have charged that it was Gorbachev's political liberalization and acceptance of pluralism that led to ethnic rioting throughout the Soviet republics, as well as to the surge of corruption, crime, prostitution, and other heretofore hidden or muted social disorders.

It is the economic difficulties, however, that have generated most of the bitterness and criticism against Gorbachev. There is the very real perception in the Soviet Union that Gorbachev has brought the country close to the brink of, if not to, actual economic collapse. The majority of Soviets believe that under Gorbachev, the economic revival he had promised not only failed to take place, but conditions have actually deteriorated. By failing to master the country's economic problems, Gorbachev lost his chance to win the confidence of the Soviet people. That issue will be the focus of the chapters that follow.

Economic conditions began to deteriorate at an accelerating pace, particularly in late 1988. A climax of sorts occurred on May 24, 1990, less than a week before Gorbachev's scheduled departure for his important summit meeting with George Bush in Washington. Then the Soviet leadership under Prime Minister Nikolai Ryzhkov, but with Gorbachev's concurrence, announced that as of July 1, 1990, the government would raise the price of bread threefold. That was six weeks before the increase was due to take place. Additional price increases were promised for January 1, 1991. The advance notice provoked a buyers' panic. And like locusts, Soviet shoppers emptied the stores of almost anything they could find. This seemed to climax what had been and what would be a continuing series of economic miscalculations. It also provided Gorbachev with the worst of all possible sendoffs for his trip to Washington. Pictures of panicked shoppers drew attention to the economic mess facing Gorbachev at home. This graphically helped to explain why it was that by 1990, a growing number of Soviet consumers had concluded that economic conditions had become worse than they were in the Leonid Brezhnev era. If the Brezhnev era was officially referred to as a period of *zastoi,* or stagnation, then by 1990, Gorbachev had brought them *zastoi II.*

I

The bifurcated attitude toward Gorbachev was vividly highlighted in the way he was received by President George Bush and the American public during his visit to the United States for the summit in late May and early June 1990, and the reception he received when he returned to Moscow. Gorbachev and his wife Raisa probably thought once or twice about the possibility of prolonging their stay in the United States rather than return to what they undoubtedly knew would be criticism, hostility, charges of overindulgence at state expense, and even calls for his resignation. Gorbachev found himself under attack on all sides, from the public, the Communist Party, and the government. This was clearly a miscalculation because one important consideration in scheduling the summit in late May and early June was Gorbachev's desire to walk into the meeting of the 28th Communist Party Congress, set for July 2, with the sight and sound of American applause fresh in the minds of the Soviet television public. The images were there, but to Gorbachev's surprise, the delegates to the Party Congress were of a decidedly more hostile mood than he had anticipated.

He clearly had misjudged just how imperiled his standing with the Soviet people had become. Only a few months earlier, Gorbachev and his advisers had assumed that his strength was growing, and for that reason they decided to move up the date of the 28th Party Congress, which was not due to be convened until 1991. That way Gorbachev could reconstitute the membership of the Central Committee of the Communist Party sooner and more to his liking, and then accelerate the pace of his reforms.

Although Gorbachev ultimately outmaneuvered most of his opponents from both the radical and conservative wings at the 28th Party Congress, that did not stop the delegates from expressing their open hostility to Gorbachev and his allies. Nor did it prevent some of the party's most promising reform leaders from announcing their resignation. Boris Yeltsin, for example, dramatically rejected the invitation to become a member of the Central Committee once more. Announcing his resignation from the party, he walked out of the Congress Hall proceedings. Those supporting Gorbachev's reforms were often openly booed or applauded into silence. For that matter, one of the first delegates to speak on opening day called for Gorbachev's resignation along with that of other senior members of the party.[5]

In the first few years of Gorbachev's ascent to power, there were few demonstrative supporters of his efforts to reform. There were no guarantees that Gorbachev meant what he said, and even if he did, those supporting reforms were reluctant to put their necks out too far ahead for fear they might suffer a backlash if he did not succeed. Indeed, there were instances of retaliation, especially in some of the provinces where the feudal rule by party officials was still very much a fact of life. Gradually, however, some of the more daring began to take Gorbachev at his word.

In the political realm at least, Gorbachev began to call for some very bold initiatives. In a break with Soviet tradition, he started to call for pluralism and local initiatives, not only within but outside the party. After some initial resistance, he even came to support the idea that the Soviet Union could be a multi-party state. That led him in early 1990 to advocate the amendment of Article 6 of the Soviet Constitution, the article that ordained a monopoly for the Communist Party inside the country. Gorbachev's expectation was that only with a grass-roots involvement would any of his reforms succeed.

As anticipated, once some of these reforms took hold, the role of both the party and the central government did begin to erode. That was exactly what Gorbachev had set out to accomplish. But in the eyes of his critics, Gorbachev succeeded too well. As many of the country's governing institutions began to weaken, parts of the society began to disintegrate. Suddenly institutions which had always subordinated themselves to the party and the center began to act on their own. This included not only the republics, but the army, the KGB, and even industrial managers. Gorbachev discovered that he was starting to lose control. In effect, he began to suffer because of his own initiatives. The attackers had become dizzy with success. In response, by 1991 there were urgent calls for the party to "reassert direct control over industry and agriculture."[6] Others extended those calls to include the army and the KGB.

Gorbachev faced a paradox. He understood that he could not singlehandedly order the reforms that he wanted. The Soviet Union is too large, the kinds of reforms that must be undertaken too complicated, and the people involved too numerous for all initiatives to come from a central source. But after seven decades of being told what to do, often in needlessly petty detail, there was a natural reluctance to do anything until everyone else was doing the same thing. In the economic sphere at least, that meant reform could only come very slowly. Had Gorbachev been willing to impose Stalin-like dictatorial edicts backed by force and terror, he might have been able to break out of the impasse and accelerate the process of reform. Hence the paradox: to get his reforms, Gorbachev could have forced them through; but in the long run, he realized that for his reforms to be self-sustaining, they would have to be backed by local initiatives.

Gorbachev is certainly not the first leader in Russian or Soviet history to seek to reform his country. As we shall see, the effort to modernize Russia or westernize it is a recurrent theme in Russian history. Russia's past is dominated by the drama of leaders struggling to bring their country up to European standards. Through heroic efforts, these czars and general secretaries sometimes succeeded, at least temporarily. In almost every instance, however, the measures they took were so draconic in scope that they served to indenture or encumber future generations.

In the early stages of his reform effort, Gorbachev seemed determined to avoid such pitfalls. For that reason he sought to reduce rather than increase political and economic controls and police repressions. However, when finally, at least in the political arena, local leaders and groups began to take initiatives on their own, Gorbachev was not too happy with the results. He was especially discomfited just before his meeting with President Bush in early summer 1990. Literally on the eve of his departure, he decided to call in a large number of delegates to the Supreme Soviet of the Russian Republic. He urged them to vote against Boris Yeltsin, who was running as chairman of the Russian Supreme Soviet. For a time Gorbachev even sought to bring in new candidates who might defeat Yeltsin. If elected, Yeltsin would in effect have become the president of the largest republic in the Soviet Union. Gorbachev did not relish a rival in that post. Ever since Gorbachev had supported Yeltsin's expulsion from his non-voting membership in the Politburo of the All Union Communist Party, Yeltsin had been determined to redeem himself, and wherever possible, at Gorbachev's expense. Gorbachev knew it would not only be politically embarrassing to have one of his most outspoken critics elected to such an important position, but that Yeltsin could complicate Gorbachev's plans for reform. Heretofore the presidency of the Supreme Soviet of the Russian Republic had always been a pro forma job with virtually no meaningful functions. However, unlike his predecessors, Yeltsin had been elected as a delegate to the Supreme Soviet in an open election and he received more than 80 percent of the votes cast. Since Gorbachev had never risked a popular election for any government position, this was far more than he himself could claim. Given his popular mandate, there was every reason to anticipate that Yeltsin, if elected, would embark on his own agenda and that it probably would differ significantly from what Gorbachev planned to do.

Despite Gorbachev's intensive efforts, however, Yeltsin won. Wasting no time, Yeltsin immediately called a press conference, which incidentally took place at the very time Gorbachev was on his way to the United States. Yeltsin spelled out his plans for the sovereignty of the Russian Republic, which went far beyond what Gorbachev had been advocating. Yeltsin's call for the economic subordination of the industry and raw materials located within the Russian Republic to the control of authorities in the Russian federation (rather than by ministries and planners at the All Union level) was not at all what Gorbachev had in mind. Gorbachev wanted instead to continue the status quo with the ministries and planners at the All Union level retaining their authority.[7] More than that, Yeltsin's comments dealt with day-to-day problems in the republic. Naturally this diverted attention in the Russian Republic from Gorbachev's visit, and for that matter forced Gorbachev, while in Washington, to respond to questions about Yeltsin and Gorbachev's feelings about what he was doing. To the outside observer there was every evidence that Yeltsin's timing was *ne sluchaino,* or not coincidental, as the Soviets would say. With the same mischievousness, Yeltsin decided to convene the Supreme Soviet of the Russian Republic on Monday evening, July 2, 1990. That happened to be the first day of the 28th Party Congress and at a time when Russian television viewers would normally have been watching the proceedings of the Communist Party Congress. Instead, Yeltsin was shown presiding over the Russian Supreme Soviet.

Before long, Yeltsin began to make real Gorbachev's worst nightmares. Yeltsin issued explicit calls for the political and economic sovereignty of the Russian Republic. If implemented, that would leave almost no role for Gorbachev and the Soviet government in over one half of the country. Moreover, once such demands began to come from the Russian Republic, it was only natural that other republics would demand the same privileges and rights. Eventually all fifteen republics began to issue calls for either economic sovereignty or political independence. Even the Belorussian Supreme Soviet, heretofore one of the most compliant of all governing groups in the Soviet Union, began to insist on the right to determine its own economic actions. Going beyond that, the Ukrainian Supreme Soviet called for the return of all Ukrainian soldiers from the Soviet Army. They were to be put instead into a new Ukrainian army.

Nor were Gorbachev's problems confined to the governments in the different republics. Upon his return from Washington, he found himself confronted with a similar siphoning off of power within the party itself. Gorbachev's efforts to induce local groups to take initiative on their own were being implemented, but not always in the way he had anticipated. Ever since Stalin, subordinate party leaders have acted as vassals of the central party authorities in Moscow. "Democratic centralism," an operating procedure designed to explain away the absence of elections and grass-roots initiatives, served to put decisions as to personnel appointments and operational behavior in the hands of the Moscow leaders. Meetings of lower-level republic or *oblast* party organizations and committees, just like their counterparts in the government, echoed the actions of their higher-ranking superiors. That in large part explained why for so long, no one seemed to notice the absence of a Russian Communist Party. All the other republics had their own party apparatus and constituency, but not the Russians. There was no function for it. Since Russians made up about 60 percent of the membership of the All Union Communist Party, a Russian Communist Party would have been redundant. That all changed, however, when local groups began to take actual power into their hands.

As the lack of confidence in the leadership of the Soviet Union began to grow, local groups began to organize and fill the rapidly growing vacuum. Upon his return from Washington, one of Gorbachev's first chores was to participate in the convening of an organizing session of the just created Communist Party of the Russian Republic. To the evident surprise of a large number of observers, the elected leader of the new party was Ivan Polizhkov, an outspoken critic of many of Gorbachev's reforms. Polizhkov, formerly the party chief in the Krasnodar *oblast,* had been fiercely critical of such basic reform initiatives as the establishment of cooperatives. He had also attacked mainline reformers such as Anatoly Sobchak (subsequently mayor of Leningrad) for what was said to be the selling of permits and licenses for private profit. Until his election as general secretary of the Russian Communist Party, one of Polizhkov's few moments in the spotlight came when Gorbachev pushed Polizhkov as a potential rival for Yeltsin's job as chairman of the Supreme Soviet of the Russian Republic. Polizhkov lost, but apparently that only fed his desire for a greater role at the center. He subsequently entered and won the race for secretary general of the Communist Party of the Russian Republic.

If Yeltsin and Polizhkov had been more subordinate and subservient to Gorbachev, he undoubtedly would have felt better about their initiatives. But despite periodic professions of cooperation and commonality of purpose, Yeltsin committed himself to what generally was a more radical reform stance (what the Soviets call leftist or reformist), while Polizhkov did his best to oppose such reforms and held to the status quo (what the Soviets call a rightist or anti-reform position). Like a two-headed Frankenstein monster, Gorbachev had created both a Yeltsin and a Polizhkov; both were byproducts of Gorbachev's reform policies, but each adopted a life and an orientation of his own. More important, each of them frequently found themselves moving at cross purposes to Gorbachev.

Undoubtedly, much of the motivation to set off on their own was a reaction to the growing perception that the Soviet economy was falling apart, particularly after the May 1990 announcement of the anticipated price increases. Whether anyone else could have provided better guidance is a debate we shall consider shortly. But by mid-1989, when more and more workers began to walk out on strike, an almost unheard-of act in the pre-Gorbachev era, and when more and more basic goods began to disappear from the store shelves, there was a growing sense of desperation and a determination by local officials to take responsibility for their own economic well-being and remove it from the hands of the Moscow authorities. Everyone, including the Russians in the Russian Republic, began to feel exploited. Each nationality and labor group concluded that they would do better on their own than as part of the whole.

There is much to be learned from contrasting the move toward political integration in Western Europe with the drive for political independence inside the Soviet Union. Why is it that in Western Europe, most members of the European Economic Community seem eager to forsake many of their long-held sovereign rights, while in the Soviet Union each republic and many regions are insisting on exercising powers they have not had for seventy years or more? Why do those in Western Europe feel that in union there is strength, while many in the Soviet Union feel that in disunion there is strength? By 1990, as we saw, parliaments in each of the fifteen Soviet republics had passed resolutions demanding control of their own sovereignty. Nor were the calls for sovereignty confined to the fifteen republics. Regional leaders in Yakutia, in the far eastern *oblast* of the Russian Republic, began to prepare their own claims for sovereignty, not only from the Soviet Union, but from the Russian Republic and from Yeltsin.[8] For that matter the mayors of some of the Soviet Union's most important cities began to make somewhat similar demands. Thus by mid-1990, the mayors of major urban centers such as Leningrad and Odessa had ordered factories within their city limits to pay higher taxes and rent to the city, and to produce and price their goods more in response to local market conditions and dictates. In the absence of any resolute action at the center, some of the local officials also decided to move on their own to market reform. Ultimately Gorbachev decided to accept the inevitable and join in and follow some of those republic efforts. In late 1990, Gorbachev even offered to change the name of the country. Reflecting the increased clamor for sovereignty, he suggested that the Union of Soviet Socialist Republics (USSR) be called instead the Union of Sovereign Soviet Republics (USSR). Although he eventually prevailed, at first his proposal was not successful. Some say he might have had more success if he had offered to call it the UFFR (the Union of Fewer and Fewer Republics).

Gorbachev's willingness to follow rather than lead is another illustration of his political flexibility. As much as it may hurt, when necessary he has sometimes been willing to play second fiddle, even if it must be under Yeltsin's direction. At other times he has found it entirely fitting to join in the singing of the *Internationale,* the rallying theme of the Communist Party, as he did so enthusiastically at the conclusion of the 28th Communist Party Congress. How incongruent it was. This agglomeration of bureaucrats and generals (of whom less than 10 percent of the total 4,700 delegates were workers), most of them reactionary, anti-reform, middle-aged, and overweight, singing a song calling for the radical upheaval of the Soviet economic system and the transfer of power to the proletariat.[9] From girth and demeanor, they resembled not so much the proletariat as a convention of the National Association of Manufacturers, with whom they probably had more in common.

While each compromise and adjustment demonstrates Gorbachev's domestic and international political skills, unfortunately he has yet to prove himself as an economic reformer. In fact, it is his failure as an economic reformer that forces him into such complicated political maneuvering. Nonetheless, as impressive as his political survival has been, the majority of his compromises have been short-run expedients, which only serve to compound the problems he must deal with in the next round.

Almost no one could have foretold that despite the best of intentions, Gorbachev's efforts would eventually bring the Soviet Union to the brink of collapse. By 1991, the Soviet Union found itself with what in the West would be called a depression. When the drop in Soviet GNP began to exceed 10 percent as it did in 1991, there is no other word for it.

But just as Gorbachev is an original thinker and doer, so his depression is also unique and probably the first of its kind in economic history. Heretofore the world's depressions have been largely the consequence of inadequate demand. As the depression builds, consumers and manufacturers cut back on their purchases and, as a result, more and more businesses close down or go bankrupt. But Gorbachev's depression is not due to a drop in demand or anything like it. There are millions of Soviet consumers eager and able to spend rubles on anything that appears in Soviet shops.

For Gorbachev the problem is very different in nature; the economy has been plunged into a depression because of inadequate supplies. This is a consequence of several factors. The powers of the central planners were intentionally shorn by Gorbachev, and then once inflation became a factor, factory managers had even more reason to disregard orders from the center. Inflation and the availability of private and cooperative shops, which could charge higher prices, served to suck goods out of state shops, which in turn caused labor unrest. Labor unrest led to further disruption of supplies, as did ethnic assertiveness. Because of all these factors, more and more Soviet factories were forced to close down. This was an unintended consequence of a policy that did all it could to prevent "needless duplication." Thus when a factory in the Soviet Union is forced to close down because of a disruption in its flow of inputs, there is usually no substitute for its output, which means that its customers in turn are also in jeopardy. The result we will call a supply side depression; the buyers are there, the goods are not.

In the pages that will follow we will seek to explain in more detail why it is that the initial enthusiasm for Gorbachev inside the Soviet Union quickly waned, and how Gorbachev's policies precipitated this unique supply side collapse. The supply side analysis should help provide us with a framework for explaining why Gorbachev's problems seem to intensify so quickly.

To help understand what Gorbachev had to deal with, we will begin in Chapters 2 and 3 by providing a look at the economic and political conditions in the pre-Gorbachev era. As already noted, Gorbachev is not the first reformer in Soviet history nor for that matter in Russia. As we also see, however, rarely did those who accepted the task achieve a complete overhaul, and when more ambitious leaders did try, they often found themselves encumbering the country's future growth. To pay for that one massive step forward, they often found themselves taking two steps backward.

Chapter 4 examines Gorbachev's background and his rise through the ranks, and considers what there was in his experience that led him to attempt such a bold break with the past and a willingness to embark on such an ambitious effort. Unfortunately, while Gorbachev's spirit was willing, his strategy of concentrating on the machine-tool industry was faulty. After approximately two years, Gorbachev, as discussed in Chapter 5, came to realize that he had made a mistake. Then he began to introduce new reforms. However, by the time corrective measures were actually promulgated, they were too little and too late. As we see in Chapter 6, the result was a growing budget deficit and inflation, which in turn precipitated an emptying of shelves in state stores and a disruption in production and ultimately a fall in the Soviet GNP.

Once committed to reforming his economy, Gorbachev also concluded that he would have to reduce political repression and encourage a period of openness unequaled in the Soviet era. But after seventy years of repression, several of the ethnic groups decided that they would take advantage of this new political openness to assert their political independence and sovereignty. The collapse of the economy hastened what eventually became a process of political disintegration. Different republics and regions began to insist on their political and economic sovereignty.

Unable to believe that Gorbachev would take his reform effort seriously, the traditionalists and hard-liners were slow to react. Chapter 7 analyzes what happened when they did respond, and how they ultimately managed to edge out Gorbachev's internal reformers and with them some of Gorbachev's more promising reforms. In Chapters 7 and 8 we will examine some of the various comprehensive reforms that have subsequently been proposed and why almost all of these undertakings have been rejected.

Like a coroner's report, our goal is to conduct what might be called an economic and political autopsy of perestroika. Why did such a noble effort fail? What we will be looking for are answers to why Gorbachev had so many problems at home, why there was such resistance to his determined effort at economic reform, and why he has had so little to show for his efforts. How much of Gorbachev's difficulty was due to problems and the structure of the economic system that he inherited and how much of it was his own doing? What were his options? Why did his mid-course corrections fail? Is the Soviet Union's supply-side economic crisis unique and why is it so serious? And finally, does the Gorbachev experience have relevance for other centrally planned societies?

If we are successful, we may be able to provide guidance about what to avoid and what to emphasize for future reformers. One of Gorbachev's biggest handicaps was that no one in the Soviet Union had ever thought through exactly what had to be done to convert the Soviet Union from a centrally planned command economy emphasizing heavy industry to a market-oriented decentralized economy emphasizing consumer goods. He had no road map to guide him. It was no wonder that Gorbachev kept switching policies as he tried to find a solution for his problems.

Whatever the ultimate fate of the original Gorbachev reform, undoubtedly the reform process will continue. By examining where Gorbachev went wrong, we may be able to provide guidance for those subsequent reformers and their advisers so that they can avoid similar mistakes.

2

The Pre-Gorbachev Era
—Trying to Modernize
—An Old Story

Russian history is marked by the drama of trying to catch up with the West and then falling back. Thoughtful analysts like Alexander Gerschenkron have commented on the schizophrenic nature of that effort.[1] Humiliated by some military defeat or provoked by some travel experience, leader after leader in what was once Russia and subsequently the Soviet Union determined that his or her mission in life was to transform that backward country into a modernized society equal to those in the West. Yet, no leader wanted to make Russia a carbon copy of the West—that would deny Russia its distinctive essence. This uniqueness is usually defined to encompass among other features the Russian Orthodox Church, the Russian peasantry, and the Russian "soul." It seeks to avoid some of the grosser aspects of democracy or what to some traditionalists is "mob rule."

Combining Russia's unique characteristics with Western pluralism, modernization, democratization, individualism, and industrialization has seldom if ever been easy. Perhaps this combination cannot work, or as economists like to say, it is overdetermined. In the same way that adding too many condiments can sour the salad, it may be that holding onto all the old and traditional complicates and distorts the modernization process. Russian nationalists take offense at this, but it may well be that by their uniqueness, the old social, economic, political, and cultural traditions are the source of the problem and explain why Russia fell behind in the first place.

In addition to trying to find the proper chemical balance between the old and the new, any would-be reformers of the Russian, and later the Soviet empires, must also ensure that the cures they prescribe do not produce new disabilities. All too often that is what happened. In his effort to westernize Russia, Czar Peter the Great decided to create a capital city on the site of a swamp. To do this properly, he decided he had to have dozens of Western architects and artists spend millions of rubles on designing a Russian industrial infrastructure, including a shipbuilding industry. But to finance such a massive undertaking, he had to mobilize thousands of laborers and raise the necessary funds to sustain the domestic work force and pay the guest artisans.

Russia in Peter's day was a poor and backward country. To expedite the transformation and generate the resources he needed, Peter put great pressure on his domestic work force. In addition to dragooning large numbers of peasants to work in the swamps, he squeezed the country's nobility for extra extractions to pay for his grandiose scheme. To satisfy Peter's demands, the nobility in turn insisted on imposing more controls over the peasants within their jurisdiction. The result was the creation of a magnificent city, St. Petersburg, and a more rigorous enserfdom of the peasants.

Within limits, Peter left his country more westernized than he found it—but the effort necessitated and came at an enormous cost. Like Faust, Peter exchanged a promise of growth for a mortgage on his country's future, an encumbered peasantry. In a reversal of the usual scenario, he and his fellow reformers took one step forward but found that to pay for it they had to take two steps backward.

Two and a half centuries later, Joseph Stalin did much the same thing.[2] One of his overriding objectives was to industrialize the Soviet Union as quickly as possible. But given the hostility in the outside world to the Bolshevik takeover, Stalin concluded that the financial and investment support he needed would have to come from within the country.

Like Peter, Stalin did not have much to work with. Eighty percent of the Soviet population lived and worked on the farm. Thus to obtain the resources for investment that he needed, Stalin was all but forced to turn to the agricultural sector—the peasants. But peasants in general are notorious for their reluctance to part with their savings. Thus it seemed unlikely that the peasants living in the Soviet Union would be any more responsive.

Because Stalin was in a hurry, he had no time for normal market and tax procedures. He wanted industrialization and he wanted it immediately. In a radical departure from existing practice, he decided he could only achieve his objective by nationalizing all agriculture, as well as commerce and industry. In quick-march fashion, he collectivized almost all private agriculture and killed off the more prosperous farmers who resisted. He also inaugurated a series of five-year plans which regulated both industry and agriculture.

The collectivization of private farms provided a way for Stalin to mobilize the investment funds he wanted to build up his industry. By asserting control of agriculture this way, he could siphon off what would otherwise have gone to private consumption, and divert it instead to state use in the city and in industry. Consolidating private farms into large collective farms also made sense economically because it made for economies of scale, and opened the way for the use of large tractors and mechanization that would have been impossible on smaller plots of land. And it made sense politically. The peasants could be more easily controlled if they were herded together into larger entities.

Stalin's moves in the commercial and industrial spheres were equally far-reaching. He assumed state control of virtually all economic activity. He not only nationalized the firms, he instituted a planning process that circumscribed and for all intents and purposes determined almost all the operating decisions of the factory and commercial enterprise managers. Yearly and five-year plans also provided for the disbursement of those investment resources that were accumulated by the state.

Like Peter the Great, Stalin managed to jump-start Soviet economic growth and advance it along the path to westernization. Industrial output rose rapidly and soon exceeded 10 percent annually. By the time of Hitler's invasion of the Soviet Union in 1941, the Soviet Union had become an economic power that could not be ignored. While still economically behind Germany and much of Western Europe, nonetheless it was able to produce large quantities of heavy industrial machines and the military equipment needed to equip a respectable army.

Stalin paid a high price to do this. Following in Peter's footsteps, he, too, made a Faustian bargain: rapid growth in the short run in exchange for what would become encumbrances to growth in the future. (It is more than coincidental that Stalin's present-day defenders justify his behavior by likening his approach to Peter's.) In agriculture, the collective farm system became a modern-day form of serfdom.[3] The main difference was that, instead of being under control of a landlord as in the nineteenth century, the modern-day Soviet peasant was subject to the dictates of the collective and state farm chairman. The peasants as a class were not issued internal passports. For three decades or more under Stalin, only peasants with special permission could leave their farms. In reality, the peasant became indentured to his collective or state farm. In addition, individual enterprise was stifled—the most resourceful peasants were liquidated. Just as intended, resources were squeezed out of the countryside and transferred to the city.

It took two centuries for Russia to undo the legacy of Peter the Great's reforms. Peter had ill prepared Russia to compete in the era of the Industrial Revolution. Prior to the nineteenth century, Russia produced twice as much steel as Great Britain. By 1840, it produced one twentieth of what Great Britain did. Only in the late nineteenth century did Russian industry show any sign of self-reliance and independence from the state. In the same way, the creation of a class of independent middle-income peasants had to await the introduction of the Stolypin reforms of 1906–11. As prime minister, Pyotr Stolypin understood the need to encourage strong, hardworking, and sober peasants in their effort to enrich themselves. For a time Russia became one of the world's largest exporters of grain—the breadbasket of Europe, as some called it. This role changed dramatically under Stalin's heavy-handed agricultural policy. Largely as a result of collectivization and the resulting peasant resistance, the Soviet Union transformed itself again. By the 1970s, what had been one of the world's largest grain exporters became one of the world's largest importers.

The five-year plans and the nationalization of all Soviet industry had a similar negative impact. What had been record-breaking rates of industrial growth in the 1930s, by the mid- and late 1980s became transformed into a good old-fashioned economic crisis and depression. State ownership and centrally planned guidance which in the 1950s had seemed to produce impressive results, by the 1970s and 1980s seemed to stifle initiative and innovative ideas. The Soviet Union began falling further and further behind the high technology being mastered in much of the rest of the Western world, as well as in countries (such as Taiwan and South Korea) that were relatively more backward than the Soviet Union had been a decade or two ago. One of Gorbachev's prime challenges was to catch up with this technological advance in industry and agriculture without setting in motion forces that would jeopardize the future.

I

There is a view that because of its past and because of the way the Soviet Union is set apart from the rest of Europe, most Soviet people are too lethargic and need the strong-arm pressure of a Peter or Stalin to move them. Others insist that Russians, and for that matter all of the Soviet people, are capable of igniting and sustaining ongoing economic growth if given the appropriate material incentives. Gorbachev initially acted upon this latter assumption. There was reason to believe such a course was feasible. For a time under Nikita Khrushchev in the 1950s the Soviet Union seemed to be moving in that direction. There had been shortages of many goods and a complete absence of others, but economic life in the Khrushchev era seemed to be approaching Western standards. In comparison with the present-day Soviet Union, lines for consumer goods were shorter and prices were lower. Industry was still periodically overdosing on machine tools, but there was reason to believe that the system was on its way to becoming more responsive. The launching of a Sputnik in 1957 signaled the growing prowess of Soviet technology. Indeed, the Soviet Union seemed capable of carrying out Khrushchev's boast that it would overtake and surpass the United States within a decade or two, what became known as the "We will bury you" boast.

Yet the Khrushchev program was unable to nourish the Soviet economy enough so that it could free itself from overdependence on the state for subsidies and guidance. In part, Khrushchev's task was complicated by the rapid changes in the nature of international technology, which preordained that the Soviet Union would fall behind. The Soviet central planning system was at its best when it was dealing with slow-moving basic technology.[4] As the development of new high technology began to accelerate, Soviet central planners were simply unable to keep up with the speed with which one innovation superseded another. Khrushchev seemed to understand what was happening but could do nothing about it. In his inimitable way, Khrushchev exclaimed: "Some officials have put on steel . . . blinders; they do everything as they were taught in their day. The material appears which is superior to steel and is cheaper, but they keep on shouting, 'steel . . . steel.' "[5]

Not all of Khrushchev's problems were due to factors beyond his immediate control. To some extent he was carried away by his own impetuousness and by what seemed to be his initial success, an occupational hazard that has bedeviled all Soviet leaders. Because so much power in the Soviet central planning system is concentrated in the hands of the Soviet leadership, there were no meaningful checks and balances either within the government or from the society as a whole to restrain its impetuousness. No one person or group felt bold or independent enough to challenge the dictates of the leadership. The absence of restraints inevitably created a sense of hubris among the leaders—a feeling they could do no wrong. When they became aware of a mistake, they sought some new panacea to resolve the problem. Consequently, for over seventy years the Soviet economy has lurched from one new policy campaign to the next, all emanating from the center. The assumption has always been that salvation comes from on high, with little if any initiative or diversity from below. The main consequence of this is that with time these policy shifts become increasingly ineffective and at times they lead to deepening alienation among the people.

Khrushchev's economic record is replete with such ill-fated shifts in policy. His decision in the early 1960s, for example, to raise retail food prices "temporarily" in order, supposedly, to provide extra investment in agriculture and food processing, is considered today to be one of his more serious mistakes. At the same time, he also decided to cut back the opportunities of the peasants to earn extra income. He ordered that peasants turn their cows over to the collective farms and he reduced the size of the private garden plot that a peasant could farm legally on his own. Khrushchev was concerned that some peasants were spending too much time on their own private farming activity at the expense of the collective or state farm effort. When combined with some other economic reforms he was attempting, these "reforms" caused a crisis of confidence in Khrushchev's leadership. Since prices were never decreased, the "temporary" increases were treated as a big lie and the confiscation of the peasants' most precious asset was regarded as a betrayal. They had saved and invested in the anticipation of an increased return in the future.

Khrushchev's actions have not been forgotten and are used to this day to explain why the population is so hostile to price increases and so reluctant to invest any of its income in building up the productivity of the land it cultivates. Khrushchev's actions, along with the suppression of the so-called kulaks or wealthier peasants in the 1920s and 1930s also help explain why Soviet peasants are not eager to set up their own family or cooperative units. Soviet economists lament that such actions have not only soured the peasants on setting off on their own, but have also made it difficult to move toward economic equilibrium in the market. As a consequence, the imbalance in the market has seemed to increase bit by bit each year.

The campaign-type way of instituting change from the top down in the Soviet Union reflects the basically conservative nature of pre-revolutionary Russia and its successor the Soviet Union. Rarely does change come gradually or in an evolutionary way from the bottom up. There is a reluctance to take initiative without guidance from on high. The proclivity for instant solutions is reflected in a story: A peasant finds that his chickens are dying. He asks his local priest for advice. The priest tells him to feed the chickens aspirin. The peasant does and in a few days seeks out the priest again. The priest asks what happened and the peasant answers that another fifty chickens died. The priest shakes his head and suggests a new approach. "Feed them penicillin," says the priest. Another week passes and once again the peasant consults the priest. "Another hundred died," laments the peasant. "What should I do now?" The priest shakes his head and says, "This time feed them castor oil." The peasant does as he is told, but when he next sees the priest he reports that this time, "they all died!" Shaking his head, the priest says, "What a pity. I had so many other ideas I wanted you to try."

Just as in the story, change in the Soviet Union tends to come from the top down. Moreover, it often comes in fits and starts and usually encounters great resistance. Given the aversion to change, needed adjustments tend to be postponed, so that when change can be delayed no longer, there is a danger that it will be accompanied by disorder and violence. If change is held back too long, there may be assassination or attempts at revolution.

The ever present possibility of disorder haunts not only the leadership but the general public. There is always the fear that change will get out of hand. This aversion to change may also explain why the Russian and Soviet people put up with czarist and Stalinist regimes over such lengthy periods. Of course not everyone in either the pre-revolutionary or the communist era was happy with their leadership, but the majority of the Russian population nevertheless complied with the decrees of their rulers. There are those who argue that if anything, because of their fear of chaos and anarchy, the Russian people in fact seem comfortable with, and indeed seem to prefer, tight rigid controls. That was the import of Fyodor Dostoyevsky's sequence between the Grand Inquisitor and Jesus in *The Brothers Karamazov*. As the Grand Inquisitor says to Jesus:

Oh we shall persuade them that they will only become free when they renounce their freedom to us and submit to us. . . . Too, too well they know the value of complete submission! And until men know that, they will be unhappy. . . .

Thou wouldst go into the world, and art going with empty hands, with some promise of freedom which men in their simplicity and their natural unruliness cannot even understand, which they fear and dread—for nothing has ever been more insupportable for a man and for a human society than freedom. . . .

No science will give them bread so long as they remain free. In the end they will lay their freedom at our feet and say to us, "Make us your slaves, but feed us."[6]

Over the centuries there have been remarkably few open or evolutionary attempts to change the country's leadership and its political system. This assertion will undoubtedly be challenged by many Russians. Yuri Orlov, the dissident physicist who was jailed and then exiled from the Soviet Union to the United States, for example, insists that there were many inside the Soviet Union who sought to change and reform the system from within. His own efforts are a good illustration. However, that is just the point; Orlov was one of the very few people who dared to risk an open challenge. For that matter, until Gorbachev came along there was no institutional provision for systematic regularized turnover of leadership. Just as under the czars, almost all Soviet leaders except Khrushchev and Malenkov served what in effect was lifetime tenure. They assumed that it was only at death that they would be replaced.

One of the main characteristics of democracy is that there must be a regularized procedure for checking power and switching leaders. That means holding him or her to account and establishing periodic reviews in the form of elections for reappointment. There must also be some institutional form of checks and balances that limits the leader's ability to tax and spend and also adjudicates when differences arise between the leaders and other branches of the government. The Magna Carta was a critical document in the evolution of democracy in the Anglo-Saxon world because, for the first time, it established bounds on the king's powers. The impetus for the Magna Carta came from below. Somehow, even in the Gorbachev era, it is hard to imagine that a document like the Magna Carta could evolve out of a grass-roots effort by the Soviet people or their representatives.

There may be exceptions, but communist societies in general seem to have trouble with the concept of pluralism and diversifying the sources of power. Lack of unanimity is usually viewed as a dangerous thing. Leaders insist on being loved. Like the evil queen in Snow White, they are always asking the mirror for a status report, although in this case it is not who is the fairest in the land but who is the most popular. Thus, when Gorbachev heard that the weekly newspaper *Argumenty i fakti* published a poll which showed that he trailed several others in popularity, Gorbachev ordered that the editor, Vladislav A. Starkov, be fired.[7] However, Starkov refused to quit and continues as editor of the newspaper. Yet until there are viable and independent power bases in these societies, there will continue to be abuses of power. All too often reformers in the communist world assume that all they have to do is duplicate the surface manifestations of Western political and economic life and their prob-

lems will be solved. This, as we shall see, is particularly dangerous when attempting to create a market system in a centrally
planned communist society, but it also can be beguiling when
trying to recreate a democracy with its restraints on the abuses
of power.

How hard it can be is reflected in a story that Professor Alan
Dershowitz, of the Harvard Law School, relates. In the aftermath of China's Cultural Revolution of the 1970s, there was
widespread agreement that the Chinese people must never
allow anything like the cult of personality to recur. It seemed
as if almost everyone had suffered in one way or another, and
there was general consensus that the pain and loss suffered
during the Cultural Revolution was not only bad for the people
but for the country. Looking to the United States as an alternative model where human rights abuses seemed to have been held
in check, Chinese officials noticed that the United States had an
unusually large number of lawyers. Perhaps, it was reasoned,
if lawyers could also play an increased role in China, China
would be spared future cultural revolutions and personality
cults.

To help them understand how the Americans did it, the
Chinese invited Professor Dershowitz to stage a series of mock
trials. He agreed, and with the aid of another lawyer who acted
as the prosecutor, and his son who acted as the defendant,
Professor Dershowitz attempted to demonstrate what functions
a lawyer for the defense performs in a democracy. According
to Professor Dershowitz, the Chinese audience was very appreciative of his dramatic defense of his client. But at the end of
each trial, they invariably responded the same way. "Your
presentation was superb," they agreed, "but why do you waste
so much time on a guilty man?"

The Soviets seem to suffer from the same lack of understanding. Like the Chinese, the Soviets insist they will never tolerate
another cult of personality. Like the Chinese (at least until the
crackdown in Tiananmen Square in June 1989), the common
Soviet refrain is "We remember the abuses of the cult of personality and will never tolerate that again." But memories fade,

and without some underlying institutional change that establishes pluralism, separation of power, and economic independence from the state, there is no institutional mechanism for preventing a recurrence of the type of abuses that were particularly blatant under Mao in China and under Stalin in the Soviet Union.

Stalin's regime illustrates, as much as anything can, where the absence of checks and balances, and restrictions on the power of the head of the party or government, can lead. That is not to ignore political and economic life under Khrushchev and Brezhnev, nor for that matter under Andropov or Chernenko or the first few months under Gorbachev. They all acted abusively with varying degrees of brutality.

II

In the aftermath of seven decades of almost unrestrained power, the Soviet people had accumulated an unusually large and overdue bill of political, social, and economic grievances. Despite its claims to be a revolutionary power, the Soviet system had instead become one of the most conservative regimes of the twentieth century. Certainly the 1917 Revolution brought with it radical change. But after Stalin's introduction of collectivization and central planning, the Soviet Union's system became one of the most conservative regimes in modern history. In effect, it claimed to be exactly the opposite of what it really was, and it often managed to mask its problems as strengths or even successes of its system. Radicals outside the Soviet Union as well as some inside convinced themselves that this was the case. It was a bit like the speculative tulip craze of the early seventeenth century. There were doubtless skeptics, but in the frenzy of the time, it seemed as if the price of tulip bulbs could only increase. In the same way, there were many, not only within the Soviet Union, but also outside it, who convinced themselves of the superiority of the Soviet system. As they saw it, this was the only correct path to socialism. According to that prescription, the dictates of the leader and plan must be accepted by everyone. Those ethnic minorities and dissenters who protest must be repressed. In addition, if the Soviet Union wanted to be the superpower that many thought it should be, it followed that 15 percent or more of the GNP would have to be allocated for military expenditures, and that additional large sums would have to be diverted for use in Eastern Europe and the Third World.

When this approach proved increasingly inappropriate in an age of advanced technology and increasing consumer demands, Soviet leaders also began to search for a new approach within the communist system. At the same time those who had been repressed began to demand compensation for past wrongs. This of course complicated any effort to redress those mistakes, particularly since many of the demands were presented at once. In Eastern Europe where the same reevaluation began, those demands included the imprisonment and even execution of the onetime dictators and their clique. It was Mikhail Gorbachev's fate to question the past and attempt to undo seventy years of such abuse. No wonder his path has been so difficult.

III

Before we look more closely at the various options a reformer might choose, it is necessary to spell out in more detail the political and economic legacy of the cult of personality. If Gorbachev had done the same thing, he might now have a better understanding not only of the reason for some of the problems he has had to contend with, but also of some of the remedies that were open to him.

Lenin was the first to move to silence critics. For a time, differences were tolerated among the Bolsheviks, but other parties were silenced. It was under Stalin, however, that virtually all disagreement within the party became a challenge to Stalin and ultimately a crime. This fostered the myth that only Uncle Joe or Nikita or Leonid knew best. Admittedly, too many leaders with too many opinions can result in endless talk and limited action; but some procedure for debate and some allowance for dissent and disagreement is more likely to avoid serious mistakes than conformity and intimidation. Suppression of debate and dissent is also likely to mean that the path of leadership will be very narrow and restricted. Until Gorbachev, the only route to leadership was through authorized party channels. Gorbachev opened the door to differing points of view. By 1990, alternate leaders had begun to emerge from non-party and even anti-party local movements. Yet it is striking that no one of any substance was willing or available to challenge Gorbachev when he ran for the new post of chairman of the Supreme Soviet of the Soviet Union (incorrectly referred to as the president of the Soviet Union) in May 1989, or for general secretary of the Communist Party of the Soviet Union a year later, in July 1990.

The consequences of suppressing ethnic and national yearnings for all those years have been much less subtle. Admittedly there are anti-social aspects of the nationalist movement that should be controlled, but the heavy hand used to intimidate any meaningful expression of differing cultures and aspirations was bound someday to entail a heavy cost. That cost would occur two ways. The affected population would become alienated and therefore sooner or later more susceptible to radical or even violent alternatives, and the Russian leadership, including Gorbachev, would find itself at a loss as to how to deal with such matters. It had no opportunity to see others deal with such problems, because for decades it was taboo even to acknowledge that there might be a similar problem in the Soviet Union. Since there was no such problem, there was no need to study it. This should explain, at least in part, why Gorbachev and his aides as well seem to be so inept in dealing with the Soviet Union's exploding ethnic problems.

The repression of dissent has also entailed a cost, although so far the bills do not appear as high as those arising from the suppression of nationalism. Dissidents, by their nature, seem to be less subject to intimidation, and therefore once released from prison or exile, they are more likely to resume their outspoken habits. Indeed, one of the most praiseworthy aspects of the

Gorbachev era is how quickly, and with what little inhibition, critics have begun to speak out. That is not to say that all restraints disappeared at once. On the contrary, there were still secrets such as the size of the money supply that in other societies would have been treated as open, even essential data. Nor were all the prisons immediately emptied of their political dissidents (although the number shrank impressively in a relatively short period of time), nor were all those seeking to emigrate automatically issued visas (although those allowed to emigrate rose by 1990 to record highs of over 400,000 a year).[8] Also there were some subjects that were still off limits, such as the military and for a time at least, the KGB. But for a while each day seemed to bring with it more boldness and less repression.

That does not necessarily mean that the liberalization process will be able to avoid more extremist recriminations. As open as the decision has been, so far there have been very few voices demanding that those responsible for some of the more blatant excesses of the past be called to account. The Soviet Union has thus far had no kangaroo court trials like those held in Romania for Nikolae Ceausescu. Nor have leaders like Vladimir Shcherbitski, until 1989 the longtime head of the Communist Party in the Ukraine, been called to account to explain their mismanagement and use of police brutality, as happened to Erich Honecker in East Germany and Todor Zhivkov in Bulgaria. That day may still come in the Soviet Union, and with it, public calls for revenge and punishment.

IV

It was the economy, however, that seems to have been most seriously deranged by the excesses of the cult of personality. There is bound to be trouble when an individual or a small group of individuals preempts for itself monopolistic authority over the entire economy. Deluded by the scope of their authority, they begin to have trouble differentiating between what would have happened anyway and what is the specific consequence of their unique insight and talents. As long as they are in power, everything good is presented as the result of the latter, that is, their specific efforts. Economic planning in the communist world offers case after case where the central planners established planning targets that could only be achieved at enormous human cost and sacrifice. The Stalinist model leads to overinvestment in heavy industry and underinvestment in consumer goods and light industry. Since communist leaders and planners are freed of having to stand for elections or to read a free press, they lack an effective feedback mechanism.

Heavy industry and machine tools are regarded as the hallmark of economic modernization in a communist state, so significant increases in output in the heavy industrial sphere have been the key to managerial premiums and achievement. Given the pressure, most managers report statistical successes even when there are few in fact. But there were some built-in statistical pitfalls that should have reduced the meaningfulness of even the most scrupulous statistical analysis.[9] For example, because of a statistical quirk called the Gerschenkron effect, attempts to measure change in GNP over a prolonged period of time result in a much higher rate of growth if price weights of the beginning year are used, in contrast to a calculation which uses price weights of the most recent year.[10]

Given everything else that has happened in the Gorbachev years, perhaps it was inevitable that sooner or later some Soviet scholars would begin to call into question their official statistical reports. This too is a reaction to the puffery and pressure of the earlier era. Yet recently there has been a tendency to bend over backwards to criticize. In fact, some estimates of the extent of the overreporting are a bit unsettling to most American Sovietologists, including those in the CIA, who in recent years have become more accepting of Soviet statistical reports—at least the industrial output reports. For example, Victor Belkin of the Soviet Academy of Sciences calculates that the Soviet GNP is in fact no more than 28 percent of the U.S. GNP, and perhaps as low as 14 percent.[11] That contrasts with the CIA estimate, which puts Soviet GNP at about 50 percent of the

American counterpart. If Belkin is correct, it would mean the Soviet GNP is not much more than India's.

Since little of the statistical underpinning that went into such computations has been published, it is difficult to judge how valid such sensational findings are. Some careful American economists like Abram Bergson are highly skeptical of what he calls the "back of the envelope" efforts by Belkin and Gregory Khanin, another outspoken critic. All agree, however, that Soviet statistics are in serious need of repair. The absence of certain data which in the past we attributed to secrecy may be as much a function of incompetence. Accurate data, for instance, about the rate of inflation may simply not exist. In other instances Belkin relates how some economic decisions have no basis in reality. For example, he describes how after careful and lengthy calculations after World War II to determine what the rate of exchange should be between the dollar and the ruble, Stalin felt that the figures suggested to him by specialists were an insult to the Soviet economy. Therefore, he arbitrarily set the rate of exchange at 4 rubles to the dollar, when in fact the ruble was much weaker and probably should have been set closer to 10 rubles to the dollar.[12]

Whatever the statistical niceties, all partners to the debate now agree that the Soviet economy is in serious trouble. The faulty judgments of the past are taking their toll all at once. The public has expressed enormous discontent with the consumer goods and services both as to quality and quantity. Even the official Soviet statistical agency recorded that Soviet GNP fell in 1990 by 2 percent. That was the first drop since World War II, and the 2 percent decline does not reflect the impact of inflation. If it did, the drop in GNP would probably come closer to 8–10 percent. Initial reports in 1991 indicated that GNP was down by 14 percent or more. It is not only that fewer goods are being produced. Those goods that are produced somehow or other quickly find their way out of the official state channel distribution system into the black market. There is a sense not only of decline but of disintegration.

V

Whenever a Sovietologist makes a critical analysis of Soviet economic performance, he or she is immediately asked to explain why it is that, if the Soviet economy is so inept, it nonetheless has produced such a great military threat. How can its scientific breakthroughs be explained if the economy is in such chaos and disrepair?

Admittedly the Soviets have made some impressive technical and military achievements, but on closer examination it usually turns out that such accomplishments are long on theory and short on technical sophistication. The Soviets, for example, have had a difficult time mastering miniaturization. They have also had trouble in fields which require sophisticated and large supplies of laboratory equipment. When the Soviets do well in science, it is mostly in the theoretical area or blackboard analysis where the absence of equipment is not a constraint.

But lest we become beguiled by Soviet failures, we should remember that in fact in some areas the Soviets have made important scientific and engineering breakthroughs.[13] Since the Soviet Union devotes a large percentage of its GNP to education and research, it should be able to make scientific advances. Perhaps the best way to explain what seems to be the schizophrenic capability of the Soviet Union's economic system is to compare it to the dual economy frequently found in Third World countries. While the backward sector relies on barter, labor-intensive inputs, and primitive technology, an advanced sector that is integrated into the economy of the outside developed world has sophisticated technologies, skilled labor, and access to convertible currencies. Those laboratories that do have such privileges often do very well. But the norm is far less impressive. Perhaps nothing symbolizes this dual nature better than the portals to the entrance of the Soviet Academy of Sciences at 14 Leninsky Prospect in Moscow. Like the Tower of Pisa—they slant. They are not perpendicular to the ground. Yet at the address work some of the country's best scientists, presumably bred on precision.

If the Soviet system has been so beset by all these inadequacies for years, why hasn't it fallen apart sooner? In the early Stalin period, it was brute force and fear that kept it going. For instance, Stalin introduced regulations that decreed that those who arrived late or were absent from work were subject to arrest. But the threat of force was not always necessary. During World War II the workers were motivated by a true sense of patriotism and sacrifice. Moreover, the country is rich in fertile soil and natural resources. Hitler wanted to conquer the Soviet Union for its oil, and we have noted its potential as the onetime breadbasket of Europe.

It could be argued, however, that the very richness of its resources has also been its curse. Because it was such a large country with a relatively light population density, and was so rich in natural resources, it was always assumed that there would be new deposits over the horizon whenever the existing deposits were depleted. As a consequence, Soviet authorities, like their pre-revolutionary predecessors, never attached much value to raw materials. The prices of raw materials, including oil, were set at what most economists agree have been misleadingly low levels. Because they were so cheap—absolutely as well as relatively to other inputs—Soviet factory managers tended to use these raw materials carelessly, without much concern for waste. This wasteful usage had nothing to do with Marxist value theory. As a matter of fact, what would the communist value system have been if Lenin, instead of disembarking in Petrograd from his sealed train from Switzerland, had gone on to Tokyo to make his revolution there? It is unlikely that a "Japanese Soviet Socialist Republic" with its paucity of raw materials would have priced those raw materials as cheaply as they were priced in the Soviet Union.

Given its abundant resources, the Soviet Union was able to mask its basic structural shortcomings. Through the 1970s and early 1980s, the Soviet Union generated over $170 billion from the export of its petroleum.[14] Unfortunately, today no one seems to know where most of that money went. (It brings to mind the U.S. savings and loan fiasco.) Some of the Soviet oil money went for the purchase of imported machinery and some for the expansion of the Soviet military industrial complex. But most of the machinery was poorly used, as were the excessive military expenditures, and so this did little to enhance the country's productivity or competitiveness. As a consequence, the country's export windfall was squandered.

Some oil earnings were also used to import food products. Rather than introduce meaningful agricultural reforms, the Soviet Union protected its misconceived collective and state farming network and made up for its agricultural ineptness by importing up to 20 percent of the grain it needed. Some Western economists argued at the time that because Soviet oil was so abundant and cheap, the Soviet Union should be encouraged to import even more grain.[15] But Soviet energy was not cheap either in terms of exploration or replacement. Moreover, with the proper incentives, there was a good chance that much of the waste on Soviet farms could have been eliminated. The peasants have poor incentives and work habits, and central planners in Moscow seldom know in advance what needs to be done in the different regions of the country. Because of this, 30 and sometimes as much as 40 to 50 percent of some crops rot in the field or in the distribution process—this is more or less equivalent to what the Soviets have to import.

Given the Soviet Union's northerly location and inhospitable climate, it may be that there was nothing authorities could have done that would have made possible a larger yield from their harvest. However, there were those who said the same thing about the Chinese agricultural communes under Mao, but decollectivization in the early 1980s made possible a startling increase in yield and delivery. The Chinese even reached the point where they were able to export grain to the Soviet Union.

Although some were aware of what was happening, the extent of the social and moral decline that accompanied the economic stagnation came as a surprise to many. There was some knowledge of the corruption, the serious problem with alcoholism, and the decline in the health system, but the apparent military strength of the Soviet Union along with its accomplishments in space made it appear that the nation was the industrial powerhouse it claimed to be. The Soviet military industrial complex was real and intimidating enough. Some skeptics argued that the Soviet Union would undermine itself economically in any prolonged arms race. Yet to those of us on the outside it looked like the Soviets could continue to sustain expenditures of at least 15 percent or more of their GNP on their military effort. That might cause the Soviets concern but it made us very nervous. By spending that much or more, they had achieved military parity—some say superiority. If unchecked, they had more than enough military equipment to destroy the United States several times over. That was why it was so scary when in November 1983, Yuri Andropov, then the general secretary, ordered Soviet negotiators to walk out of the arms control talks in Geneva, and on November 8 or 9, 1983, the KGB was reported to have issued a flash telegram warning of an impending American first strike.[16] The Soviets would not return to the arms talks, they insisted, until the United States agreed to halt its expenditures on its Strategic Defense Initiative (SDI or "Star Wars") and cease the installation of Pershing II missiles in West Germany. It was an extremely tense period.

The Soviet Union may have been nothing more than a paper power, but it was easy to be misled. The overexpansion of the Soviet military might also explain why some Sovietologists had such difficulty with the notion that the Soviet Union was in a state of crisis.[17] Those who said the Soviet Union was in a crisis were often written off as being anti-Soviet.[18] The debate continued until Mikhail Gorbachev's accession to the post of general secretary, when he himself acknowledged the semi-crisis and later the crisis condition of the Soviet Union.

3

Patch and Procrastination —If It's Broke, Don't Fix It

American Sovietologists were not the only ones who failed to comprehend just how serious the Soviet economic situation was. Many within the Soviet leadership in the 1980s were convinced that a little patchwork here and there would remedy whatever ailed the economy at the time. Both Yuri Andropov in 1982 and Konstantin Chernenko, who succeeded him in February 1984 as general secretary, seemed relatively relaxed about the state of the Soviet economy. Admittedly, neither man was in office for more than a year and a half. Moreover, they might have adopted a more radical approach if they had lived longer; but given the way the Soviet Union chooses its leaders, the odds were high that Brezhnev's immediate successors were not likely to stray far from the traditional approach.

The general secretary has almost always been chosen from among the narrow ranks of those who hold appointments in both the Politburo and the Secretariat of the party. This meant that there were seldom more than three or four candidates to choose from, and in no case was it likely that anyone would be chosen who was not a member of at least one of these groups. In other words, there was virtually no chance for a dark horse. Those who were eligible were almost certain to be well known to those making the selection. Moreover, elevation to the ranks of the Politburo and Secretariat was not an unstructured process. Those eligible first rose through the ranks of the party organization—initially the Komsomol for younger members, and then an apprenticeship served in the local, *oblast,* and ultimately republic bureaucracies. This winnowing process and the close working relationships of those involved provided countless opportunities to observe one another under fire. Those with quirks, sparks of genius, or unpredictable tendencies were almost certainly weeded out early in the game.

It would have been considered heresy if anyone during the Brezhnev era had so much as hinted at the possibility of switching from central planning to a market system. The thought of favoring private property would have been equally disturbing. When Soviet officialdom spoke about the superiority of their communist economic system, there was the sense that they were sincere in their protestations. It helped, of course, that the leadership or the *nomenklatura,* the elite members of the Central Committee and bureaucratic managerial classes, were protected from the day-to-day rigors of life by a network of specially provided provisions, shops, limousines, and dachas. Yet whatever their own privileges, they could correctly point to the inequalities in capitalism as well as the callousness and materialism of life in the West and properly feel their defense of the system was justified and not all that hypocritical. Just like many Russian intellectuals in the nineteenth century, many modern-day Soviet intellectuals along with the ideologically driven bureaucrats sincerely desired to avoid the excesses associated with capitalism. The challenge as they saw it, and as expressed in the official party line, was not to abandon but to perfect the Soviet system.

The Soviet system seemed to bring with it several benefits. It could mobilize effectively the resources of a poor country. Look, its supporters insisted, how the Soviet Union had provided its people with public amenities lacking in richer nations, such as an efficient, attractive subway commuter network without comparison in the West. The Soviet system had transformed a basically illiterate society into one of the world's scientific leaders. It moved in the same way to improve public health conditions.

Yet most Soviet spokesmen even then acknowledged that all was not perfect. What was needed, it was agreed, was to improve productivity as well as life for the consumer. Not surprisingly, that was also the focus of most reformers. Some thought they could find a remedy simply by reorganizing the administrative system. Such an approach had provided some temporary help in the past.

For example, when Nikita Khrushchev created a system of *sovnarkhozy* or regional economic councils in 1957, economic life did seem to improve. The advantage of the *sovnarkhozy* was that they allowed economically related enterprises in a locality to deal directly with one another rather than having to go through a central ministry first. Under the traditional ministry system, which Khrushchev sought to displace, decisions within an industry were organized and implemented vertically. Thus, iron ore mines and steel mills did all their business with the Ministry of Steel in Moscow. If they needed coal or machinery, they had to requisition their superiors in Moscow, who would then negotiate with their counterparts in Moscow at the Ministry of Coal and the Ministry of Machine Building. That was the procedure, even though the steel mill might be the next-door neighbor of a coal mine or machine-tool factory. When Khrushchev suddenly made it possible for a steel mill to negotiate directly with its neighbors, it facilitated the production process, and for a time at least, reduced the paper flow to Moscow significantly.

Like most Soviet administrative reforms, however, the initial improvements were not due to any fundamental overhaul of the system, but a result of eliminating abuses and inefficiencies of the old system. Some of these inefficiencies arose from the need to coordinate each move in Moscow, but some were also an inevitable product of the stagnation that takes place when a bureaucrat stays in his job too long.

While Khrushchev's reforms helped for a time, eventually the *sovnarkhoz* reforms began to develop their own shortcomings. Although there are real advantages to horizontal decision making and negotiating, there are also certain decisions that do indeed have to be made in Moscow. Left to themselves, some local authorities, especially those in the smaller republics, began to act as if they were their own bosses. They simply ignored Moscow and ordered cutbacks in shipments to other republics and to Moscow itself. Without pressure to do otherwise, they kept a greater share of their production for themselves.

In addition to the efforts at structural reorganization, occasionally some people sought to refine the incentive system. The proposals associated in the West with the name of Yevsei Liberman, an economist from Kharkov, are a good example. Liberman had been toying with the notion of reducing the Soviet system's incentive emphasis on quantity of production. He, along with several other economists, had been working on new approaches to incentives for some time. His ideas, which had previously been confined safely to obscure academic journals, in September 1962 suddenly began to appear in places like *Pravda.* Liberman did not advocate anything so radical as the abandonment of the planning system or state ownership of the means of production. Even so, his proposal to give state enterprise managers more authority to act on their own was considered a brazen attack on the existing system. Performance would be judged by whether or not the manager made a profit, and the amount of the profit, not by how much he had increased production. Managers would also have to pay a charge for the capital they used. In exchange for bearing those costs, the managers would have more freedom in determining what to produce and how.

It was not a retreat to capitalism because the state retained ownership and control of the means of production. Rather, it was an effort to transplant Western economic decision-making techniques to the Soviet Union. There was no ideological reason why placing a premium on more efficient use of the factors of production, including capital assets, was a technique that could only be used by capitalists. True, such procedures had been attacked periodically by defenders of Soviet morality, but there was nothing in Marxism or Leninism that precluded their use by socialist or communist managers.

Even though they were not ideologically incorrect, Liberman's proposals came to naught. At first there were two or three experiments to see if the concepts would work, but gradually the proposals were watered down. By the time Aleksei Kosygin, who had become prime minister in 1964, agreed to use some of Liberman's ideas to reform Soviet industry, the reforms had become meaningless. Nevertheless, Liberman's proposals were not the last. In the subsequent two decades, there were all manner of proposals; but as before, after some initial enthusiasm, interest quickly waned. Even when the enthusiasm did not dissipate immediately, few of the reforms were implemented. Like its czarist predecessor, the Soviet bureaucracy is well trained at embracing reforms and then quickly eviscerating them, so that after a short time there is little or nothing to show for the effort.

Discouraged by the failure of earlier reform efforts at home, many Soviet economists in the 1980s began to look elsewhere, particularly to Hungary, China, and the German Democratic Republic, for inspiration. Depending on their preferences, there were two differing approaches. Those favoring centralization turned to the German Democratic Republic, while those seeking reduction in government control and less centralization looked to Hungary and China.

Germany has always provoked a love/hate reaction among most Russians. The Russians vividly remember German brutality in World War II. Simultaneously, however, German efficiency, cleanliness, discipline, and managerial rigor are admired and held out as models of what Russians themselves might someday attain. Soviets looked to this efficiency when considering economic reforms. But was East German economic efficiency really all that it was claimed to be? In other words, was it the East German model that made the German Democratic Republic the most advanced and envied member of the Council of Mutual Economic Assistance (CMEA—the economic organization composed of most of the Communist bloc nations), or did the German work ethic and fraternal support from West Germany make it more or less irrelevant what kind of system the East Germans were using?

The East Germans organized a series of vertically organized structures called the *Kombinate*. There were about 130 *Kombinates* at the national level, each with an average of 25,000 employees.[1] The *Kombinate* tended to operate as a monopoly, combining related enterprises all producing components of a specified product. Within that organizational umbrella, there were also included units specializing in foreign trade, services, and research. The top-down nature of the *Kombinate* seemed well suited to the German penchant for order taking and discipline.

Admittedly for years the East Germans received substantial subsidies from their cousins in West Germany, over $1 billion annually. Furthermore, out of deference to the West Germans, the European Common Market allowed East German goods to be sent into West Germany without invoking Common Market trade restraints or tariffs. None of these opportunities was available to other East European countries. Nevertheless, in the mid-1980s, some in the Soviet Union argued strongly that German culture and fraternal help notwithstanding, East Germany's success was due to the *Kombinate* model. As they saw it, the reform that the Soviet Union needed was not horizontal decentralization, but *Kombinate* forms of vertical control.[2] The East German approach became particularly attractive when growth in most of the countries of CMEA ceased but the East Germans continued to report economic gains.

But once the Berlin Wall was breached and unification became a reality, except for a few pockets of success, the East German economy as a whole seemed to disintegrate. It may have been the bright shining star of the Communist bloc, but once exposed to the fresh air and strains of the competitive capitalist world, it collapsed. As Soviet reformers contemplated the prospects for their own economic transition, the East German debacle must have added to their confusion.

Those worried that the Soviet Union would be unable to replicate either the East German discipline or organizational skills began to look elsewhere for a model. They were joined by others who had come to distrust overcentralized control. For that reason they looked to Hungary and China, both of which at various periods in the 1970s and 1980s seemed to have made important economic breakthroughs.

The Hungarians began their effort in 1968 with the New Economic Mechanism (NEM), which was designed to curb the role of the central planning authorities. Simultaneously an effort was made to expand pricing flexibility over what was expected to be a growing selection of goods. This, it was assumed, would allow enterprises to respond more rapidly and appropriately to changes in economic circumstances. In agriculture, Hungarian peasants were allowed to form cooperatives where they were also given more decision-making power over what to produce and how to share the proceeds. While a number of these reforms led to a general improvement in production, which some called the "golden age" of economic life in Hungary, the changes were not significant enough to offset the impact of rising prices due to the OPEC 1973 oil embargo. Because of agreements with the Soviet Union, Hungary was protected somewhat from any major disruption or price hikes on oil shipments; but to the extent that it imported manufactured products from outside the Socialist bloc, Hungary found it had to pay higher prices for its purchases. In addition, Hungary like other former centrally planned economies has not been able to break up the monopolies created by its state enterprises and generate internal price competitiveness. This imported inflation and the absence of domestic competition precipitated serious economic dislocation within the country and ultimately provoked calls for more government interference to protect the ordinary consumer. Eventually anti-reformers in Hungary gained ascendency, and from 1972 to 1979 the conservatives reclaimed their power and brought the reform process to a temporary halt. Since 1979, Hungary's economy has been subjected to a series of reform starts and stops.

Despite its homogeneity and relatively small size, Hungary has still been unable to revitalize its economy or establish a viable and competitive economic entity comparable to countries such as Finland and Austria that most resemble it. While the quality of Hungarian life and the stocks of consumer goods in the warehouses make it appear that the Hungarian standard of living is considerably more attractive than it is in the Soviet Union, by any objective standards, Hungarian economic reform is not a success story, and the adoption of the Hungarian model is hardly likely to bring a solution to the Soviet Union's economic problems.

In retrospect, Soviet reformers should have looked more to the economic reforms going on in China. Of all the countries that have attempted to work their way out from the morass of the Stalinist-type economic model, China has made the greatest progress and achieved the greatest economic growth. With economic growth close to 9 or 10 percent a year, almost equal to the record set by its East Asian neighbors, China's growth was real, not a statistical sleight of hand. There were measurable and objective improvements in the standard of living of most peasants. The monopoly of the state in agriculture, commerce, and industry was broken. Change in the countryside was particularly impressive. By 1989, agricultural products made up less than 50 percent of the output emanating from the countryside, and most of the remainder was produced by a variety of rural industries. Equally impressive, by early 1989, the state sector's share of industrial output accounted for only 59 percent of the total (a sharp drop from 81 percent in 1979 before the reforms began) and 100 million people (or almost one tenth of the entire population) were working outside of and competing with government industrial and service enterprises.[3]

If anything, the growth was too rapid and too far-reaching. The acceleration brought with it dislocations. It was very difficult to manage growth at 9–10 percent a year and still avoid inflation and social upheaval. In some counties near Canton or Guangzhou, industrial production rose nearly 40 percent a year. The change from year to year was staggering. Such rapid growth sooner or later was bound to provoke a violent reaction.

Another difficulty was that not all groups in China benefited equally. Initially there were little or no salary increases for the party cadre or officials in the cities, intellectuals, the military, and some workers in state factories. These groups continued to function much as they had before Deng Xiaoping. Unlike the workers in new industrial enterprises and agricultural activities, there was no measurable increase in their productivity. As a consequence, the incomes of these traditional groups remained relatively constant, which meant that they suffered as prices began to rise. With time they began to feel that they were losing social status as the newly rich were able to use their money to upgrade their housing and material comforts, aspects of life that prior to Deng Xiaoping's reforms tended to favor the bureaucrats. The white-collar groups were particularly upset with the rise in wealth of the private businessmen and traders, whose acquisition of consumer goods and services became increasingly apparent with the emergence of dance halls and restaurants designed to cater to their taste.

The newly created disparities would ultimately give rise to considerable tension. Strikes among Chinese urban industrial workers began to occur in increasing numbers. There was also a growing feeling that many of the moral values of the early years of the revolution had been displaced by materialism. This source of moral degeneration was intensified by reports of extortion and payoffs among leading officials and their children.

The protests in Tiananmen Square were not initially or primarily economic in nature. Although the students called for political reform, pluralism, and the right to express dissenting points of view, using as a benchmark the far-reaching political reforms inaugurated by Gorbachev in the Soviet Union, they called even more loudly for the end of corruption and economic favoritism exercised by the country's leaders and their children. However, after the first few days, the students found their ranks enhanced by the addition of workers complaining not only about corruption but about inflation and their deteriorating economic status. The prospect that the workers would link up with and fall under the influence of the protesting students terrified Deng Xiaoping and the other elders of the revolution. That fear as much as anything led them on May 20 to impose martial law.

By 1989, large numbers of pilgrims from the Soviet Union had made their way to China to see what they could learn from the Chinese economic reforms. Upon their return, they filled the Soviet press with praise for what they found. Proposals were made to copy many of the Chinese economic reforms. And some, such as joint ventures and special economic zones, were actually adopted. However, none of them seem to have had the impact they did in China. In part that was because the bureaucracy was even more entrenched and resistant in the Soviet Union than in China, but in part the Chinese also seem more diligent. As the Soviet economist Nikolai Shmelev put it during a discussion in September 1988, "The Chinese work hard. The Russians talk hard."

It may also have something to do with pride of place. As the leader of the Socialist bloc, most Soviet officials did not like the idea of copying the Chinese. In addition, there were probably residual doubts about the suitability of the Chinese approach for the Soviet Union. Until about mid-1986, the Chinese reforms were bitterly attacked in the Soviet Union.[4] The order had come to criticize the Chinese reforms, and Soviet journalists at that time did as they were told. Some reforms may have warranted criticism; but the Soviet press attacked everything, even the very impressive growth that was taking place in the Chinese countryside.

Gradually Soviet authorities came to realize they had made a serious mistake. When I visited Moscow in January 1986, several Soviet Sinologists told me that they had been ordered to go back to China and take a second look. Soon thereafter, the Soviet view of the Chinese reforms became much more positive.[5] But valuable time had been lost. What was unique about the Chinese reforms was that they began in the countryside and took place at the start of the reform process. In fact, allowing the peasants more control over the land and their daily work activities defined the reform. Quick success in the early days enhanced the credibility of Chinese leaders and made it easier for them to move forward with their reforms.

Because Gorbachev failed to begin his reforms in the countryside, he was unable in the early days of reform efforts to gain the credibility that probably would have come if there had been an initial period of economic renewal and transformation comparable to what occurred in China. Of course it may well have been that even if he had begun in the countryside, the Soviet peasants would not have responded as enthusiastically as their Chinese counterparts. When Gorbachev began to encourage Soviet peasants to set up their own farms in 1989, there were disappointingly few takers. Yet there is reason to believe that if, like Deng Xiaoping, Gorbachev had begun in the countryside, he would have found more takers. For example, when the German armies invaded the Ukraine in 1941 and announced that they had come to liberate the peasants from the Bolsheviks, the peasants immediately reclaimed their old lands. They did the same thing in 1930 when Stalin announced what turned out to be a temporary suspension of the collectivization process.[6]

The violent halt to many of the Chinese reform efforts on June 4, 1989, must certainly have given reformers in the Soviet Union considerable pause, particularly because many of the Chinese demonstrators looked to Gorbachev as their inspiration, at least in the realm of political reforms. Those in the Soviet Union opposed to the Chinese reforms undoubtedly felt vindicated by the crackdown in Tiananmen Square. Yet opponents of the East German approach must have felt equally satisfied after the breaching of the Berlin Wall and the collapse of the East German economy. Unfortunately, the division inside the Soviet Union as to which economic approach to take has been a major impediment to any clear break with the past. This division is another reason why Soviet leaders have tended to temporize and patch rather than attempt fundamental restructuring.

Given so many constraints, it was all but ordained that

Brezhnev's immediate successors would not veer too far from the existing system. There were a few who warned that the Soviet Union was in need of something more than minor repair.[7] After all, by late 1982 there was already clear evidence (except as we saw within the Soviet Union itself) that the radical economic reforms in the Chinese countryside were producing impressive economic results and that something comparable in the Soviet Union might be especially effective.

Yet, while almost everyone in the Soviet senior leadership knew about the increasing seriousness of the economic situation, they did not know what to do about it. Not only had agricultural output been declining for several years running, but economic growth and production in several of the country's most important industries had begun to fall. Thus the harvest, which was reported to be 237 million tons in 1978, had fallen to 158 million tons in 1981. It improved somewhat to 187 million tons in 1982, but that was still a disappointment. In the same way, steel production, which hit a peak of 151 million tons in 1978, fell to 147 million tons in 1982. There had always been fluctuations in the harvest (although the drop in 1981 was an extreme one), but except for World War II there had almost never been a decline in steel production.

In addition to the economic decline, there was also widespread embarrassment over the corruption that had become so endemic that it reached into Brezhnev's family itself. It was well known, for example, that his son-in-law, Yuri Churbanov, the deputy minister of the interior, was taking bribes from a mafia-like operation in Uzbekistan and that his wife, Brezhnev's daughter, was running around with a circus clown who also was a diamond smuggler. Most of all there was shame over Brezhnev himself. It was impossible to have hidden the fact that he was seriously ill. He seemed to have suffered a heart attack in 1974 and perhaps a stroke in early 1982, which left him with a pacemaker and the need for daily medication.[8] His slurred speech and unsteady walk appeared to confirm the rumors that he had been declared brain dead several years before he actually died in November 1982. As Arkady N. Shevchenko put it,

"During his last years in power, he was a feeble invalid, able to work only a few hours a week, kept alive by sophisticated drugs and modern medical techniques."[9]

Yuri Andropov's selection as general secretary in November 1982 produced a sigh of relief and great expectations from most of the population. I could sense the renewal of enthusiasm during a visit to Moscow in January 1983. A no-nonsense disciplinarian, who as head of the KGB knew how to dig out the rot, he was just the man to take charge. As anticipated, he moved quickly. Within days of his assumption of power, Andropov launched a tough campaign against corruption and alcoholism. Patrols were sent into drinking halls and shops in search of any patrons during working hours who were there without proper authorization. Those caught were reported to their places of employment and their bosses criticized for not exercising closer supervision.

There were also signs that Andropov might be more amenable to making changes. He showed more than the usual concern about the economy, and a few months before he died, he commissioned several studies about the long-run prospects for the Soviet economy.[10]

One of the reports, written by Tatiana Zaslavskaia, a researcher at the Siberian division of the Academy of Sciences, boldly called for radical surgery. Somehow her analysis found its way into *The Washington Post* and became an overnight target of attack by Soviet bureaucrats, who sought to protect their own jobs and to reassure themselves and others that nothing serious was wrong with the Soviet economy.[11]

Andropov also launched an exploratory effort to provide more decision-making powers for enterprise managers. Andropov's proposals effective as of July 26, 1983, however, fell far short of the earlier Liberman reforms. While Andropov was certainly not content with the status quo, most of his solutions went no further than the old patchwork approach to the Soviet economy. It is doubtful that Andropov had in mind anything far-reaching. Conceivably if he had lived and stayed in office another decade or so, he might have backed himself into more radical changes, as Gorbachev would later do.

But while Andropov was Gorbachev's mentor, there were some crucial distinctions between the two men which made it unlikely that Andropov would have followed the Gorbachev route. However flexible about economic reform Andropov might ultimately have proven to be, he was very rigid about political matters, both internal and external. According to a onetime major general in the KGB, "Andropov was a controversial figure. Indeed with his arrival at the KGB, the struggle against political dissent was stepped up and kept increasing. The system of political detection escalated under Andropov's chairmanship of the KGB."[12] Under the circumstances, that suggests that Andropov would probably have been much less receptive to political reform. Yet to be effective, far-reaching economic reform must ultimately be accompanied by political reform. Admittedly, there is a danger that the political reforms may come too fast and lead to anarchy, but a refusal to relax politically is an equally serious threat to the overall success of any reform effort.

Gorbachev did not immediately throw open the prison doors to political prisoners or increase the quota for emigration the day after he became general secretary, but he did not clamp down on human rights as Andropov had done. Moreover, within less than two years Gorbachev's policies on these issues became distinctly more responsive. Beginning in late 1986, for example, Gorbachev began to release all but a relatively small number of political prisoners imprisoned while Andropov was the head of the KGB. Their policies toward emigration also differed. Andropov cut the number of Jews allowed to emigrate to 1,314 in 1983, the lowest it had been since 1970. In contrast, while keeping the numbers down in 1985 and 1986, Gorbachev began to relax controls in 1987 so that by 1990 alone almost 200,000 Jews were allowed to leave. The contrast between Andropov's and Gorbachev's treatment of dissent was even more dramatic. As the head of the KGB, Andropov led the charge on dissidents and groups like Helsinki Watch. The press was purged and critical articles all but disappeared.

Andropov was equally hard-line on the issue of international affairs. When the Soviet Air Force downed the Korean Airlines Flight 007 on September 1, 1983, with a loss of 269 lives, Andropov called the Boeing 747 a spy plane and blamed the United States for the tragedy. Eventually the Soviet Union reorganized its defense procedures in the Far East, but Andropov was unyielding in his unwillingness to acknowledge Soviet responsibility. He was equally uncompromising in his attitude toward arms talks with the United States, refusing to acknowledge that the Soviet Union had gone beyond parity to superiority in its installation of missiles in Eastern Europe. By 1987, the Soviet Union under Gorbachev would come to acknowledge that its forces were larger than those of its American counterpart. Following that logic, the Soviet Union subsequently agreed to reduce its European missile strength by a larger amount than the United States. Against the opposition of some members of the Soviet general staff, it would later make the same concession about conventional weaponry. At the time, however, Andropov conceded no such thing. Instead, he threatened dire consequences if the United States, under Ronald Reagan, did anything to redress that disadvantage. Andropov warned that the Soviet Union would walk out of the U.S.-Soviet arms talks in Geneva unless Reagan halted the shipment of Pershing II missiles to West Germany and curbed future expenditures on the program for the Strategic Defense Initiative. Reagan refused to do either. In response, on November 23, 1983, Andropov honored his threat and ordered his negotiators to leave Geneva until such time as Reagan complied with the Soviet demand.

It is important to remind ourselves that such attitudes persisted into the post-Brezhnev era. In the euphoria which swept the world after Gorbachev's accession to power and eventually led to his receipt of the Nobel Prize, there were some who insisted that the reform process that began under Gorbachev would have taken place with or without a Gorbachev in charge. In the political sphere, at least, Andropov's behavior suggests that Gorbachev's actions were instead a discontinuity, not an evolving process, and that if he had lived, Andropov might have adhered to very different domestic and international policies from Gorbachev's. Would the result have been any different if someone other than Andropov had been selected? It is difficult to say, especially since almost no one at the time predicted that Gorbachev would do what he ultimately did. The other choices were even less promising. Chernenko, for example, was already known to be seriously ill before he was selected to succeed Andropov. Thus there was never much chance that he would do anything substantial in the way of reform. Admittedly the decision to return to the Geneva arms talks with the United States in January 1985 was made shortly before Chernenko died in February 1985. We don't know precisely who made that decision. We do know, however, that when Chernenko was no longer able to attend Politburo sessions, Gorbachev presided in his place. It is logical to assume therefore that Gorbachev had a major role in the decision to resume the negotiations, even though at that point President Reagan had not backed down from his Pershing II and SDI program.

As for the other members of the Politburo, it is hard to find any who might pass as reformers. The average age of the ten succeeding members was sixty-seven, with one half over seventy years old. The younger ones, that is those in their sixties, such as Geydar Aliyev, Grigori Romanov, or Vladimir Shcherbitski, were corrupt, alcoholic, or tyrannical. Gorbachev, at age fifty-four, and Vitali Vorotnikov, at fifty-nine, were the youngest members, but Vorotnikov had been a Politburo member for less than a year and a half. Others, such as Viktor Grishin, a corrupt leader of Moscow, and hardly a person likely to pursue a reform policy, contended for the post of general secretary, but lost after Andrei Gromyko swung his support to Gorbachev.

It is hard to see, therefore, that there would have been much of a reform program if Gorbachev had not been selected. Other members of the leadership group were probably even less prepared temperamentally than Gorbachev. For that matter there was little to indicate that Gorbachev himself had any interest in, much less a passion for, reform. And as we have come to see, even Gorbachev's patience has its limits. But whatever Gorbachev's ultimate commitment to the market and democracy, his fellow members of the Politburo at the time were even less predisposed to deal with the resistance of the bureaucracy and the general public and to make changes of any sort, much less introduce substantive reforms. For that matter, any changes that might have broken the implicit social contract between the state and the general population would have been considered provocative. Although there was no formal document spelling out the rights and obligations, beginning in the late 1920s the Soviet public had gradually come to accept the idea that in exchange for full employment and little or no inflation, they would put up with a shortage of consumer goods and an overzealous police state. Anyone threatening that order had better be not only ambitious and self-confident but willing to risk the viability of the contract itself. At the time there were few if any hints that Gorbachev would be significantly different from his predecessors. What was there in Gorbachev's background that led him to undertake such risks and in effect to break the contract he had been so carefully trained to uphold?

4

Mikhail Sergeevich Gorbachev Goes to Moscow: A Learner's Progress

It is a long way from the tiny village of Privolnoe to Moscow. In terms of distance, the Stavropol *oblast* in which Privolnoe is located is slightly less than 900 miles away, but as a ladder to power it seems even further, and a most unlikely first rung. Privolnoe is a backwater but rich black earth farming area of about 3,000 peasants, some 100 miles northwest of Stavropol. Simply to visit Moscow, much less aspire to rise to the head of the Communist Party or the presidency of the Soviet Union, would be considered overreaching; but Mikhail Gorbachev did just that.

However unlikely this region may appear as a breeding ground for Soviet leaders, it turns out that several were born or did most of their early party work in the immediate vicinity. Yuri Andropov, for example, was born a few kilometers away; Mikhail Suslov, a longtime member of the Politburo and ideological hard-liner, was assigned to party work in the provincial capital in the late 1930s; and Fyodor Kulakov, who headed the Stavropol party *krai* (regional) organization, went off to Moscow in 1964 and ultimately to membership in the Politburo.[1] Because so many other leaders preceded him from this particular region, Gorbachev undoubtedly received help in his rise to the top. But whether Gorbachev had help or not, before anyone could climb out of the Privolnoe backwater, he or she had to show considerable initiative and leadership. Mikhail Gorbachev did just that. He managed to lift himself out of a provincial area that even lacked its own high school. He went on from this agricultural region to become the leader of what at the time was viewed as the number-two industrial and maybe number-one military power in the world.[2]

Gorbachev's progress is a testimony to how mobile the Soviet Union occasionally can be, and to his natural talents and hard work as well as his luck. According to those who have studied his childhood and visited his birthplace, there was little to suggest in his formative years that Gorbachev was destined to have such an impact on his country and the world.[3] Although the region from which he came had been a refuge for free farmers seeking to escape the peasant serfdom, which in Russia prevailed until 1861, there is nothing to suggest that Gorbachev's forbears were particularly innovative or nonconformist. In fact, one of Gorbachev's grandfathers agreed to become the chairman of one of the first collective farms in the region. That was probably before Mikhail Sergeevich Gorbachev was born on March 2, 1931.[4] Shortly thereafter, in 1933, Gorbachev's other grandfather was arrested for "failing to fulfill the sowing plans."[5] With the husband sent off to Irkutsk, half of the family died of starvation. Given the massive bloodletting that marked those years of collectivization and famine, before too long the grandfather who headed the collective farm was also sent to prison. He was interrogated for fourteen months and his family was ostracized for having housed "an enemy of the people."[6] Not having heard from him, the family thought at the time that he had been executed.[7] While this experience was by no means unique, there is no doubt that it affected Gorbachev very deeply. He would later refer to it when he explained why he had decided to embark on a program of political and economic liberalization. (It should be noted, however, that despite such traumatic associations, Gorbachev has continued to support the collectivization of agriculture.)

Too young to go to war, Gorbachev remained on the farm,

including the five-month period when the region was occupied by the Germans. When it came time to go to high school, he had to walk ten miles or so a day to the regional center at Krasnogvardeiskoe.[8] During the summer, Gorbachev began to work as a temporary employee at the local machine tractor station.[9] It was a wartime requirement that all young people work on some farm in the area, a practice that continued into the postwar period. After graduation in 1949, Gorbachev worked for a year as an assistant combine operator.[10] Ultimately the job on the farm provided Gorbachev with a very important opportunity. Working very hard, Gorbachev's farm combine group managed to bring in an exceptionally large harvest during the summer of 1949. As a reward, he was presented the Order of the Red Banner of Labor, an unusual achievement for one so young.[11] At the same time, Gorbachev managed to do very well in school. In a regional academic competition, he won second place and was awarded a silver medal for academic achievement.

These accomplishments, plus the fact that in 1950 he apparently also applied for membership in the Communist Party, undoubtedly helped draw attention to Gorbachev when he applied for admission to the Moscow State University (MGU). It was as if an all-state football captain, a farmboy from a small town in Idaho, was also the number-two ranking scholar in the state. If he applied to Harvard, the odds are that he would have been admitted, especially if Harvard, like MGU in 1950, had just been ordered to increase the number of rural farmboys admitted as first-year students.*

What made Gorbachev even more unique was his decision to study law. The law profession in the Soviet Union has never been a prestigious one. In 1950, at the height of the Stalinist era, neither public prosecutors *(prokurators)* nor public defenders were well regarded. Law was also an unusual profession for a small-town farmboy. But it was one of the few courses at the university where a student could be trained in public speaking

---

*Having taught at MGU, I can testify that orders or not, students from the agricultural provinces were usually few in number.

and the writing of laws. Some suggest that Gorbachev originally wanted to be a physicist (that is where the out-of-towners usually excelled) until he failed to pass the qualifying examination.

A lawyer's training, however, was ultimately very useful for Gorbachev. Upon his graduation from MGU in 1955, he was offered entrance into graduate school or a position in law in Moscow. Instead, he returned home briefly as an investigator in the local prosecutor's office. Because he had been active in the party before he went to Moscow and involved himself with party affairs while at the university, it seemed only natural that before long Gorbachev would be assigned to do organizational work for the Komsomol (the Communist Youth organization) in Stavropol.[12] Within a year of his return to Stavropol, Raisa, the woman he had met and married while at the university in Moscow, gave birth to their daughter Irina. Raisa, who had won the gold medal in academic competition in her local province a year after Gorbachev's less prestiguous silver medal, would become an important influence on Gorbachev, and her advice significantly contributed to his rise.

It was almost inevitable that Gorbachev would rise rapidly through the ranks. After all, he was a rare bureaucrat—a local boy who was willing to start at the bottom, unafraid of hard work, who was also a graduate of the best university in the country. It was like a graduate of the Harvard Business School returning to his hometown to work as a teller in the local bank. He was quickly taken under the wing of a string of local leaders who would bring Gorbachev along with them. Two of the most important officials in the Stavropol area were Vsevolod Murakhovsky and Fyodor Kulakov. Murakhovsky was the first secretary (the chairman) of the Stavropol Komsomol in 1955 and the man who hired Gorbachev to work in the Komsomol. Murakhovsky pulled Gorbachev after him as he moved up the party hierarchy. In 1956, for example, he recommended Gorbachev as his successor for secretary of the Stavropol City Komsomol.[13] Within five years Gorbachev would become the head of the Komsomol in the whole Stavropol region.[14] By 1970, he had leapfrogged over Murakhovsky and in a turnabout suggested Murakhovsky as his own replacement. Ultimately, in November 1985, after he had become general secretary, Gorbachev brought Murakhovsky to Moscow and made him a deputy first minister in the Ministry of Agriculture and thereafter head of the new superministry dealing with agriculture, Gosagroprom. That proved to be a mistake. Because they had been so close, Gorbachev found it difficult to criticize his old friend and onetime mentor. But Gosagroprom needed criticism. The agricultural bureaucracy was particularly resistant to far-reaching reform and proved to be a major roadblock to the whole reform process.

Kulakov played an even more important role in Gorbachev's career. In 1960, Kulakov became the first secretary of the Communist Party in the Stavropol *krai.* [15] To be sent down to the countryside must have been a big disappointment for one who had been a minister of grain procurement in the Russian Republic stationed in Moscow. The transfer was not a reflection of Kulakov's abilities so much as a byproduct of Khrushchev's decision to close down a number of the ministries in Moscow and send the bureaucrats to the provinces so they could associate on site with the people they had been ordering around for so many years. Since the Stavropol area is one of the country's most important grain-producing regions, Kulakov's assignment, at least from Khrushchev's point of view, was a logical move.

Having Kulakov as a mentor brought important advantages to Gorbachev. Kulakov was an intelligent and able official, who retained influential contacts in Moscow. For example, he arranged for Gorbachev's election as a delegate to the 22nd Communist Party Congress in 1961. [16] The following year Gorbachev left the Komsomol to do party organizational work in one of the rural regions. This meant leaving the city of Stavropol and moving into the countryside. To do his job well, Gorbachev also decided he would have to learn more about agriculture. For that reason he took a five-year extension course in agriculture at the Stavropol Agricultural Institute. [17]

Through a series of other assignments within the party, Gorbachev continued his rise. After returning to Stavropol, he was promoted to first secretary of the Stravropol City Communist Party, and by 1970 became the first secretary for the whole Stavropol regional party organization.

This appointment meant that Gorbachev had become a senior official in the party. Thus it was not surprising that he would next become a full member of the Central Committee, which he did in 1971. That same year Kulakov was made a full member of the Politburo in Moscow. This did nothing to diminish Gorbachev's influence.[18] Kulakov had been serving as the head of the Agricultural Department in the Central Committee since November 1964 and continued that responsibility once in the Politburo.[19]*

Having completed his degree work in agriculture, Gorbachev decided to try out some of his ideas on a few of the farms under his jurisdiction in Stavropol. In 1971, he set up what later would come to be referred to as the "contract system." Selected groups of farmers agreed to enter into contracts with their collective farms for the delivery of a specified crop.[22] Once they met their contractual obligations, they were entitled to keep what remained for their own use or sale. The results were reportedly very promising. The new system was said to have increased output by as much as 50 percent. For that reason, in 1976 Gorbachev tried to induce all the farms in the Stavropol region to adopt it.

But in a pattern that would later come to typify his approach to the reform process, Gorbachev reversed himself in 1977. Working in conjunction with Kulakov, he proposed instead a system involving a centralized agro-industrial combination.[23] This too turned out to be a success, at least for the first year. It almost seemed that whatever the experiment, even if it was

---

*Kulakov died a mysterious death in July 1978.[20] According to the official report, "his heart stopped beating." Because there were growing signs that Kulakov had become more popular in the party than Brezhnev, and because everyone in the Politburo attended the funeral except for Brezhnev, Aleksei Kosygin, and Mikhail Suslov, the ruling triumvirate, there were rumors that Kulakov's death (it was not a heart attack as such) may not have been the result of natural causes.[21]

just the opposite of what had been tried before, it worked. This may have been the local version of the Hawthorne effect, named after the Hawthorne plant of Western Electric, where it didn't matter which procedures were introduced. The important thing was that someone was watching and cared about what the workers were doing. After he left the Stavropol area, Gorbachev would often switch his agricultural policy back and forth between differing extremes. These actions suggest flexibility and an openness to new ideas or criticisms, but Gorbachev's continuing experimentation and backtracking also indicates a lack of commitment and appreciation for the effect of frequent changes on morale and efficiency.

His experiences in Stavropol helped to shape his work in other ways as well. While serving as first secretary of the Stavropol party organization, he had several opportunities to travel outside the Soviet Union to the West, an experience unavailable to most ordinary Soviet citizens at the time. These trips (often with Raisa) to Belgium, Italy, West Germany, and France undoubtedly made it possible for him to contrast firsthand how much more efficient and productive non-communist political and economic systems could be.[24] It should also have allowed him to see the West firsthand, undistorted by Soviet propaganda. This did not mean that he suddenly developed a more favorable view of capitalism or capitalists. On the contrary, advisers to President Ronald Reagan who were present during the Geneva summit meetings in November 1985 when the two men first met reported that Gorbachev attacked capitalism just as Stalin had done. Yet with time, Gorbachev seemed to mellow. The fact that he was able to see the economic accomplishments of Western Europe with his own eyes may have had a tempering impact on his ideological stance.

More problematic is the effect his party job had on his ability to lead the Soviet Union. While his "hands-on" work in agriculture certainly added to his credibility, he did not have a similar experience in industry. Like many American politicians, he was a lawyer, a government servant, and eventually the chief administrator of a major political subdivision, not necessarily the best experience for undertaking economic reform. Theoretically at least, it might have helped Gorbachev in his understanding of what needed to be done if at some point he had also worked in industry and acquired some managerial responsibility. This lack of experience—he never had to meet a payroll—probably made it more difficult for him to deal with industrial reform.

At the same time it remains uncertain whether or not experience as a Soviet factory manager, especially in a large enterprise, is necessarily the kind of exposure a reformer in the Soviet Union should have. Serving as a Soviet manager in one of the large conglomerates of the Soviet military industrial complex tends to breed an overdependence on the role of the state and the central plan. This dependence was vividly reflected during several meetings Gorbachev held with hundreds of managers from the country's largest factories.[25] These managers were all but unanimous in expressing their dismay at the chaos and spontaneity they were convinced they would have to deal with if the Soviet economy allowed itself to be governed by market forces. It is easy to see why it often seems that Soviet industrial managers have been among the most resistant to any meaningful reform. This perception is reinforced by the fact that the vast preponderance of Soviet managers have been educated as engineers. Their training may help explain why former managers such as the onetime prime minister Nikolai Ryzhkov (who prior to going to Moscow was the director of the Uralmash heavy machinery plant in Sverdlovsk) become permanently scarred by the experience. An engineering perspective imparts the sense that there is usually a solution to every problem and that satisfying Soviet consumers is merely a matter of increasing production. This leaves them with little understanding, if not outright contempt, for market forces. They seem unable to entertain the notion that perhaps the market-oriented system, which involves raising and lowering market-prices, might solve the economic problems more effectively than edicts from the center. Against this backdrop, perhaps Gorbachev's lack of industrial experience was not such a shortcoming after all.

It may well be that there is no good preparation available

within the Soviet Union for someone about to attempt a market reform. Gorbachev has acknowledged that as the chief administrator of the Stavropol region, he had the advantage of a rather complete if fragmented view of the country's problems.[26] If nothing else, this at least provided him with an appreciation of just how poorly the economy was functioning. But it did not provide him with the insight or the experience he would ultimately need to remedy these deficiencies and implement market and democratic reforms. For that matter, it is unclear just what if any experience might be available within the Soviet Union for an undertaking of that magnitude and complexity.

It was his agricultural experience, however, that paved his way to Moscow. Kulakov's death meant that Gorbachev lost his most supportive patron in Moscow, but it also meant that Moscow needed someone to replace Kulakov as an agricultural specialist. His death opened the door for Gorbachev and for those who were to become his new mentors, Yuri Andropov and Mikhail Suslov, perhaps the two most influential members of the Politburo and coincidently both alumni of Stavropol.

In addition to being an agricultural center, the Stavropol region was also the regional hub of several of the country's more popular resorts. The local mineral water was thought to be a good cure for chronic diseases such as kidney problems. These resorts, particularly Kislovodsk, were often visited by senior members of the Communist Party, including Andropov and Suslov, both of whom had such ailments.[27] Since it was expected that the local party chief would be on hand to welcome Politburo members, Gorbachev, this *oblast* regional party leader with a university education, had many opportunities to meet Andropov and Suslov. While Gorbachev was not the only candidate for the job as agriculture overseer in the Central Committee in Moscow, his qualifications and his sponsorship combined to make him the choice.

His return to Moscow in November 1978 coincided with the news that the Soviet Union had reaped its largest harvest ever, 237 million tons, a tough record to match. Thereafter, as Table 1 indicates, it was downhill. In no year while Gorbachev was the Central Committee secretary responsible for agriculture did the harvest exceed 192 million tons. In 1981, the harvest dropped to 158 million tons, which except for the disastrous year of 1975 was the poorest harvest since 1962. To ensure that there would be enough grain to feed its people, the Soviet Union made up the difference by increasing grain imports. Soviet purchases, which totaled approximately 15.5 million tons in 1978, rose to an estimated 46 million tons in 1981 and ultimately hit a peak of approximately 56 million tons in 1984. That was a new record, amounting to over 30 percent of the Soviet Union's harvest.

In an earlier era, anyone with such a dismal performance would probably have been banished from a position of leadership. But partly because of the prominence of his patrons, Gorbachev remained in his post. In fact, due to Andropov's patronage, Gorbachev's responsibilities were significantly enhanced. For example, in November 1979, virtually a year after moving to Moscow, Gorbachev was made a candidate member of the Politburo, and the next year he was elevated to full membership. It was as if one's performance were no criterion for promotion.

In fairness to Gorbachev, it should be pointed out that he was not the only one responsible for the sad state of Soviet agriculture. The minister of agriculture, Valentin K. Mesyats, presumably had day-to-day operational responsibility. Then there was Brezhnev himself, who continued to play a key role in formulating agricultural policy. He took the lead in introducing the much-acclaimed "Food Program" in May 1982 at a Communist Party plenum. The presentation of this cure-all of the Soviet Union's food problems was only notable because there was virtually nothing new about it and because Gorbachev, the party representative presumably responsible for agriculture, said nothing official during the presentation of the program at the plenum. It was not that Gorbachev was bereft of proposals for reform. In December 1978, shortly after assuming his agricultural responsibilities in the Central Committee, he gave a speech proposing an increase in the size of the private garden

TABLE 1

Soviet Grain Harvest, Exports and Imports
(million metric tons)

Year	Harvest	Exports	Imports
1960	126	6.8	.2
1961	131	7.5	.7
1962	140	7.8	—
1963	108	6.3	3.1
1964	152	3.5	7.3
1965	121	4.3	6.4
1966	171	3.6	7.7
1967	148	6.2	2.2
1968	170	5.4	1.6
1969	162	7.2	.6
1970	187	5.7	2.2
1971	181	8.6	3.5
1972	168	4.6	15.5
1973	223	4.9	23.9
1974	196	7.0	7.1
1975	140	3.6	15.9
1976	224	1.5	20.6
1977	196	2.3*	18.9*
1978	237	2.8*	15.6*
1979	179	0.8*	31.0*
1980	189	1.7	27.8
1981	158	0.5*	46.0*
1982	187	0.5*	32.5*
1983	192	0.5*	32.9*
1984	173	1.0*	55.5*
1985	192	1.8	44.2
1986	210	1.5	26.8
1987	211	1.8	30.4
1988	195	1.8	35.0
1989	210	1.3	37.0
1990	240		32.0

SOURCE: Various Soviet statistical reports.

*U.S. Department of Agriculture Estimate.

plots that the peasants were allowed to farm on their own.[28] Apparently nothing came of this idea.

Zhores Medvedev argues that had it not been for Brezhnev's death, Gorbachev would have been called to account for the problems of agriculture and might have lost his position in the Politburo.[29] According to Medvedev, Brezhnev and his allies were especially disappointed that the 1982 harvest was also far below expectations. The first year of the vaunted Food Program had turned out to be no more productive than earlier years. Personally embarrassing for Brezhnev, there were rumors that he would take remedial measures immediately after the November 7, 1982, Revolutionary Day celebration.[30] Whatever the substance of such rumors, fortunately for Gorbachev, Brezhnev caught a cold during the Red Square Parade and died three days later.

Gorbachev's responsibilities increased when Andropov succeeded Brezhnev to the post of general secretary. Because of his overt loyalty to Andropov, however, Gorbachev's status suffered a year and a quarter later when Andropov died and Chernenko became general secretary. Gorbachev was not deprived of all his power. In fact, as Chernenko's absences became more and more frequent, Gorbachev, who had become second secretary, began to preside regularly over the Politburo and also the Secretariat even before Chernenko's death.[31]

Chernenko's coolness toward Gorbachev in part was an extension of his differences with Gorbachev's onetime sponsors, Andropov and Suslov. By contrast, Chernenko had a considerably more relaxed attitude toward discipline and ideological rigor. While Chernenko was not as tolerant of corruption as Brezhnev, Andropov's death and Chernenko's succession were good news for many of the seamier segments of Soviet society.

Whatever the reaction of the party hacks and black marketeers, Chernenko's selection as general secretary, even for a brief time, provoked wide disillusionment among the general public. Foreign visitors to Moscow were told openly by their hosts of their disquiet that the Soviet leadership seemed unable to find anything but superannuated leaders (Andropov was sixty-eight and Chernenko seventy-two when they assumed power) and even more important, one who was not on the brink of death. Between 1982 and 1985, the Soviet people were forced to contend with four different leaders, the first three of whom would have been better suited for a retirement home than the Kremlin.*

Given his pedigree, it was not surprising that Gorbachev picked up where Andropov left off. While Gorbachev never went as far as Andropov, who in one speech used the word "discipline" *(distsiplina)* thirteen times, Gorbachev was nonetheless a strong believer in tighter control. In his speech to his election district on February 20, 1985, for example, and reiterated a month later at a meeting of the Central Committee as well as in virtually every one of his many published statements during his first year, he repeated the theme of "strengthening of discipline."[32] Although not as relentless as Andropov in his crackdown on labor absenteeism, he made a special effort to expose corruption and self-dealing. Gorbachev went even further, however, in his crackdown on alcoholism. Urged on by Politburo members Yegor Ligachev and Mikhail Solomentsev, on May 17 he decided to meet this problem head on. Since alcoholism has been an integral part of the Russian way of life for centuries, this was not an easy decision. His first act was to curb the output and sale of alcoholic beverages, going so far as to order the destruction of many of the country's best vineyards. He also banned the sale of alcohol before 2:00 P.M. and warned that government officials who drank excessively would be penalized. When Andrei Gromyko reportedly said of Gorba-

---

*I remember my own reaction to the procession of the elderly and infirmed Soviet leaders. My one close encounter with Leonid Brezhnev took place at a Kremlin dinner in December 1978, where he spoke with a slur and appeared very unsteady on his feet. For this reason he was constantly attended by two mafia-type valets, who helped Brezhnev stand up to make his toasts and then sit down. They stood on either side of him as he walked out to prevent his falling. That was almost four years before his death. Again, I was startled when about seven months into Andropov's term, the same two attendants resumed their place behind him; and sure enough, they reappeared a year or so later when Chernenko's health also began to fail. They were probably among the few in the Soviet Union who were unhappy to see the fifty-two-year-old Gorbachev take over in March 1985.

chev, "This man has a nice smile, but he has iron teeth," he was alluding to more than Gorbachev's political doggedness.[33] This was also a reflection of Gorbachev's concern about the economy and his country's social problems, and his willingness to use stern and forceful measures to resolve them, at least initially.

We now know that Gorbachev was a man in a hurry. It turns out that he had already worked out the major features of what would become his program before his final election as general secretary. Few of us noticed it at the time, because of course Gorbachev was just one of many members of the Politburo, but in a speech to an ideological meeting on December 10, 1984, he spelled out the major themes that were to shape the Soviet Union for the next several years.[34] This speech was a remarkable guide to what was to come. At the time, Chernenko was still general secretary, failing fast, it is true, but that was not known for certain by the outside world. So Gorbachev's speech seemed to be nothing more than just another bureaucratic harangue by another member of the party apparatus. For those hardened by the usual Soviet rhetoric, not much seemed to be new. There were some unusual terms such as "intensification" *(intensifikatsiia),* "acceleration" *(uskoreniie),* "reconstruction," and "openness," but none of this seemed much different from the pious platitudes of his predecessors. Like communism and motherhood, they were concepts that were hard to oppose. Moreover, if experience was any guide, tomorrow there would be a new set of pious generalizations, and perhaps even new leaders.

To Gorbachev, however, his speech was more than a string of empty offerings. In retrospect, it seems clear that Gorbachev was preparing himself not only to succeed Chernenko, but to shift the Soviet Union in a new direction. Almost everything that Gorbachev had to say at the time would come to constitute the heart of his reform program in the years ahead. For example, what we translated as "reconstruction" and "openness", Gorbachev in Russian called *perestroika* and *glasnost'*—words that would soon become part of every language. Yet given Gorbachev's origins, his echoing of the Andropov line, and the pedestrian nature of what heretofore had been his few initiatives, there seemed to be little reason to anticipate that were Gorbachev to be chosen as Chernenko's successor, he would do anything unusual. As one who had risen through the ranks and rarely shown any noticeable inclination for innovation, it seemed unlikely that he would break out of the mold. If proof were needed, look at the 1982 Food Program. Agriculture had been Gorbachev's chief responsibility and that "new" program only seemed to be more of the same. The fact that Gorbachev did not speak up at the party plenum when Brezhnev chose to make the formal presentation and that his input into the program may have been limited seemed to demonstrate his ineffectuality. Based on his record, it was hard to see how any of the reforms Gorbachev might ultimately decide to promote would involve anything more daring than the Food Program.

How then can Gorbachev's subsequent radical proposals be explained? In an unusually revealing encounter with a group of intellectuals, Gorbachev himself has described his intellectual odyssey to perestroika and glasnost. In December 1984, during a walk along the beach at Pitsunda in Georgia, Gorbachev and Eduard Shevardnadze began to reminisce about their experiences as chief administrators of their home regions, Gorbachev at Stavropol *krai* and Shevardnadze in the Republic of Georgia.[35] After some reflection, Shevardnadze confessed that "it had all gone rotten." Gorbachev agreed. Because of the arrest of both of his grandfathers, Gorbachev knew firsthand what suffering had been inflicted on the Soviet people. He also noted that one of those grandfathers was forced to "confess to things he had not done."[36]

Shevardnadze and Gorbachev concluded, in Gorbachev's words, "that it was impossible to live that way. We began looking for an answer to the question: How should we live? A concept appeared for the country and for the world. For internal problems we call it perestroika. And we put forward a simple formula: more democracy, more glasnost, more humanity. On the whole, everything must develop so that the person in this society feels like a human being. There you have it—a simple formula of life." Yet it was that same formula that Gorbachev made the centerpiece of his December 1984 speech on ideology, delivered not coincidentally at about the same time as the Gorbachev-Shevardnadze stroll on the beach at Pitsunda.

While those of us outside the Soviet Union were unaware of Gorbachev's conversation with Shevardnadze until several years after it occurred, there were still a few early clues that despite his background, Gorbachev might end up leading the Soviet Union in a new direction, though in no way did they prepare us for the radical reforms that were to come. The decision to return to the Geneva arms talks with the United States was made as we saw, in late 1984 under Chernenko, but while Gorbachev was chairing the Politburo. Since the United States had not met any of Andropov's terms, this was a major reversal of the Andropov hard line. Evidently Gorbachev realized that Andropov's threats were not working. President Reagan did not back off from his program of installing Pershing II missiles in Europe or his pursuit of a SDI program. However, unless something was done quickly, the Soviet Union would find that it had not only lost its superior nuclear strength relative to that of the United States, but it would not even be able to sustain the parity it had fought so hard to attain. In the meantime, the Soviet Union was losing its battle for world public opinion because of its refusal to discuss arms control measures in Geneva.

For anyone concerned with the Soviet Union's excessive expenditures on weapons and missiles, this was an eminently rational decision. The CIA at the time estimated that the Soviet Union was spending 15–17 percent of its GNP on military expenditures.[37] Some Soviet economists argued that this was actually an understatement, and the Soviet Union was in fact spending 20 percent or more of its GNP on such non-productive efforts. But however sensible such a decision ultimately was to be, at a time of jingoistic rhetoric against the United States and its hostile intentions it took some courage to back off. At the time I heard almost no one, even in the Soviet intellectual community, suggest such a potentially heretical course. Gorbachev's uniqueness can also be seen in the kind of academic specialists he sought out for advice. His mentor Andropov had called in the heads of some of the Academy of Science Institutes, such as Georgii Arbatov of the Institute of the United States and Canada, and Nikita Khrushchev had used some thoughtful journalists such as Fyodor Burlatsky as speechwriters. Gorbachev also came to rely on some of these more politically and strategically inclined specialists. He even brought back Alexander Yakovlev, who had been banished to Canada as Soviet ambassador for a daring but impolitic attack on Russian nationalists. He first installed him as director of the Institute of World Economics and International Relations of the Academy of Sciences in late 1985, and then put him in charge of propaganda in the Central Committee. Gorbachev also began to seek advice from a succession of scholars from the Academy of Sciences. But Gorbachev went further than his predecessors. He reached out beyond Moscow to seek out academics less directly involved in party and government matters, an approach more akin to that of Franklin D. Roosevelt and John F. Kennedy than to the actions of previous czars and general secretaries.

His willingness to seek out academic specialists may have been a consequence of his own university training and his wife Raisa's even more extensive involvement in university affairs. Tatiana Zaslavskaia, the sociologist attached to the Institute of Economics and Organization of Industrial Production at the Siberian branch of the Academy of Sciences and an expert on agriculture, was one of the first specialists consulted by Gorbachev. As early as the preparation and discussion of the Food Program in 1982, Gorbachev decided to seek out some fresh ideas, and so he summoned her to Moscow from her home in Novosibirsk.[38] With time Gorbachev expanded the scope of his discussions to include broader economic issues. Academician Zaslavskaia began inviting others to attend such meetings, including the head of the Institute of Economics in the Siberian Academy, Abel Aganbegyan.[39] Before long, under Aganbegyan's influence, Gorbachev managed to sketch out what eventually came to be the main outlines of his early reform programs.

At the time, Aganbegyan seemed like a good choice. From the relative safety of Novosibirsk and its nearby university town, Academgorodok, Aganbegyan had developed a remarkably independent and candid perspective about the Soviet Union's economy. At times his outspokenness precipitated the wrath of authorities in Moscow, who prevented him from traveling outside the Soviet Union, except for brief trips to Bulgaria and Hungary. In fact, until Gorbachev came to power in 1985, Aganbegyan was precluded from visiting the West.[40] He and his colleagues published their views regularly in Aganbegyan's journal *EKO,* a major outlet for some of the best critical analysis of what was wrong with the Soviet economy. Much of that criticism was not only edited but written by Aganbegyan. One of Aganbegyan's main concerns was the Soviet Union's falling capital productivity. But despite his criticisms, Aganbegyan adhered to the Soviet Union's conventional wisdom that machinery would solve all economic problems.[41] In his own words, "Machine building lies at the heart of the technical reconstruction of the economy."[42]

Traditionally, Soviet planners had subjected the Soviet people to savings ratios of as high as 25 percent, the preponderant share of which was for the machine-tool industry. This forced-march investment policy was regarded as the source of the Soviet Union's rapid economic growth in the Stalinist era. The pace was somewhat relaxed after Stalin's death; but on the whole, investment in the machine-tool industry at the expense of consumer goods was still the policy of choice in the early 1980s.

To the extent that Aganbegyan took a different approach, he switched the emphasis away from investment for investment's sake to a stress on a more intensive form of specific investment. He regarded Soviet planners' preference for new factory construction, in effect the building of new facilities, as a mistake. This overemphasis on brick and concrete at the expense of machine tools explained why some estimated that 30–40 percent of the Soviet industrial stock had been in use fifteen to twenty years, the highest percentage in the world.[43] According to Aganbegyan, two thirds of the Soviet machine-tool stock was obsolete.[44] No wonder the Soviet Union found itself spending so much on repairs and enduring so many disruptions in the production process. What they should have done instead, according to Aganbegyan, was to adopt a more intensive form of investment that would have diverted the money to "retooling and refurbishing."[45] Instead of building new factories, they should have instituted three shifts a day and used existing facilities more effectively. According to Aganbegyan, these changes would accelerate scientific and technological progress, or what he came to call the intensification of economic growth. It was not that too much was being spent on investment in the heavy industrial sector; rather, it was being spent on buildings, not machine tools. He seemed generally pleased that while investment in machine tools had increased by a mere 24 percent in the eleventh five-year plan (1980–85) over the tenth five-year plan, it would come into its own again and would increase by 80 percent in the twelfth five-year plan (1986–90).[46]

Given the fact that every Soviet leader since the revolution had also granted pride of place to the machine-tool industry, Aganbegyan probably found Gorbachev a willing disciple. It is hard to know exactly why Soviet leaders are so obsessed by the machine-tool industry. It may have been that earlier Soviet officials, principally Stalin, were determined to build up their military strength and to do that they first had to develop a heavy machinery sector. But the pride that Soviet officials have always had in boasting about their big factories, big drill presses, big tractors, and big microprocessors suggests that there is something more involved (the Soviets didn't seem to understand that having the world's largest microprocessor was not the most sensible economic strategy to follow). Because of our own overabsorption with consumption and unwillingness to save, from the perspective of the United States, it sometimes seems that Soviet leaders have a fetish about machine tools.

(Indeed it sometimes seems that machine tools are to Soviet leaders what sex is to the average American, and the bigger the machine tool, the more satisfying.)

A look at what Gorbachev was saying even before he became general secretary indicates that he had studied Aganbegyan's lessons well. In the December 12, 1984, speech mentioned earlier, as well as a February 1985 speech in his election district, Gorbachev referred to "intensification" at least five times.[47] Once installed as general secretary, *intensifikatsiia* (intensification) and *uskoreniie* (acceleration) became a constant theme, more so at first than *perestroika* and *glasnost'*. Gorbachev even called for intensification and acceleration at the first meeting he chaired of the Central Committee on April 1, 1985, and thereafter almost constantly repeated the theme until 1987.[48]

It is not that Gorbachev invented words such as *intensifikatsiia* and *uskoreniie*. Others occasionally have used them as part of the rhetoric, but few took them seriously.[49] Until Gorbachev they were like background noise, similar to the sort that dentists use to mask the pain.

Unfortunately, another part of Gorbachev's initial December 10, 1984, speech about *perestroika* seemed to fall by the wayside. Included in that early version was a concept which can be translated as "the distribution of wealth," or literally, "the distributive relation" *(raspredelitel'nye otnosheniia),* which Gorbachev considered to be crucial to the achievement of social justice. Presumably this referred to an increased and more equal distribution of consumer goods. If he had devoted more effort to this side of Soviet economic life rather than to the heavy industrial side, it is possible that the Soviet population would be more supportive of Gorbachev and the reform process today. But Gorbachev restricted himself to the more traditional Soviet approach. In the first one and a half to two years of his efforts, he adhered to his and Aganbegyan's emphasis on machine tools, with little or no mention of anything more far-reaching than discipline and some superficial reorganization. That was a crucial mistake. Ultimately *perestroika* and especially *glasnost'* came to have broader and more radical implications. As we shall see in the next chapter, that is because Gorbachev came to realize how misguided his initial approach to reform had been.

In the early period, there was little discussion of the desirability of private property, an end to central planning, the need to concentrate on consumer goods, food, production, or private business, and the right of individuals to hire private labor. On the contrary, the Soviet Union embarked on a draconic crackdown on private trade, effective as of July 1, 1986. This seemed to be a step backward, not forward. The Chinese economic reforms, although over six years old at the time and eminently successful, were rejected as unsuited for the Soviet Union. That attitude would soon soften, but for the time being the East German approach with its *Kombinate* seemed to be the model preferred by Aganbegyan and in turn by Gorbachev.[50] After all, the East Germans in 1985 seemed to have the best of both worlds: successful economic growth and communism. It was beyond belief that East Germany would ever disintegrate, much less do so in four years' time. The trick as Aganbegyan and Gorbachev saw it was to make Soviet planning more disciplined, not to give it up. For that reason Aganbegyan came to advocate the formation of superministries, a Soviet variation of the *Kombinate*. Gorbachev in turn in a June 11, 1985, speech praised the idea of superministries. With superministries, Soviet planners could eliminate intermediate bureaucracies and concentrate on overall strategic planning. Day-to-day functions would then be delegated to the industrial enterprises.[51]

As promised, Gorbachev created a superministry for machine tools in October 1985. Aganbegyan, as late as 1988, insisted, "our strategy is to insure in the first place an increase in machine building."[52] In November 1985, Gorbachev also created Gosagroprom, and as we saw, installed his old friend Vsevolod Murakhovsky from Stavropol as the chairman. Gosagroprom, modeled on U.S. agro-business corporations, was to take charge of everything having to do with agriculture. It combined five former ministries and one state committee, all of which had previously been responsible for one aspect or another of the food-growing and food-processing cycle. In March 1986, he formed a super bureau for fuel and energy. In addition, Gorbachev also established a brand new organization called Gospriemka. Translated as the State Quality Acceptance Committee, this agency's function was to bring about a radical improvement in the quality of goods, a persistent shortcoming of Soviet economic life. Even before the formal establishment of Gospriemka, inspectors in 1985 were assigned by Moscow authorities to nineteen enterprises with the power to accept or reject output. By October 1, 1986, factories producing 20 to 30 percent of all Soviet output were assigned Gospriemka inspectors. By January 1, 1987, representatives from Gospriemka began to inspect the output of almost all major Soviet industries.[53]

As Gorbachev came to rely more and more on his economic advice, Aganbegyan moved from Novosibirsk in the summer of 1985 to Moscow, where Gorbachev arranged for him to be chairman of the Economic Commission of the Scientific Center in the Academy of Sciences.[54] Such confidence appeared warranted because initially these reforms seemed to be working. As Table 2 indicates, industrial growth seemed to rebound. After Gorbachev's on-site visit in September 1985 to the Tyumen oil fields, even oil production—which had been declining since late 1983—started to grow again. Although Tyumen is the Soviet Union's main oil-producing center, many complaints have been heard over the years about its inept organization. After some unprecedentedly frank discussions, Gorbachev demanded remedial measures and a purge of local administrators and managers. The turnaround was almost immediate. Petroleum production increased markedly in January 1986. What better proof was there that inspired leadership, close supervision, anti-alcohol campaigning, and administrative house cleaning could make a difference? Finally the Soviet Union had a leader who seemed able to provide the country with a sense of direction and discipline.

At the same time, Gorbachev continued to experiment. He sought to decentralize as well as centralize. If his superministry

TABLE 2

Industrial Production Figures
*January–February production as a percentage of preceding
January–February*

Product	Brezhnev 1982 1981	Andropov 1983 1982	Chernenko 1985 1984	Gorbachev 1986 1985
	(percent)			
Electricity	103.4	103.0	103.3	104
Petroleum (incl. gas condensate)	99.8	102.0	96.3	101
Natural Gas	106.4	108.0	109.1	107
Coal	99.3	100.5	98.4	106
Steel	95.6	104.0	92.2	111
Fertilizer	97.7	111.0	98.0	116
Metal-cutting tools	101.5	104.0	103.6	114
Robots	—	147.0	100.0	142
Computer technology	76.8	109.0	110.0	123
Tractors	99.6	102.0	104.0	105
Paper	93.3	108.0	93.7	113
Cement	88.3	113.0	93.7	111
Meat	93.6	106.0	106.3	113
Margarine	100.0	110.0	92.6	108
Watches	100.0	105.0	96.4	108
Radios	98.9	111.0	93.0	106
Television sets	99.9	108.0	100.0	106

SOURCES: Figures are taken from *Ekonomicheskaia gazeta.* For 1982 over 1981: March 1982, no. 12, p. 4; for 1983 over 1982: March 1983, no. 12, p. 4; for 1985 over 1984: March 1985, no. 11, p. 15; for 1986 over 1985: March 1986, no. 12, p. 4.

construct was to succeed, the underlying Soviet industrial enterprises just like their East European prototypes would have to be stimulated to make more decisions for themselves. To see if that would work, the Soviet government in May 1985 announced that three important factories would be assigned extraordinary authority and would be allowed to operate as semi-independent financial entities. The enterprises were the Volga automobile plant in Togliatti, which produces the Lada; the Saransk semiconductor factory; and the Frunze Scientific Production-Combine in Sumy.[55]

Eventually only the Sumy and Togliatti combines were kept in the program, but even they did not fully implement the experiment. The plan was that each factory could keep a portion of any profit it made over a set amount which had been agreed to five years in advance. This was to prevent Moscow's financial ministries from jacking up the tax collection the minute the factory increased its profitability. Soviet authorities also promised to reduce the number of targets imposed on the enterprise management. And they were told that they could keep a share of any hard currency export earnings they made, as well as a share of the savings from any reduction in the size of the labor force.[56]

The intent of the planners was honorable; but as happens so often with promised reforms, the promise exceeded the reforms.[57] Initially, the two enterprises were told they could keep up to 40 percent of the hard currency they earned from exports, but a few months later the enterprise's share was reduced to 20 percent.[58] And there were complaints that Gosbank, the official state bank, would not allow them to keep even that much.

Gorbachev was equally active and ultimately more successful in the field of international diplomacy. As a follow-up to the January 1985 meeting between Secretary of State George Schultz and Minister of Foreign Affairs Andrei Gromyko, Gorbachev agreed to meet in November 1985 with Ronald Reagan in Geneva. No concrete agreement about arms reduction was reached at that particular summit. Yet both men spent five and a half hours alone (plus their translators) sounding out each other, breaking through the ice of the Cold War, and setting the foundation for important initiatives that would soon follow: not only a reduction in the arms race, but a cutback in the military buildup and eventually in budget expenditures for weapons, making possible greater attention to the civilian economy. Gorbachev's efforts at economic reform and international understanding and relaxation of tensions were winning support both at home and in the outside world. Gorbachev was making a difference.

5

Mid-Course Correction

Despite all his enthusiasm and energy, Mikhail Gorbachev's initial approach to economic reform was doomed to fail. There was little chance that Gorbachev's stress on intensification, *uskoreniie,* Gospriemka, and the superministries would produce the far-reaching reform of the Soviet economy that he sought. It took him almost a year and a half to realize that his approach would not work. That lost time was critical. Gorbachev aroused the population with his call for a complete overhaul of Soviet society—but in the economic realm at least, complete overhaul turned out for the most part to be not much more than a minor lubrication job. By the time he was well enough aware of the ineffectiveness of his original approach, the damage had already been done. Gorbachev's failure to embark on a truly radical course cost him his credibility. He had nothing to show. In effect, he had squandered his honeymoon when the expectant public was more tolerant and prepared for sacrifice. Because of decisions Gorbachev made in 1985 and 1986, economic forces had been set in motion that would prove counterproductive to the efforts to reform the economy.

The realization that it was necessary to implement far more radical political and economic initiatives dawned on Gorbachev bit by bit as he traveled around the country trying to whip up support for his original remedies. At the January 27, 1987, Central Committee meeting, Gorbachev acknowledged that the challenge was greater than he anticipated. As he explained it, when he took over, he was unaware of the depth of the crisis facing the Soviet Union. "The problems that have accumulated in society are more deeply rooted than we first thought. The further we go with our reorganization, the clearer its scope and significance; more and more unresolved problems inherited from the past come out."[1]

Reluctantly Gorbachev came to understand that he had to do more than simply improve the way Communist central planning operates. In other words, he and his advisers would have to forsake their search for that magic lubricant that if applied properly would eliminate the squeaking or the breakdown of socialism. In the absence of such lubricant, he had settled for glue and patches. Gorbachev was unwilling to consider abandoning communism or the Stalinist emphasis on central control and heavy industry altogether. Even a few years later when he began to consider more market-type functions, he continued to limit himself to discussions about "a *regulated* market economy." "Regulated" was the governing word, with its implications for an ongoing role for government bureaucrats and limitations on the legalization of private property. Unlike Deng Xiaoping, who in practice at least seemed to be much more economically pragmatic, Gorbachev seemed unwilling to break out of his ideological cocoon. Gorbachev never echoed Deng's proclamation that "It is good to be rich," or what some consider his underlying spur to China's 1980s economic miracle: "It matters not what color the cat is, as long as it catches mice."

During the first year or so, Gorbachev made explicit his limited aspirations for economic reforms. He even appeared to have trouble with the words "economic reform," because he rarely used them. There is no question that radical economic reforms can be destabilizing, especially during the first one hundred days when a new leader may not have the political support needed to change the status quo. But while Gorbachev may have been new, he certainly did not appear to be weak. For example, he moved rapidly to purge his political rivals—faster in fact than any other previous general secretary. Grigori Romanov from Leningrad was dismissed in July 1985, and Andrei Gromyko was pushed upstairs to the honorary post of president, which then left open the post of minister of foreign affairs for Eduard Shevardnadze, whom, as we saw, Gorbachev credits with being the godfather of perestroika. This was a change critical for the opening to the West Gorbachev wanted to pursue. In October 1985, Nikolai Tikhonov was forced to resign from the Politburo as prime minister; and in December 1985, Viktor Grishin, perhaps Gorbachev's main rival, was also pushed off the Politburo. All this occurred in less than one year. Despite these dismissals, Gorbachev appeared to have felt the need for even more political support.

Yet with or without a comfortable majority, many innovative leaders, including Franklin Roosevelt and Deng Xiaoping, have chosen to make their moves early in their administrations while there is still the good feeling that usually comes with a change in leadership and before those likely to suffer understand the full implications and move to frustrate the planned changes. In other words, many leaders take their losses early. That allows them to blame their predecessors for the accumulated problems. Early action assumes of course that the new leader has a clear vision of what he or she plans to do, not just in the short run but over a longer period of time as well. Gorbachev thought he knew what he wanted to do, as seen in the early emphasis on intensification, *uskoreniie,* discipline, superministries, the machine-tool industry, perestroika, and glasnost, but some of these ideas quickly proved to be harmful. In the end, Gorbachev found himself with the worst of both worlds. He moved too fast in instituting machinery intensification and creating superministries, but not fast enough in supporting privatization and markets at all levels, as well as the significantly higher output of food and consumer goods.

One eventual casualty of this agonizing reappraisal was Gorbachev's adviser, Abel Aganbegyan. Aganbegyan came to bear the brunt of some very angry criticism from fellow economists.[2]

Ultimately Aganbegyan himself began to criticize the early economic decisions of the Gorbachev administration without acknowledging that he, Aganbegyan, had helped shape much of Gorbachev's early program.[3] Others were more forthright, in particular Vasilii Seliunin, who repeatedly noted that Aganbegyan with his continued insistence on heavy industry and the machine-tool industry had led Gorbachev astray. In Seliunin's view, Aganbegyan's approach actually deepened the structural disproportions in the Soviet economy instead of ameliorating them.[4]

Although it would be some time before he would come up with an alternative approach, gradually Gorbachev came to understand that his efforts were less productive than he had anticipated. In fact, some Soviet economists began to argue that whatever the initial success, the momentum or what was left of it could not be sustained. According to Stanislav Shatalin, one of the Soviet Union's most respected economists and one of the authors of the Five Hundred Day Plan, per capita consumption in 1986 rose only 2 percent; allowing for inflation, the more appropriate figure was probably a drop of 1 percent.[5]

It was bad enough that the Soviet Union's economic growth seemed to be lagging; but like investors in American investment firms, Soviet planners had become addicted to quarterly and yearly economic reports, at which time they were pressured to show satisfactory rates of growth. Gorbachev, however, came to understand that to be successful, the Soviet Union would have to do more than merely show improvement over the preceding period. After a few months in office he began touring around the Soviet Union. What he saw surprised and depressed him. As a member of the Politburo, presumably Gorbachev had received frequent and relatively accurate briefings, but after he became general secretary, his journeys confirmed his suspicion that even Politburo members had been shielded from reality. Gorbachev later confirmed that despite the fact that he was a member of the Politburo, he was denied "access to the Soviet budget or information on questions of expenditure."[6] His friend Andropov told Gorbachev that he and other members of the

Politburo were "youngsters meddling where they shouldn't." That means that even members of the Politburo have been unable to escape what the Russians traditionally have called *pokazuka* or Potemkin villages, models and sham representations passed off as the real thing. The peasants and workers with smiling faces were in fact angry and suffering badly. Gorbachev began to insist on meeting real people and engaging in honest give and take; he was often surprised if not shocked. On a July 29, 1986, tour of the far eastern city of Komsomolsk on the Amur River, for example, Gorbachev was told by a worker that "the cold water supply keeps failing."[7] Gorbachev then asked, "Is this on every floor? In general I can see a lot of problems have accumulated here."

In a speech he gave on September 6, 1985, in Nizhnevartovsk in the Tyumin region of West Siberia, the site of the country's largest oil field deposits, he was shocked among other things to discover that the city of 200,000 people had no movie theater. Other service facilities, such as medical care and recreation, were in equally short supply, or in *deficity,* as the Soviets would say. After his visit Gorbachev reportedly told Aganbegyan, who had urged him to visit the Siberian region, "Abel, it is even worse than you told me."[8]

His visits around the country evidently not only made Gorbachev aware of deteriorating economic conditions, but of a populace deeply alienated from the Soviet political and economic system. As long as the overall system remained unchanged, Gorbachev concluded that the Soviet people would not respond to his call for hard work and discipline. Why should they work hard, when there were so few desirable goods to buy with the rubles with which they were paid? This was true in good times and even more so in the post-Brezhnev era. To some it was a charade, as described by a widely held view: "Soviet leaders pretend to pay the workers with worthless rubles; in exchange, the workers pretend to work."

The profits, when there were any, went to what the Soviets call the *nomenklatura,* members of the Central Committee along with senior government, industry officials, and technocrats who lived in a world of their own. They had special shops with goods not available to the masses. They had special dachas, special hospitals and clinics, special limousines, chauffeurs, and even special lanes on the highway reserved for their cars. Once one became a member of the *nomenklatura* (or *shiski,* as the ordinary people called them), it was like being made a tenured professor—it usually meant tenure for life. This was also true for the country's leaders. Even when Brezhnev, Andropov, and Chernenko became incapacitated, they remained in office until they died.

As he traveled around the countryside, Gorbachev also came to appreciate that this bureaucratic tenure system had become another impediment to any kind of meaningful reform. After all those years in office, Soviet officials had become corrupt and abusive. Not only were the workers and peasants enormously resentful of the *nomenklatura* class, but the *nomenklatura* system itself had become a serious obstacle to reform. Since reforms threatened their jobs and privileges, they fought furiously against them. Consequently, Gorbachev's reforms encountered tremendous obstacles, because to implement the reform he had to rely upon the very people he wanted to get rid of. In effect, he was asking them to destroy themselves as a class, to give up their power and prerogatives. It is not surprising that they resisted so strenuously.

I

Despite the obstacles, Gorbachev was determined to move ahead. His goal was nothing less than uprooting the system, or as he put it, "bringing a bulldozer to remove" the problems. "Leaders must not think that . . . now I have my job I am the king of the castle. They have been choosen by the people [but] they are servants of the people and thus this is how they should be judged."[9] But with a few exceptions, the *nomenklatura* tended to become abusive and arrogant. This was a natural consequence of the political system of democratic centralism. Democratic centralism was predicated on the assumption that victory in the revolution was a sign the people had spoken. Thus there was no need to verify their continued support. That obviated the need for future elections. Consequently, the leaders could choose their own successors and subordinates. Such a system all but guaranteed the continued abuse of power and the consequent inevitable alienation of the population.

Gorbachev sought to ameliorate this situation by purging the ranks of the *nomenklatura* as he had purged members of the Politburo. He continued the process that his mentor Andropov had begun. Within a year, more than 20 to 30 percent of the ranks of the Central Committee *oblast* or county leaders and industrial ministers had been purged. Gorbachev expected that these purges would rouse the remaining members of the *nomenklatura* to support perestroika in order to forestall subsequent purges. He also hoped to signal the Soviet people that tenure was no longer an enduring privilege.

During most of 1985, the term *glasnost'* was used primarily in the context of exposing corrupt and wasteful leadership. But that sort of criticism and subsequent purges were nothing unique or novel to Gorbachev. As with so much of the Soviet reform effort, the full dimensions of the glasnost process took some time to unfold. Initially Gorbachev used the word for several months with little noticeable new discussion of subjects that had been traditionally off limits. Gradually, however, particularly at the 27th Party Congress of the Communist Party in February 1986, he pushed for more criticism of subjects heretofore considered sacrosanct. But glasnost in those early times did not permit too detailed a look at the Soviet past. Reflecting the cautious nature of the process, Gorbachev told a reporter for *L'Humanité* that "Stalinism was a concept made up by opponents of communism and used on a large scale to smear the Soviet Union and socialism as a whole." A few months later at a meeting with thirty writers in June 1986, Gorbachev warned that "if we start trying to deal with the past, we will dissipate our energy."[10] Similar initial silence after the April 1986 Chernobyl explosion revealed that glasnost was still an arbitrary concept.

Gorbachev continued, however, to stress the need to expose incompetent and corrupt officials, and glasnost was well suited for that purpose. Slowly at first, but then with accelerating frequency and daring, a growing number of ordinary people and local and provincial newspapers began to criticize corrupt local officials. But increasingly Gorbachev came to see that there were severe limitations to glasnost as it was then understood. Once drawn to his attention, Gorbachev usually was able to purge the ranks of incompetent ideological diehards. Yet there were some major exceptions, such as Vladimir Shcherbitski, the head of the Communist Party of the Ukraine. Gorbachev was almost a one-man band. He could only purge when he became aware of a problem and when he had enough power to act. The Shcherbitski situation illustrated that when there was a regional leader firmly in control, critical pressure from below was of little avail. In fact, the critics often had cause to regret their own outspokenness. As Gorbachev pointed out at a plenum of the Central Committee of the Communist Party in June 1986, criticism can be risky. "A Communist voices his personal opinion in a city or district party committee or shares his thoughts, but instead of giving him a substantial answer, they say, 'Do not forget your place.' " "Later in the year, during an August trip to the Soviet Far East, a young man from a wholesale fishery processing plant in Khabarovsk asked Gorbachev "A simple question. They said at the Communist Party Plenum that we should criticize all of them Lenin-style. I risked doing so, about the manager of the fisheries processing plant at a meeting of the trade union committee. Today I am out of a job."[12]

Initially Gorbachev seemed to think that the whistle-blowers would be protected if he could induce the Soviet press, especially the local press, to pursue his policy of glasnost. He was realistic enough to understand, however, that it was not easy for the local editors to criticize local party officials. " 'We have seen what the central press writes and what the local newspapers write and we see that in the local ones there is peace and quiet and plenty of it. What is wrong? Does not the Secretary of the *raikon* [regional council] or the *gorkom* [city council], the *obkom* [*oblast* committee] and *krai* [regional committee] give permission for strong criticism?' (Laughter follows.)"[13]

The thought did not leave him. Two days later, while meeting with a group of party officials in Khabarovsk, he berated local party and government bureaucrats who tried to suppress criticism.[14] What we need, he insisted, is "glasnost in order to ensure the fulfillment of the tasks of the Party Congress." But he complained that the local newspaper people were timid when they did speak out, because the local party officials harassed them. Therefore, he said, self-criticism was all the more necessary because "We do not have any opposition parties."[15] Since there was no other way to prevent or correct power abuse by local party officials, glasnost was required as a restraint. Later he would agree to end the monopoly of the Communist Party, but even then Gorbachev acknowledged that as long as such abuses went unchecked, the workers would have no interest in perestroika. "A home could be put in order only by a person who feels he owns his house."[16] Thus, changes in political as well as economic conditions were necessary.

This series of encounters evidently caused Gorbachev once again to expand his ideas. He came to realize that while glasnost as then interpreted could be helpful, it clearly had its limits. By February 1987, Gorbachev had come around to the idea that the restraints on glasnost had to be relaxed. He needed a much fuller airing of the mistakes of the past. This represented a complete about-face from his stance six months earlier, when he warned about digging up the past. Thus in a meeting with heads of the mass media, Gorbachev expressed this switch in approach by boldly asserting: "There must be no forgotten names, no blank spaces, either in history or in literature."[17]

Greater glasnost was one form of a check on power, but there had to be other checks as well to limit the power that naturally evolved in a one-party state. It was as if he were reinventing the American constitutional concept of checks and balances and discovering for himself the arguments spelled out in *The Federalist Papers:* "A dependence on the people is no doubt the primary control on the government but experience has taught mankind the necessity of auxiliary precautions."[18] Gorbachev's language was not as flowery, but eventually it would come to much the same thing. A month and a half later, on September 18, 1986, during a visit to the party officials in Krasnodar, Gorbachev argued that "perestroika would be more dynamic if we focused greater attention on the question of expanding democratization in our society."[19] In his December 1984 conversation with Eduard Shevardnadze on the beach in Georgia, Gorbachev did include democracy along with glasnost and humanity in his "simple formula of life," but this was his first use of the word "democratization" in a public forum. Pursuing this concept, he added, "All of us comrades must start learning to work in conditions of extended democracy."[20] Heeding his own advice, he broadened his campaign for glasnost to include with it "democratization." " 'Democratization' will not weaken our society but on the contrary, it will strengthen it. It will not only *not* undermine discipline and order, but on the contrary all this will be taking place on the basis of awareness. This is how we will rectify our shortcomings."[21]

Gorbachev needed to provide some institutionalized procedure so that the disgruntled and abused could hold the bureaucrats to account. It was that quest that led Gorbachev to his call for democratization. He then called for multi-candidate elections and a secret ballot. To protect himself, however, he took care to ensure that these elections did not reach up to the republic level nor to the party secretary himself. Yet with that exception it was an enormous step forward. Elections do not guarantee honesty nor an end to abuses of power, but they do serve to constrain officials who hitherto operated with little accountability. Gorbachev also added a touch that went beyond the normal election process in the West. He extended secret, multi-candidate elections to include the determination of managers and shop foremen. This carried the procedure to the grass-root level again in order to curb abuse and generate popular public involvement.

Gorbachev's call for democratization a year and a half into

his term and his further elaboration of that concept seemed to be the logical way to win the Soviet masses over to his side. Until the man in the street could feel he had some check on the behavior of the party, government, or enterprise, he would never believe that he had a stake in perestroika.

His supporters echoed these views. Tatiana Zaslavskaia, for example, emphasized the close link between reform of the economy and glasnost and democracy: "Worker apathy can only be overcome if politicians give an honest explanation of why the Soviet economy is in such a poor state."[22] Once this logic was accepted, the ramifications were far-reaching. In Zaslavskaia's words, "The habit of half-truths . . . in a certain sense is worse than lies. If you conceal from people . . . information about the conditions of their own life, you cannot expect them to become more effective in either the economic or political sphere. People's trust and support can be obtained only in response to the trust placed in them."[23]

Others argued that only with information and some form of accountability would it be possible to avoid a return to the cult of personality. "Today we have one person in control and things run this way, tomorrow we shall have another and things might change completely. Our party and the whole country are now thinking of a mechanism that should necessarily be based on the laws of socialist democracy."[24]

It is not surprising that such radical reforms of the Leninist party-state encountered obstacles. Gorbachev in a speech to the Trade Union Congress on February 25, 1987, acknowledged that "greater democratization might prompt some people to ask if we are not disorganizing society, if we should not weaken management, and lower the standards for discipline, order and responsibility. This is an extremely important question. We must have complete clarity on it. I will put it bluntly. Those who have doubts about the expediency of further democratization apparently suffer from a serious drawback that is of great political significance and meaning: they do not believe in our people. They claim that democracy would be used by our people to disorganize society and undermine discipline, to undermine the strength of the system."[25]

Given that he was addressing what seemed to be one of the most conservative segments of Soviet society, the trade unions, this was one of Gorbachev's most daring speeches. Continuing the argument, he insisted, "Democracy is not the opposite of order. . . . Democracy is not the antithesis of responsibility." In full acknowledgment of the importance of some system of checks and balances, Gorbachev added: "Instead democracy means self-control by society."[26]

That was Gorbachev's remedy for power abuse and, by extension, a precondition for effective economic reform. "The more democracy we have, the faster we shall advance along that road of reorganization to social revival and the more order and discipline we shall have in our socialist home. So! It is either democracy or social inertia and conservatism."[27]

Had he reflected on these thoughts two or three years after he made them, Gorbachev might very well have realized that democracy, while necessary, may also have been his undoing. The democracy Gorbachev had in mind was narrow in scope. It held in check the power abusers and incompetents from the old era while at the same time it energized the supporters of perestroika and glasnost. There might be criticism, but it would be constructive and disciplined and would serve to help, not hurt, the reform process.

In the past, Soviet citizens had experienced discipline, but it had been the wrong kind. Gorbachev had a very different form of discipline in mind—one where votes were taken and there were differences, but the majority would then prevail. Those in the minority would honor that majority and not take to the street every time they lost a vote. Gorbachev assumed that the overwhelming percentage of the population would observe that discipline and share his vision of reform. His problems began when lack of custom and disappointment with his reforms led a growing number of critics to disregard his notion of discipline.

In the early days of Gorbachev's reform efforts, however, his confidence in himself and his program increased daily. His growing emphasis on glasnost and democratization ultimately led him to reconsider his government's policy toward dissidents and refuseniks. It was illogical if not hypocritical to campaign for glasnost while continuing the exile or imprisonment of those who had spoken out in the pre-Gorbachev days, but it took some time for him to come to that conclusion. After all, he was a protégé of Yuri Andropov.

Unlikely as it seemed at the time, the arrest by the KGB on August 30, 1986, of the American journalist Nicholas Daniloff was the spark that triggered a complete about face in the Soviet Union's human rights policy. Only then did Gorbachev's deeds begin to reflect his words. Deep in the midst of his glasnost campaign, Gorbachev suddenly found himself in a rapidly escalating confrontation with the United States over the U.S. arrest of Gennady Zakharov, a KGB agent in New York City. Glasnost or no glasnost, Gorbachev seemed determined to stick by the KGB in the defense of its spies. From the looks of it, the arrest of Daniloff threatened to set off an expulsion match similar to the one he had engaged in when Margaret Thatcher expelled several dozen spies from Great Britain in 1985. Gorbachev reciprocated by expelling a large number of Englishmen from the Soviet Union. Ultimately Mrs. Thatcher cried "uncle" and the match was declared a tie.

After a tense standoff with the United States, a compromise of sorts was reached. The Soviets agreed to release Daniloff first and threw in Yuri Orlov, the physicist who had been arrested and exiled for his leadership of the Soviet Helsinki Committee. Orlov had been a close friend of his fellow physicist, Andrei Sakharov. His release from jail and "expulsion" to the United States served as a prelude to the release of Zakharov and ultimately to the end of exile for Sakharov himself.

Reflecting on the exile of these two brilliant men, Orlov in Siberia and Sakharov in Gorky, Gorbachev undoubtedly must have come to question the kinds of policies that led the Soviet Union to imprison or exile its best minds. These were the kind of thinkers the Soviet Union needed to become a world leader.

What if they criticized Soviet policy? After all, Gorbachev's policies now not only welcomed but encouraged criticism or glasnost of all sorts. How did the Soviet Union come up with such a counterproductive policy of intimidation and imprisonment? It could only have been foisted on the Soviet Union by its enemies, not its friends. A mole from the CIA bent on sabotage and disinformation must have penetrated the Politburo; the traditional Soviet policy of repression is hard to explain in any other way.

Yet, as counterproductive as such actions might have been, it was not easy to reverse them. Sakharov's work on the hydrogen bomb notwithstanding, the Soviet people had been bombarded for years with "irrefutable" evidence about Sakharov's disloyalty and anti-Soviet tendencies. Nevertheless, Gorbachev moved quickly and decisively to rehabilitate him. Since Sakharov had been in exile in the city of Gorky and since it would have been too inconvenient for Gorbachev to fly to Gorky to speak with him, Gorbachev decided to talk by phone with Sakharov. But even though Sakharov had tried for six years to obtain a phone, the KGB had always prevented it. Thus, according to Sakharov's account, he was considerably surprised when on December 15, 1986, two telephone men and a KGB agent suddenly came to his apartment to install a phone. Even more of a surprise, the next afternoon the telephone rang. Who had the phone number? "Hello, this is Mikhail Sergeevich Gorbachev. I want you to come to Moscow to work in your laboratory for the national good."[28] Shortly thereafter virtually all the country's dissidents were released from prison and internal exile, and four years later even those exiled outside the Soviet Union were notified that their citizenship had been restored.

Equally far-reaching was Gorbachev's decision to end the Cold War. The Soviet Union would not be able to address its internal needs as long as it was spending 15 to 20 percent or more of its GNP on its military sector. The estimates are approximate because as we have seen neither we nor Soviet economists have meaningful estimates of how much was spent or what the Soviet GNP is by international standards. Despite

occasional lower estimates, a growing consensus has concluded
(even among Soviet economists who used to insist that the
Soviet Union spent no more than 2 to 3 percent of its GNP on
the military budget) that the Soviet military burden was closer
to 20 rather than 10 percent of the GNP, and needlessly large.[29]

Failure to reach some accommodation with the United States
would have set off another round of expenditures on new and
more expensive weapons. President Ronald Reagan was committed to his Strategic Defense Initiative. It may very well be
that no one understood what that meant except Ronald Reagan
and his science adviser, Edward Teller. But the Soviet leadership, unlike most Americans, believed in American technology,
and the Politburo sought to forestall the American effort. Given
Reagan's determination to end Soviet superiority in weaponry
and his deep ideological hostility to communism, that would
not be easy to do, but Gorbachev realized he did not have much
choice. The desire to cut back expenditure on the military in
large part explains the Soviet Union's reversal of Andropov's
decision to walk out of Geneva and the summits that subsequently have taken place at least once a year beginning in 1985.

Reagan was a tough bargainer. While negotiations were not
entirely one-sided, Gorbachev seemed to yield the most. As an
official in the offices of the Central Committee of the Communist Party told me at a meeting there in September 1988, "From
a hard-liner's point of view, it always seems that when Reagan
and Gorbachev meet, Gorbachev comes home without his
shirt." That view is understandable given Gorbachev's willingness to concede a disproportionate reduction of Soviet arms
compared with the American reduction, a willingness to allow
on-site inspection, and an agreement to withdraw Soviet troops
from Afghanistan. By contrast, while the United States agreed
to cease installation and remove the Pershing II missiles, it did
not agree to halt the SDI program. True, Congress cut back its
funding, but neither President Reagan nor President Bush
abandoned the program.

The one-sided nature of the bargaining negotiations reminded me of a story my father-in-law used to tell about his

arrival as an immigrant at Ellis Island. Penniless, all he had was a train ticket to St. Louis to stay with his cousin, the only person he knew in the United States. The next morning he joined another immigrant on the train in saying his morning prayers. Suddenly the train came to an abrupt halt and my father-in-law hit his head on the seat in front and started bleeding. The conductor came by, saw the bleeding, and offered my father-in-law $25 as compensation. But he was at the point in the prayer where Orthodox Jews are precluded from speaking, so he could not answer. Not understanding, the conductor increased the offer to $50. His cousin in St. Louis can be forgiven for failing to understand how my father-in-law could start out penniless in New York but arrive with $50 in St. Louis. Only in America.

There were times when Gorbachev, like the conductor, must have felt similarly stymied. Gorbachev wanted a general agreement to relax American-Soviet tensions from Reagan, but given Reagan's hearing problem, Reagan may well have asked, "What did you say?"

"Okay, I will destroy two or three missiles for every one the United States destroys," answered Gorbachev.

"What did you say?"

"Okay, I will agree to mutual inspection."

"What did you say?"

"Okay, I will withdraw Soviet troops from Afghanistan as well as Eastern Europe, reduce the size of the army, and cut Soviet aid and interference in the Third World."

Of course, this was not the scenario. Nonetheless, Gorbachev's flexibility in reaching arms accords astonished everyone, including his generals, many of whom did little to disguise their disagreement. In their eyes the Soviet Union was making itself vulnerable to the United States and throwing away all its gains from World War II, while the United States seemed to be going about its business as usual.

Whatever the grousing within the Soviet general staff, the United States also began to cut back. If for no other reason, the U.S. Congress began to cut the American defense budget. While mutual suspicion and distrust may never disappear, in a remarkably short period of time much of the hostility was transformed into an unprecedented degree of cooperation. Both sides talked of conversion and peace dividends. The invasion of Kuwait by Iraq squandered much of that dividend, but even then the United States and the Soviet Union found themselves voting on the same side of an issue dealing with the Middle East in one of the few if not first times in forty years.

The importance of the arms accords was that it allowed Gorbachev to defend his military budget cuts, which by 1990 amounted to 8–10 percent a year. To be successful in perestroika, he had to stop the drain of resources away from the civilian sector and reduce the inflationary pressure that was compounded by such large military expenditures. But that was dependent on a relaxation of American-Soviet tensions. For that reason Gorbachev began to head in this direction even before he took office in 1985, but it was not until 1987 that such policies could be implemented.

II

There were many reasons for Gorbachev's shifts in domestic and international policies, but certainly a primary one was motivated by his desire for economic reforms. At the same time, beginning in late 1986 and 1987, he also came to realize the errors in his initial economic reform efforts. Thus, like most everything else he was doing in 1987, he reoriented his concept of economic reform. His subsequent economic reform proposals were as far-reaching or at least had the potential to be as far-reaching as his political reforms, but because of indecision, inconsistency, and a poor understanding of the underlying economic forces involved, his amended economic reforms also failed to produce the intended results. In fact, because of the reluctant and halfhearted nature of many of these economic efforts, more harm than good was done. The effect was to discredit such efforts altogether and complicate subsequent economic reform initiatives that other reformers (both Gorbachev and his successors) might attempt.

The second round of economic proposals unveiled in 1987 initially evoked general excitement. Unlike the first batch of economic reforms in 1985, the second set seemed to reflect a turning away from the Stalinist economic system. Gorbachev adopted a more tolerant, even a more supportive attitude toward market mechanisms. While he had not given up his determination to remain a socialist he saw the need for far-reaching remedies.

One of the first indications of the new orientation was the decision to legalize the establishment of individual farming and cooperative businesses effective as of May 1, 1987. This represented a complete about-face from the July 1, 1986, law implemented less than a year earlier, which banned anyone from deriving unearned income from the sale of products produced and grown by any third party. Some Soviet economists explain that the 1986 crackdown was enacted against Gorbachev's better judgment and that the 1987 decision was a better reflection of his true instincts.[30] They insist that Gorbachev had been forced to yield to Politburo conservatives like Yegor Ligachev because Gorbachev had lacked sufficient political power to push through his real agenda and move to market liberalization. He may have been hedged in by conservative forces, but how then was he able to launch his political reforms and Politburo purges described earlier? Gorbachev did not seem to lack for power. His continued shifting between anti-reform and reform measures might be explained as the inevitable consequence of the fact that he had no road map. He knew where he wanted to end up, with a more productive, consumer-oriented economy (Japan would do), but he did not know how to get there. Moreover, since no socialist country had ever made the journey successfully before and since the road was poorly marked, he tried one approach for a while and, if that did not produce results quickly, he then tried something else or reversed himself, only to end up in another dead end.

This weaving back and forth was also a natural result of Gorbachev's style of coalition building. Repeatedly he sought to involve people with widely varied attitudes toward the reform process. This included those explicitly opposed to his goals. He would hear them out, but after a time purge them. Thus, despite his outspoken determination to preserve the *kolkhozy* (collective farms) and *sovkhozy* (state farms) and his expressed doubts about encouraging private and family farming, Ligachev was selected by Gorbachev to oversee the country's agricultural reforms. However, after the 28th Party Congress in July 1990, Ligachev was eased out of his central party position, including membership in the Politburo. At the same time, Gorbachev lobbied for the creation of a new center of power, the Presidential Council. This Council was part of his effort to curb party influence and replace it with governmentally constituted bodies. But to everyone's surprise, Gorbachev's council appointments included Veniamin Yarin, the founder and head of the anti-reform United Russian Workers Front, and Valentin Rasputin, an outspoken populist who was one of the spiritual godfathers of *Pamyat* or Memory, an avowedly semi-Fascist, anti-Semitic advocate of Russian nationalism. (The origins of *Pamyat* are described at greater length in Chapter 7.) Their presence probably explains why despite great anticipation, the Presidential Council was a relatively inert and shortlived body. Gorbachev also included liberal reformers such as the economist Stanislav Shatalin in the Presidential Council, but it is hard to see how there could have been anything but split votes on the important issues dealing with reform.

Given Gorbachev's indecisiveness, his coalition politics, the continuing prominence of anti-reform advocates, as well as his insistence on improving, not abandoning, socialism, it is not surprising that even when a law such as the 1987 reform supporting private and cooperative trade was passed, it, like the effort to legalize private and family farming, was considerably flawed. Initially there were all kinds of restraints on what could be sold and who could sell it. A literal reading of the private and cooperative trade law limited full-time participation in cooperatives to pensioners and students. Others could only participate after normal work hours or on weekends. These restrictions were designed to prevent members of the regular state work force from deserting their factory jobs in state enterprises and forming their own cooperatives.

This halfhearted toleration of cooperatives and private trade was guaranteed to sabotage the whole effort. Given the continuing prominence of anti-reform voices and Gorbachev's own ambiguity, it was understandable why he sought to prevent workers from abandoning state enterprises. By tying one hand behind the market's back, however, Gorbachev prevented cooperatives and private trade ventures from fulfilling one of their two most important functions—an increase in the supply of goods offered. At the same time, the other function of the market, providing an outlet for consumers to bid for the goods they want, worked only too well. Given the failure to increase most supplies adequately, it was inevitable that prices would rise. In government stores where fixed prices were established by decree, that could not have happened. Consumers could buy as long as the supply lasted or until shelves were empty. But private and cooperative businesses initially at least responded to the demand pressures of long lines by increasing their prices.[31]

Because of such behavior, cooperatives came to be viewed as either institutions owned by the Soviet version of the mafia or opportunities for illegal action by state institutions.* One of the most notorious examples of state interference involved the cooperative called Aftomatika-Nauka-Tekhnika (Automation-Science-Technology). It was set up by different government ministries, most of whom were associated with the military defense sector, and run by officials who had left government employ to make their fortune in the "private or cooperative sector." To earn hard currency, ANT went into the export business, but what it sold was Soviet military equipment. The government officials as well as the general public were in-

---

*In the Brezhnev era, what came to be called the mafia was concentrated as we saw primarily in Uzbekistan. With the advent of perestroika, however, local toughs joined by Central Asians and Georgians began to strongarm entrepreneurs all over the country. Sometimes the stronger would organize themselves into a hierarchy much like their Western counterparts. But today the term "mafia" has come to encompass any form of criminality, including young hooligans whose weapons range from fists to firebombs.

furiated when they discovered that ANT had loaded several railroad cars full of the Soviet Union's most modern tanks and sold these tanks to foreigners, presumably the French, for dollars. This was not the first time that the Soviet Union had sold its military equipment, but it was unusual to be selling such equipment to members of NATO, particularly since the bill of lading listed the tanks not as tanks but as scrap. There were some who charged that the scandal reached up to Prime Minister Ryzhkov himself. Ryzhkov denied that he was involved, but it was a serious blow to him and to the government's credibility.

On occasion the market did respond properly to economic stimuli. For example, reacting to the higher prices, flower sellers suddenly sprouted all over the Soviet Union. Flowers that once were rarely available could now be purchased at almost any time of the year and at prices not much higher than those charged at the state stores which normally were empty. For that matter, even the prices of jeans sold by cooperatives for a time fell below the price demanded on the black market. In other words, under the proper circumstances, supply and demand does work in the Soviet Union.

For the most part, however, prices of goods in the cooperatives were significantly higher than those in the state stores. After a slow start, the number of cooperatives began to increase at a respectable rate, but they met with repeated obstacles. The contrast with China is instructive. One year after they were authorized, there were only several thousand Soviet cooperatives. By July 1989, there were 133,000. That may sound impressive, but in China, where the peasants were under much less restraint, cooperatives and private enterprises beginning in the early 1980s numbered in the tens of millions and by 1988 exceeded 90 million.[32]

The relatively slower development of Soviet cooperatives had important sociological and political ramifications. Without a large number of participants the private and cooperative movement could never attain credibility. A large number of new sellers would produce a competitive environment that could hold prices down. It would also make the cooperatives more respectable, which in turn would make it more likely that others would open up their own businesses. When the number of competitors is too small and the prices are too high, the seller is viewed more as a gouger and a social deviant. Even Gorbachev joined in the verbal attack on cooperatives that buy and resell. In his eyes, "all these intermediaries are pure rogues."[33] Such a negative perception explains why by the late 1980s cooperatives were generally regarded negatively. The cooperatives also became a target of extortion by government officials and members of the mafia. Most of the public was not particularly distressed by such signs of public and private corruption— "Why bother? The cooperatives deserve what they get."

Similar attitudes deterred Soviet peasants from taking advantage of Gorbachev's initiative to set up their own family or cooperative farming efforts. Unlike China, where by the early 1980s, virtually all communes were decollectivized, in the Soviet Union the movement in this direction was slow. In both countries there was opposition from rural bureaucrats and managers of the collective and cooperative farms, but in China the party cadre were in disarray after the Cultural Revolution. Also the cadre were allowed to claim some of the choicest parcels of land and equipment. Moreover, as we saw, Deng Xiaoping had early on urged the Chinese to enrich themselves. As he put it, "It is good to be rich."

Gorbachev made no such statements. In December 1987 on Soviet television and at public meetings he encouraged peasants to establish their own farms, but the response was unenthusiastic.[34] If more had been done earlier to encourage private farming and there had been fewer contradictory signals, there might have been more takers who would have felt safer amidst the larger numbers of fellow entrepreneurs. As noted earlier, the Ukrainian peasants did reclaim their land during the German occupation in 1941. It would also have helped if Gorbachev had authorized the private ownership of land.

Until 1989, at least, the Chinese were spared the kind of backtracking and inconsistency that characterized Gorbachev's policies toward private and cooperative trade. Nor did it help when Gorbachev appointed Yegor Ligachev to oversee agricultural operations in the country. Undoubtedly this caused considerable second thinking among the peasants who might have contemplated separating themselves from the collective farms in order to set up their own farms. Repeatedly Ligachev expressed his preference for collective and state farming over private efforts.[35] How, Ligachev asked, could a socialist state abandon those poor peasants who lacked the talent needed to farm and support themselves? The farmers had no guarantee that the zigs which are permitted today would not be superseded by more restrictive zags tomorrow.

As it was, those few who did set up their own farms found themselves subjected to very unpleasant attacks. Not only were they frequently called "kulaks"—as were the 20 to 30 million peasants whom Stalin had exiled and executed in the 1920s and 1930s—but some were also physically attacked and sometimes stabbed. Others had their farms set on fire.[36] Not all this hostility is a legacy of communist indoctrination. Much of it is a remnant of pre-revolutionary attitudes as well. Family farming in Russia does not have long-established roots. Most peasants were serfs until 1861; when they were freed, they remained in their villages and worked the surrounding land as part of a commune or *obshchina*. It was only after the Stolypin reforms in 1906 and 1910 that any significant number of family farms was created. However, Stalin's subsequent collectivization drive brought the brief experiment to an end. The combination of little pre-revolutionary experience with private farming and constant attacks on private activity in the 1980s have had their impact. A Russian joke tells of a genie who offers three wishes. For his wish, the Englishman asks for a cottage overlooking the English channel. The Frenchman requests a vineyard and a château with enough rooms to house his mistresses. When the Russian is asked, he hesitates for a long time. Finally he points to his neighbor and says, "My neighbor has a goat. I don't have a goat. Kill my neighbor's goat!"

Recently there has been an increase, but as of April 1990, there were only about 20,000 private farms in all of the Soviet

Union.[37] Of those, over 12,000 were in the Republic of Georgia and 5,700 in Latvia. Not surprisingly, only 240 were registered in the Russian Republic and 4 in the Ukraine.

III

The decision to allow foreign firms to open joint ventures in the Soviet Union was as radical in its implication for Marxist ideology as was the return to private and family farms and private enterprise. New legislation spelling out the new opportunities was first published January 13, 1987, but it took until December 1988 to refine the initial joint venture legislation with subsequent amendments. In addition, bureaucratic obstructionism was often as daunting as the effort to hamstring private and cooperative business and farms. Nevertheless, the decision marked an about-face from the rejection of similar efforts that had been attempted earlier. In the mid-1970s, for example, the Bendix Corporation had lobbied hard to open up a joint venture in the Soviet Union and had prepared a plan to assist the Soviet Union in the manufacture of carburetors. It had also agreed to export a share of the output to provide for Bendix's share of the earnings. The proposal went as high as the Politburo for discussion but was ultimately rejected.

Party ideologues opposed to joint ventures with capitalist countries were fearful that capitalists would use such ventures to gain control of Soviet manufacturing, steal Soviet secrets, and exploit Soviet workers in the process.[38] Joint ventures were viewed as a form of economic and political infiltration and even espionage. In a 1982 meeting in Varna, Bulgaria, I warned East European and Soviet foreign trade officials that without joint ventures, the communists would fall hopelessly behind the developed world, but I was vehemently attacked as a provocateur by Vladimir Sushkov, who was then the Soviet deputy minister of foreign trade.[39] A few years later Sushkov was caught smuggling dollars and VCRs into the Soviet Union from Japan and was jailed. Whatever the inconsistency between his personal behavior and his ideology, he wanted to be sure that the East

Europeans at least would not succumb to the temptations of the West and corporate decadence.

Five years later, however, Soviet officials came to appreciate that their insistence on self-reliance had made it all the more likely that they would fall behind technologically. Not all the opponents had become supporters of joint ventures, but Gorbachev at least eventually concluded that the Soviet Union could only become a competitor in a world economy with an infusion from the capitalist world not only of technology but of capital and managerial skills, and that this must be a sustained effort. No one wanted to repeat the 1970s when $187 billion in oil earnings was squandered on imports of Western technology, with little to show for it. Without some ongoing Western involvement in the application and use of that technology, Gorbachev feared there would be similar waste in the 1980s.

IV

The implementation of what was called the Enterprise Law on January 1, 1988, did not involve the same kind of ideological reversal as the law on joint ventures or the law on private and cooperative efforts. Nonetheless, for many the announcement in June 1987 that an enterprise law would soon go into effect was viewed as the beginning of the first real reform effort affecting state-owned enterprises. All the other reforms we have considered so far, as far-reaching as they might be, affected only narrow segments of the Soviet economy. Some day private, cooperative, and joint ventures might become a meaningful component of the Soviet economy; but for the near future, the vast percentage of the country's productive activity would continue to revolve around state-owned enterprises. That is why, when it was announced, the Enterprise Law was regarded as the keystone of Gorbachev's economic reform.

The intent of the new law was to strike at the central planning authorities and transfer decision-making power from the center to the enterprises themselves. This would be done in stages. During 1988, enterprises accounting for 50 percent of the country's output were authorized to exercise their new powers. Managers in the remaining enterprises had to wait until January 1989. In effect this was an acknowledgment that the idea of superministries had been a bad one. Indeed, the Enterprise Law called for an ever-shrinking role for all ministries. To fill the vacuum, state enterprise managers would be encouraged to act on their own. There was no discussion about denationalizing or privatizing Soviet enterprises. That was still too radical a notion. Advocates of privatization would have to wait until 1990 before such notions could be seriously considered. Nonetheless, many of the provisions of the Enterprise Law marked a sharp departure from past thinking.

Managers were not given complete freedom of action. As before, they would still have to devote the bulk of their effort to fulfilling state orders for the delivery of goods specified by their ministries and Gosplan, the state planning organization that conceives and implements the central plan. These orders were to be called state orders—*goszakazy*. These *goszakazy* were supposed to differ from the old way of doing things because the planners were told they would have to shrink the share of *goszakazy* in the total output of the enterprise each year. The goal in 1988 was to reduce *goszakazy* to something like 85 percent of enterprise output. It was presumed that such an arrangement would appeal to the managers and workers of the enterprise because the managers would then be free to sell the remaining 15 percent of output wherever they could and at whatever price they could negotiate. Since it was assumed that the prices of the extra output would be set at a higher level than the goods delivered to the state, this supposedly would bring a windfall to the manager and his staff. And since the manager was also to be given more control of his product and wage determination, it was assumed he would move to respond to profit-making opportunities that in the past had often been ignored. To provide even more incentive, the authorities sought to reduce the financing provided as a regular subsidy to the enterprise. This would not only serve to reduce national budget expenditures and what soon was to be acknowledged as an ongoing budget deficit, it should also stimulate the manager to shift his production to more profitable fields. If implemented properly, the result would be the same as if the Soviet Union had adopted private enterprise. The attraction of higher profits would lead manufacturers to be more responsive to industrial and individual consumers. While the higher profits would reward worthy workers and managers, they would also be available to increase capital investment and expansion of the productive capabilities of those products for which consumers were prepared to pay high prices.

These measures were designed to accomplish much of what a private enterprise economy achieves, but without abandoning state ownership and/or communism. If successful, the Enterprise Law would have combined the responsiveness, feedback, and attentiveness to consumer sovereignty of the market with state ownership of the means of production. In fact, the Enterprise Law provided for one step more. Unlike most corporations in the West as well as past practices in the Soviet Union, under the Enterprise Law, Soviet factory workers were empowered to elect the manager of their enterprise. This was a complete turnabout from the past when communist and ministry officials usually chose the factory manager from a preselected and approved list of elite members of the party and government—the so-called *nomenklatura*. Many of the workers in Yugoslavia had the power to elect a workers' council which in turn elected the plant management, but within recent times few Western and virtually no Soviet labor force had been given such authority.

With all these new powers, it was easy to understand why many reformers both inside and out of the Soviet Union were so enthusiastic about the Enterprise Law. In their eyes it was the crux of the whole reform effort.[40] In the next chapter we shall see how the Enterprise Law failed to produce the expected results. If anything, it contributed to the accelerating deterioration of economic life and the supply-side depression.

V

Sensing that in the new, more relaxed political and economic environment there would be a growing demand for more decentralization of power, Gorbachev and his close adviser Alexander Yakovlev (elected to the Politburo in June 1987) decided to anticipate some of these pressures. Some of the demands would be for the overall liberalization of rights and governing procedures and some would focus specifically on more autonomy for the various ethnic groups within the USSR. Where possible, Gorbachev and Yakovlev sought to guide and shape these processes rather than be pressured into them because of political protest. However, once under way, the dynamic for change gained such momentum that it became all but impossible to stay ahead.

Ultimately both the general and the ethnic political demands would adversely affect economic stability. But because the change came so suddenly and the impact was so far-reaching, we will concentrate on the secessionist movement among the Baltic states. It provides a good case study of what is likely to happen once strict controls in a totalitarian society are relaxed, illustrating Alexis de Tocqueville's observation that "The perilous moment for a bad government is when that government tries to mend its ways."[41]

Following the Nazi-Soviet Pact of 1939, Soviet authorities gradually instituted very strict controls over the whole Baltic region. One of the first steps by the Communist government was to exile both outspoken and potential nationalists from the area. In their place, Russians were shipped in to water down the influence of the various Baltic nationality groups. Public demonstrations, the showing of the national flag, and complaints about Russification were certain to bring repression and even imprisonment. Calls for secession brought arrest as late as 1987, and demonstrations in Riga during the summer and fall of 1987 brought immediate police crackdowns.[42] The police were especially vigilant in late August 1987 to ward off the commemoration of the anniversary of the Nazi-Soviet Pact.

Recognizing the importance of the region and its economic contribution to the Soviet Union, Gorbachev made a special visit to the three republics in February 1987. Hitherto he had had little experience in dealing with ethnic issues. He held no such responsibilities either in Stavropol or in his work with agriculture while in the Central Committee. Nor did he seem unduly concerned that except for Eduard Shevardnadze, there were no representatives of the non-Slavic portion of the Soviet Union in the Politburo. An outburst of ethnic violence in Kazakhstan in December 1986 suddenly forced Gorbachev to devote more time and attention to some of the nation's different ethnic groups.

His comments during the following February visit to the Baltic states focused primarily on the overall impact of perestroika on the economy and the need for more glasnost or outspokenness in the country as a whole. As far as can be determined by his public statements at open meetings and street visits, there was no talk of independence for the area. Gorbachev's call for glasnost and more grass-roots participation, however, had set some to thinking that perhaps local autonomy and even independence should be a part of glasnost as well. Nor was it ignored that shortly after his visit to the Baltics, Gorbachev made a similar visit to Czechoslovakia in April 1987 which set off widespread public demonstrations in what was seen by most in the Soviet Union as a protest against the rigid political controls of the then very orthodox Czechoslovak Communist regime.

By mid-1988 the constraints of the past had all but disappeared. There was no official announcement to that effect. Uncertainty about a violent reaction from state authorities to protest demonstrations inhibited action for some time. Those who moved too fast and too vigorously continued to risk arrest or violence. Yet all of a sudden demonstrations began in 1988. What is it that leads someone to decide to participate in a demonstration, particularly when there have been virtually no such initiatives before? Moreover, anyone who tried to demonstrate would almost certainly be arrested. The same question has to be asked about the 1989 demonstrations in Tiananmen Square and subsequently across Eastern Europe, including Romania. Somehow the word spread that it was permissible to demonstrate and that by the summer of 1988, the communist authorities would tolerate demonstrations in the Baltic republics. Eventually the protesters became so emboldened and powerful that they were actually elected to replace those with more orthodox and restricted outlooks.

In an effort to harness this energy and diffuse the growing pressure for separatism in the Baltic states, Alexander Yakovlev decided to visit the region. He picked mid-August 1988, two weeks before the forty-ninth anniversary of the signing of the Nazi-Soviet Pact, always a flashpoint. As the most sophisticated of the Soviet republics, the Soviet leadership realized that any successful economic revitalization program would have to rely heavily on the lead of the Baltic region. Yakovlev in particular was also very sensitive to the grievances of the Baltic people against the Russians. Signaling an end to past slights, Yakovlev stressed the need for greater appreciation of ethnic differences. In Latvia he acknowledged that in the past, "The substitution of departmental 'efficiency' at the expense of the interest of the whole people has led to negative consequences for regional economies and resulted in . . . the exacerbation of social problems. . . . Perestroika opens up the way for resolving those problems. . . . In relations between nationalists, particular value is placed on caring for national interests and traditions, mutual respect, patient tolerance and a desire and ability to understand any partner and respect for the people's language and tradition. . . . There is much to do . . . to safeguard the economic autonomy and the status of republics and the national formations within the Soviet Union and to find a relationship between the Union and the republics and eliminate the numerous absurdities that exist here."[43]

Neither Yakovlev nor Gorbachev was able, however, to temper the demand for sovereignty by the Baltic peoples. If anything, Moscow's willingness to talk and negotiate was often interpreted as weakness and a signal that even more could be demanded of the Kremlin. Before long, crowds of 500,000 or more were insisting on new political and economic freedoms. Given that Estonia's population totals slightly more than 1.5 million people, Latvia's 2.5 million, and Lithuania's 3.5 million, many of whom at least in Estonia and Latvia are Russians, not Balts, turnouts of this size were a major political statement that could not go unnoticed.

Tolerating such mass turnouts in the Baltics emboldened those in other Soviet republics. They too began to demand similar concessions, which ultimately led to declarations of economic and political sovereignty and before long even political independence.

VI

The breakdown in the Soviet system highlighted by the upheaval in the Baltic region was in many ways predictable.* The simultaneous introduction of the economic reforms associated with perestroika and the political reforms referred to as glasnost all but guaranteed that chaos would follow.

There may well have been better strategies that Gorbachev should have considered. Certainly the emphasis on the machine-tool industry, discipline, and superministries was a seri-

---

*Of course, such assertions are more easily made after the fact. In addition, those who claim that they had predicted what was ultimately to take place, especially if they are prolific writers, often find it useful to protect themselves with all kinds of restrictive assumptions as well as predictions of just the opposite which they can fall back upon if the original prediction is wrong. While I too may be guilty of such devious tactics, it happens that as early as March 1987, I predicted that should he hold to the reforms he had set for himself, Gorbachev's efforts would probably fail and that it was unlikely that he would still be in office four years later, that is, by March 1991.[44]

Predicting such changes four years in advance was a rash thing to do. At the time, Gorbachev was just beginning to move into the second stage of perestroika and most observers were optimistic if not euphoric about the changes he was attempting. Occasionally there were even accusations that I was being anti-Soviet. Reportedly, Gorbachev and Yakovlev also felt that way. After my predictions were carried on Voice of America, Yakovlev called in the American chargé d'affaires from the U.S. Embassy in Moscow and demanded that American academics stay out of Soviet domestic politics.

While the prediction about Gorbachev being forced out of office may have been unduly pessimistic, even the assumption that in four years Gorbachev, then at the height of his popularity inside the Soviet Union, would soon find himself in disrepute, was not an obvious conclusion.

ous mistake. But even if Gorbachev had opted for the Chinese way, with more reliance on agriculture and consumer goods, he would still have encountered difficulties. It was unrealistic to expect people who have been deprived of political rights for seventy years to temper their demands once they are allowed to express themselves. This becomes particularly difficult if they perceive they are not improving their standard of living as quickly as they anticipated or that others are gaining at their expense. Under the circumstances, others who were less effective politicians than Gorbachev would probably have had even more problems. But as early as 1987, it was apparent that combining perestroika and glasnost was like mixing sulfuric acid and water—it would set off sparks. The lifting of strict political controls after seventy years of often ruthless enforcement was bound to cause excesses.

Given Gorbachev's approach to perestroika, it was hard to see when, if at all, there would be an outpouring of high-quality consumer goods. Moreover the high prices, the unemployment, and income inequality that sooner or later flow from the economic reforms at least initially were bound to cause economic distress, which in turn would give rise to even more acute economic disintegration.

As difficult as it might be to implement either perestroika or glasnost separately, when they are implemented simultaneously, it is of the utmost importance that public expectations never run too far ahead of what is feasible. On the one hand, with glasnost the public is urged to speak out when they feel they are being ill-served. Ventilate their complaints, they were told. That was the way to expose wrongdoing and wrongdoers. On the other hand, perestroika is bound to cause disquiet among major segments, if not the entire population. Perestroika, whether or not it succeeds, will create sharp price rises, a major increase in unemployment, and income inequality—all social disfunctions that were never overt under the old regime. Told to speak out often enough, sooner or later it is likely the public will come to believe that it is safe to do just that and eventually will begin to complain about these new phenomena even if the standard of living is improved. However, if there is no improvement in material conditions, the public will likely not only ventilate their discontent, they might even hyperventilate.

This combustible combination of perestroika and glasnost as much as anything predetermined that there would be growing ethnic, political, and social tension clashes, complicating the already difficult process of economic reform. In the end, Gorbachev ran the risk of being mocked for bringing the Soviet people words but no material benefits; glasnost but no perestroika. Moreover, once given glasnost, the public were likely to take that glasnost for granted while they focused even more on the failures of perestroika.

Reflecting their frustrations, Muscovites tell a story that seems to sum up not only their growing disappointment with Gorbachev's leadership, but the growing difficulties of their daily lives: Lenin was on a train when it suddenly came to a halt. Eager to determine what happened, he summoned the conductor. "We have run out of track," the conductor reported. Lenin thought for a moment and then announced that he would order a *subbotnik* (a "voluntary" Saturday workday imposed periodically on the population in order to squeeze an extra day's work out of them without pay) in order to build the necessary track.

A few years later, Stalin found himself on the same train. During the ride, the train again ran out of track. In response, Stalin ordered the conductor to shoot the engineer and put the engineer's family in a labor camp.

When it was Khrushchev's time, he ordered the conductor to take the track that was in back of the train and lay it down in the front.

Brezhnev had a less strenuous approach to resolving the problem. "Pull down the shades," he ordered. "Everyone bounce up and down and pretend the train is moving."

Finally it was Gorbachev's turn. When told that there was no track, Gorbachev turned to Raisa and said, "Did you hear that, there is no track!" Then he called in the Politburo. "There is no track," he said. Next he convened the Central Committee, then the Supreme Soviet. Finally he went on television. "Imagine," he said in a warm and candid manner, "there is no track!"

6

The Effort Collapses

Once having stumbled, Gorbachev found it virtually impossible to regain his balance. By mid-1987, possibly even beginning in late 1986, the damage had already been done. After two years or so of poor results, he had lost much of his credibility, at least on economic matters. Thereafter, the crisis began to build. By mid-1988 the decline was becoming evident and important economic institutions were beginning to disintegrate. Even if he had an ideal program at that point, he would have had a great deal of difficulty redressing his past mistakes. By that time only massive radical surgery could have rescued the economy.

At the core of his problem was a macro-economic difficulty of his own making. Heretofore Soviet officials, including Gorbachev and his economic advisers, thought only in terms of central plans and administrative decision making. Macro- and microeconomics were capitalist system-type issues that had no relevance for a centrally planned economy. Stalin in effect had decreed null and void the impact of taxes, expenditures, monetary policy, interest rates (macroeconomics), and supply and demand, and competition (microeconomics) played little or no role. Unaccustomed to paying attention to such matters, they ignored signs of runaway inflation until it was too late.

For decades Soviet officials had insisted that the national

budget was in balance. Even though this was not true, they did not worry about such things. And as we saw, when even a Politburo member like Gorbachev asked Andropov if there were budget deficits, he was told that it was nothing he should worry about. More important to the Soviet leadership was whether or not the five-year plans were in balance. This approach was a natural reaction from engineers who predominated in Gosplan's offices. They understood the need to balance physical supplies, but not revenues and expenditures. Consequently an unbalanced budget in their eyes would not have made much difference.

When unexpectedly in October 1988 it was announced as part of glasnost that the Soviet budget had been running a deficit since 1976, the reaction was initially more one of bemusement than one of great concern.[1] That there had been budget deficits for a long period of time and that the public had not been informed apparently seemed to have made little difference. As far as most economists could ascertain, the economy in that period operated much as it usually did. Moreover, this was not the only time the government had lied.*

According to official but untrue statistics, Boris Gosteev, the minister of finance, reported in October 1985 that the Soviet Union had generated a budget surplus of 4.1 billion rubles.[2] Belatedly in 1988, he corrected himself to reveal that on the contrary, the 1985 budget had not run a surplus but a deficit of 37 billion rubles, or about $59 billion.[3] Conditions apparently had not changed much in the early years of the Gorbachev era. Gosteev anticipated that in 1989 there would be a budget deficit of 35 billion rubles or about $56 billion, not much different from the deficit ultimately reported in 1985.[4] A few scholars in the West, particularly the émigré economist Igor Birman and subsequently Judy Shelton, who relied heavily on Birman's work, felt themselves vindicated.[5] After years of being ignored by most other Western Sovietologists for his "myopic" insistence that the Soviet Union was running a big deficit which in

*Even Gorbachev, as we saw earlier, was denied a full accounting by Andropov when he tried to find out if the Soviet Union had a budget deficit.

turn had caused an outpouring of rubles into the system, Birman in particular finally had his day.

It became quickly apparent, however, that the deficit and its magnitude involved more than a debate among Sovietologists. Some important economic issues were involved, affecting not only how the Soviet economy had been operating, but how it would operate in the future. The sudden acknowledgment of a deficit suggested there might be a cover-up on other economic matters as well. In his confession, Minister of Finance Gosteev, for example, continued to insist that the Soviet Union would spend only 20.2 billion rubles (about $33 billion), or almost 2 percent of the Soviet GNP, on the maintenance of Soviet armed forces.[6] Given that military expenditures constituted the largest single budget item in the Soviet budget, this seemed a ridiculously low figure. Subsequently Gorbachev himself acknowledged that the military budget amounted to 77 billion rubles, or some 7 percent of the Soviet GNP. Since so much more was being spent on the military, how could Gosteev report that the budget deficit in 1989 was only 35 billion rubles? Most observers in the West, including the CIA, agreed that the defense budget was closer to 15 to 20 percent of the Soviet GNP, and some Soviet critics said the military expenditures may have been as high as 25 percent of the Soviet GNP.[7]

This absence of a full accounting revealed the limits to glasnost. Equally important, because of continued quirks in the Soviet pricing system, Soviet officials really do not know how to price their military equipment. Traditionally, the military sector has received special treatment. There is a strong sense among many Soviet and Western economists that because of the subsidies provided to enterprises producing military goods, the Soviet military industrial complex claims a larger share of the country's resources than is reflected in the statistics. That means that machinery used for military prduction is priced more cheaply than comparable machinery used for civilian production. Soviet soldiers and also draftees receive a very low salary. Reinforcing that skepticism is the fact that the Soviet economists assigned to official commissions to design some of the reform programs that have been officially commissioned are also unable to obtain the official data.[8]

What had caused the rapid increase in the budget deficit? Since Ministry of Finance officials acknowledged that the budget had moved into the red in the early 1970s before Gorbachev was summoned to Moscow, it is evident that deficits are not solely due to faulty decision making on Gorbachev's part.[9] The deficit fluctuated in a relatively narrow range between 1978 and 1985 (Table 3).

But the increases in the deficit beginning in 1986 are mainly Gorbachev's doing. In one year, from 1985 to 1986, the budget deficit increased almost threefold from 17–18 billion rubles to 48–50 billion.* Of course the public was given no hint at the time, but the increase in the deficit can be attributed to Gorbachev's approach to perestroika. As we saw in Chapter 4, Gorbachev's first version of perestroika involved an increased emphasis on the role of heavy industry and machine tools, or what the Soviets call sector A. His fetish with machine tools also had a double-barreled impact on Soviet foreign trade. On the one hand, he and his advisers deliberately set out to increase imports of Western machine tools. On the other hand, to pay for these imports, Gorbachev found it necessary to reduce imports of consumer goods. This resulted in shortages and lost sales tax revenue.

As the data in Table 4 show, by 1988, the Soviet Union had increased imports of machinery by approximately 2.5 billion rubles over 1984. This was done despite the fact that due to the fall in the world price of oil, petroleum export sales to both hard and soft currency buyers fell from a high of 30.9 billion rubles in 1984 in the pre-Gorbachev period to about 20.7 billion rubles in 1988. This loss constituted a staggering drop of 10 billion rubles, or one third of the total of the Soviet Union's export earning capacity.

*Gosteev's figure for 1985 is 37 billion rubles.

TABLE 3

Estimates of Soviet Budget Deficit
(billion rubles)

	1978	'79	'80	81	'82	'83	'84	'85	'86	'87	'88	'89	'90
A	16	15	13	11	17	10	11	17	50	64	68		
B											90	90	
C											100	120	200
D								37					

Sources

Rows A & B: Central Intelligence Agency, *The USSR: Sharply Higher Budget Deficits Threaten Perestroyka* (Washington, D.C.: Sov. 88-10043U, September 1988), p. 19.

Row C: RFE/RL, September 22, 1989, p. 12 (author's estimates).

Row D: Boris Gosteev, *The Wall Street Journal*, November 2, 1988, p. A 17.

Fortunately, two good harvests in 1986 and 1987 made it possible for the Soviet Union to reduce grain imports. This allowed a reduction of 2–3 billion rubles in import expenditures, making up for some of the shrinkage in export earnings. But poor harvests in 1988 and 1989 made it necessary to increase grain imports by 50 percent in 1988 and again in 1989, thereby increasing hard currency expenditures on imports. When it became clear that oil export revenues had fallen off sharply, Gorbachev's advisers would have been prudent to recommend reducing machinery imports by a substantial amount as early as 1985 and certainly before 1987. As Table 4 shows, however, Gorbachev and his staff did just the opposite; rather than cut back on machinery imports, they actually increased them.

To compensate, Soviet officials cut imports of consumer goods. This began in 1986 and continued each year into 1989, so that by 1988 Soviet consumer goods were about 1.5 billion rubles less than they had been in 1985 (see Table 4). With sales tax and exchange rate supplements included, these imported consumer goods would have been marked up about sixfold by the time they were sold to Soviet consumers. This explains why Soviet authorities report that under Gorbachev, food and consumer good imports fell by the equivalent of 8.5 billion rubles in retail prices.[10] This slashing of consumer good imports and the resulting loss of sales tax revenue had serious fiscal implications.

The fetish with industrial machinery was further reflected in the domestic budget. Budget expenditures on capital investment for both factory construction and machinery (particularly sector A—heavy industry) continued to rise steadily throughout the Gorbachev years, with a particularly notable surge in 1986.[11]

Taken alone, the increase in budget expenditures for machine tools would probably not have been enough to precipitate the breakdown in fiscal discipline that has proven to be so difficult to control. However, when this expenditure increase was com-

TABLE 4

Soviet Exports and Imports
(million rubles)

Product	1983	1984	1985	1986	1987	1988
			Imports			
Machinery	22,747	23,944	25,683	25,455	25,155	26,584
Food (except grain) and consumer goods	11,079	12,411	13,205	12,926	11,964	11,738
Food and consumer goods plus grain	14,724	17,776	18,045	14,961	13,516	14,101
			Exports			
Petroleum, crude and refined	28,216	30,895	28,188	22,464	22,826	20,708
Natural gas	6,302	7,463	7,695	7,358	6,381	5,197

Source: *Vneshnaia Torgovlia, Statisticheskii sbornik,* annual editions, 1980 through 1988.

bined with a decision about social policy, the problem was compounded. The May 1985 crackdown on vodka sales, while regarded primarily as a laudable social policy, had serious economic implications.

The curb on the sale of vodka combined with the sale of fewer consumer good imports resulted in a drop in turnover tax receipts, the Soviet counterpart of a sales tax. From a high of 103 billion rubles in 1983 and 1984, turnover tax collections fell by nearly 13 percent to a low of 91.5 billion rubles in 1986. Overall the anti-alcohol drive was said to cost 200 billion rubles.[12]

The impact of higher budget expenditures on machine tools combined with lower turnover tax collections was dramatic. It was the main reason for the increase in the size of the deficit to 48 billion rubles in 1986. Once the 17 billion ruble deficit was breached, what little economic discipline was left seemed to dissipate. Thereafter, the deficit increased each year and continued to grow. By 1989, the budget deficit was not the 35 billion rubles that Gosteev anticipated, but at least 90 billion rubles. A new minister of finance, Valentin Pavlov, reported that the deficit in 1989 actually totalled 120 billion rubles, or 10–12 percent of the Soviet GNP.[13] Again the disparity probably reflects the continuing inability of Soviet statisticians to determine what the figures actually were.

Because of strenuous and determined efforts to cut budget subsidies, it was predicted that the deficit of 1990 would be reduced to 60 billion rubles.[14] Similar to efforts in the United States, that proved to be wishful thinking. Unofficial estimates in October 1990 indicated that instead of a shrinkage, the 1990 Soviet budget deficit had actually increased to over 150 billion rubles and maybe even 200 billion rubles.[15] Some officials in the Ministry of Finance insist the deficit was closer to 100 billion rubles, but as of 1990 most Soviet economists acknowledge in private conversation that with the size of the military budget in doubt and the various republics acting as if they are sovereign countries, no one really knows what the deficit is. Led by the Russian Republic, the republics began to withhold three quarters of the 1991 tax collections which the center had expected to collect. This caused Vladimir Orlov, then the minister of finance, to warn that the first quarter budget deficit already exceeded the planned deficit for the whole year.

Gorbachev's well-intended but misguided economic strategy was in itself enough to cripple any chance to bring about the economic revitalization he wanted so badly. But the macroeconomic implications of his budget deficit eventually came to have their own impact. Whatever their commitment to socialist economic planning, Soviet officials by 1989 and certainly by 1990 belatedly came to understand that macroeconomics and budget deficits, particularly large ones, do matter. As Gorbachev himself admitted in an October 19, 1990, speech to the Supreme Soviet of the USSR, "We lost control over the financial situation in the country. This was our most serious mistake in the years of perestroika. . . . Achieving a balanced budget today is the number one task and the most important one."[16] But Gorbachev's disregard of macroeconomics and the conventional wisdom that planning was what mattered had taken its toll. Because it had been ignored, the budget deficit had become so large that it set in motion forces that made the malfunctioning of the system all the harder to remedy. The magnitude of the deficit began to threaten the continued functioning of the national economic system.

One of the most serious consequences of the growing budget deficit was a sharp jump in inflation. For the most part, these deficits and debts were financed the old-fashioned way—by turning on the printing presses, which in turn caused the sudden inflation and goods shortages. Inflation is not an entirely new phenomenon in the Soviet Union. Because of the persistent emphasis on military expenditures and heavy industry, there has always been a tendency to pay out a wage bill that was larger than the value of the consumer goods and services available for purchase with those wages. And since most prices were carefully controlled in state shops, the result was a steady form of suppressed inflation. But the increasing size of the budget deficit and the legalization of cooperative ventures with considerably more power to set their own prices made inflation overt even in official Soviet statistics. In 1988, for the first time since World War II, prices of virtually all Soviet goods began to rise. The impact was immediate. According to the Soviet journalist-economist Vasilii Seliunin, the emphasis on heavy industry, combined with the outpouring of newly printed rubles, explained why "we have fewer goods than planned and twice as much additional money. What happens in this case? During the second half of last year [1988] trade began to fall to pieces before our eyes."[17] By 1989, many prices were increasing at a rate of 20 percent or more—that is, when one could find the goods to buy. Some Soviet economists even began to warn of hyperinflation.[18] The reports that prices on the collective farm markets had increased by almost 70 percent in early 1991 over 1990 and the threefold April 2, 1991, increase in the price of basic consumer goods in state stores seemed to validate such warnings.[19]

Gorbachev's decision to curb the sale of alcohol was particularly unpopular. From 1985 to 1986, production of alcoholic beverages was cut in half, from 600 million deciliters to 325 million deciliters.[20] No matter how laudable the decision seemed at first, the crackdown had several unintended consequences in addition to the loss of state revenues. To the working class, this was a direct assault on their main escape from socialist reality. Gorbachev's attack on vodka effectively alienated him further from the proletariat. It also engendered a shortage psychology. After a few months of effective enforcement, thousands of enterprising Russians realized that there was much money to be made in distilling home-produced vodka, moonshine, or *samogon,* as the Soviets call it. Distilling became a massive business. Moonshiners, however, found they needed large quantities of sugar for their work. In a short time it was not only vodka but sugar that had disappeared from the country's shops, even in Moscow. For the country as a whole, sugar consumption increased from 42 kilograms per capita in 1985 to

50 kilograms per capita in 1990. But the demand grew even faster and so did the sugar shortage, an almost unknown event in the pre-Gorbachev era.

The unprecedented sugar shortage combined with the decision to reduce consumer good imports, plus the surge of newly printed rubles and resultant inflation, triggered a buyers' panic. To protect themselves from any future fall in the value of the ruble, Soviet consumers began to seek out tangible items to buy in exchange for the increasingly worthless ruble. People started to hoard. One Moscow friend acknowledged that there was no more room to store the sugar that she had to buy with ration coupons. As she put it, "It has reached the point where I can no longer squeeze into my kitchen." Nonetheless, she continued to buy for fear that sugar would not be available when she needed it or that the price would be even higher. When I saw her a few months later and asked if conditions had changed any, she replied, "No. Now I have another problem. I can't move around my bedroom. It's filled with soap." In this kind of environment it was difficult to keep much on store shelves. By mid-1991 conditions had deteriorated so that her kitchen and bedroom were empty, and even with ration coupons there was almost nothing for her to buy. Most Soviet stores at various times were empty of such products as jewelry, furniture, milk products, sausage, soap, laundry detergent, pasta, tea, matches, and even salt.

The story is told about the man who walks into one of the main Moscow meat markets. "I would like two kilos of meat," he says. "We don't have any," reports the clerk. The visitor takes out his pad and notes "No meat." After a visit to a succession of stores, he writes, "No fish," "No chicken," "No eggs," "No cigarettes," and finally "No bread." At that, a beefy-looking man in a leather overcoat accosts him, demanding to know what he is writing and why he is bothering all the sales clerks. The visitor innocently replies that this was his first visit to Moscow in forty years and his wife asked him to keep a diary so that when he returned home, he could remember what he had seen. "Forty years ago you would have been shot for this," harrumphs the watchdog in the leather coat. Reflecting on that for a second, the visitor takes out his pen once more, and this time adds "No bullets!"

I

Gorbachev's efforts at reforming state-owned industry have been equally counterproductive. To many observers, the keystone of Gorbachev's reform effort was his June 1987 reform, the Enterprise Law. Of course, in 1985, intensification, *uskoreniie*, superministries, and Gosagroprom were keystones. The Shatalin Five Hundred Day Plan of 1990 and the anti-crisis plan of 1991 were other examples. Each year Gorbachev seemed to come up with at least one more final solution. But at the time, the Enterprise Law seemed to promise a solution to the most intractable sector of the Soviet economy, the big state enterprises controlled by various industrial ministries. By 1987, Gorbachev came to understand that unless these industrial enterprises acted more independently, there could be no economic reform. Under the Enterprise Law, the role of the ministers in Moscow was to be curbed and the role of the plant managers out in the field to be expanded. Within broad limits, managers were given authority to set wages, determine product mix, and finance the operation and expansion of the enterprises with bank loans and deductions from profits. To ensure that this new initiative would win the support of the work force, the enterprise workers were allowed to elect their own managers.

Most important, managers as we saw were promised that each year they could set aside a larger and larger share of production, which they could sell on their own at whatever price they could negotiate in the market. It was assumed that the attraction of higher prices and therefore higher profits would make managers eager to respond to these new opportunities. The share of output retained by the state in the form of state orders or *goszakazy* was to shrink to 70 percent. It was assumed that the opportunity to sell their output outside the control of the state plan would appeal to enterprise managers because the prices customers would be willing to pay for goods that were usually in short supply would be higher than official state prices. These prices would generate higher profits and bonuses for the managers and workers, which in turn would stimulate increased output that would serve to establish a market equilibrium at lower prices. Eventually, as the state's share continued to shrink and the freely marketed share expand, economic planning would cease to play a meaningful role. *Goszakazy* would not disappear completely; they would be available to respond to some government needs, just as the Department of Defense orders equipment in the capitalist world.

It was a good idea, but it did not work. The Enterprise Law went part of the way, but not far enough, and as usual it was too little, too late. Unwilling to attempt too much too soon, it was decided that enterprises producing 50 percent of the country's output would shift to the new guidelines as of January 1, 1988, and that the rest of the country's industries would shift a year later, in January 1989. Not surprisingly, this staggered approach caused confusion. When a similar staged reform had been proposed in the mid-1960s, cynics immediately joked about what would happen if Moscow traffic authorities behaved in the same way. As they told the story, it was reported that in order to improve traffic safety, Moscow traffic engineers suggested that the authorities switch the traffic flow in the city to the British system where traffic moves on the left side. However, one of the more cautious engineers warned that a sudden shift of such magnitude might cause difficulty for infrequent drivers who need more time to adjust. Therefore, as a compromise, it was decided that as of January, taxis and truck drivers would switch to the left side of the road while ordinary drivers would stay on the right side for at least the remainder of the year in order to have more time to prepare for the switch.

Confusion was caused not only because some enterprises were allowed to reduce their share of *goszakazy*, but also because essential parts of the traditional market infrastructure were missing. There were no wholesalers available for industrial managers to turn to for needed supplies when they wanted to go beyond the product mix authorized by the plan. Nor were there wholesalers for them to sell to. Manufacturers had to establish their own trading relations with potential suppliers and customers. There were no middlemen available to perform that function for them. Since very few manufacturers had access to the necessary information (even the ministries were not completely informed), only a few of the more venturesome enterprise managers were willing to risk setting off on their own. It was much safer to adhere to the old system. Most enterprise managers were delighted therefore when their ministries continued to insist on control of not 70 percent, but often 90 percent or even 100 percent of the factory's output. And for those ministries that tried to operate with a 70 percent share of *goszakazy,* more often than not the enterprises themselves insisted that the ministers take a larger share. It might mean lost profit opportunities, but offsetting that enterprise managers freed themselves from having to worry about finding customers, disposing of output, or obtaining adequate supplies. All of this suited the ministries, which were equally reluctant to see the enterprises become more independent. Were they to take up the challenge, there would be no need for the ministries or their bureaucrats.

Not only did the Enterprise Law fail to facilitate the move to a market system and reduce the role of planners and ministries, in many ways it contributed to the magnitude of the macro and monetary problems. This law was one of the factors that helps explain why the economic situation actually began to deteriorate under Gorbachev. With increased authority to choose their own product assortment, the managers invariably opted to increase the share of expensive goods they produced. While this provided them with higher profits, it also guaranteed the disappearance of cheaper products, thereby exacerbating the problem of shortages.

At the same time that the Enterprise Law was adding to the shortage of certain types of goods, it was fueling an increase in overall demand. To curry favor with the workers to whom they owed their jobs, managers responded readily to pressure for higher wages. As a consequence, wages rose rapidly. In 1988 average wages rose by 8 percent, and in 1989 they rose 13 percent.[21]

With hard budget constraints and rigorous self-financing limitations, there might have been fewer problems. The managers would have had to act with more restraint or face bankruptcy. But the enterprise managers knew that the state would not tolerate bankruptcy, with its resulting unemployment and abandonment of capital. As expected, the state continued to provide subsidies when asked. Because of the increased distortion in the product mix and the newly aggravated wage inflation, the subsidies required were greater than before the introduction of the Enterprise Law. Recognizing that the law had been a mistake, Gorbachev on June 11, 1990, amended it by taking away the workers' right to elect their own managers.[22] The intention was to reduce wage inflation, which may have helped somewhat; but most of the damage had already been done.

II

Despite his reluctance to turn to the market and his lack of an effective strategy, Gorbachev achieved one thing: the gradual dismantling of the planned and administrative economic system. This dismantling was not entirely intentional. As we saw, in 1985, when Gorbachev established superministries, his original goal was to strengthen the planning system by making it more effective and efficient. However, as he merged, created, and abolished a dizzying array of ministries and planning organizations, the effect was to create confusion, disarray, and ultimately ineffectiveness. Ministries and their ministers were here today and likely to be gone tomorrow. While it had never been easy, it now became increasingly difficult to find someone who could answer relevant questions. And if answers were given, there was no guarantee that they would not be reversed a few days later.

It was not that Gorbachev completely dismantled or destroyed the planning system. He did not. Nor was it certain that he wanted to destroy it completely. That became evident in the summer of 1990 as he struggled to decide on yet another reform effort. As we shall see, he could not make up his mind whether to support the far-reaching Shatalin Five Hundred Day Plan or alternative plans that were considerably less radical in scope and retained some elements of planning. Whatever Gorbachev's intentions, this continued bombarding of the planning mechanism resulted in the increased weakening of planning effectiveness. At the same time, little was being done to establish an alternative mechanism such as more reliance on the market. An inevitable result of Gorbachev's flip-flopping was that the Soviet Union had neither an effective market nor a planning system. Just as he had his doubts about central planning, he was uncertain about too much reliance on the market and private ownership. As late as April 1990, he gave a speech in Sverdlovsk in which he complained, "They say, 'let's have free enterprise and give the green light to all forms of private ownership. . . . But I cannot accept such ideas. . . . They are impossible ideas."[23]

Had he been more committed to the market and private property, however, there was still little likelihood that Gorbachev could have produced an overnight transformation. Even in countries like Poland, where the market is the goal, it takes time for the market to develop in its full complexity. As the American economists Kenneth Boulding and Joseph Berliner have noted, creating a market is a bit like trying to build a forest. The market, like a forest, is easy to destroy: just chop it down. But planting twenty trees does not create a forest, nor does opening several retail stores create a market. A forest, like a market, is an organic phenomenon, with an infrastructure of insects, animals, and underbrush, which serve as forms of supportive life, sources of supply, and servicing systems.

Once legalized, private trade can immediately provide certain basic functions, especially at the retail level. But it is too much to expect that wholesaling, let alone sophisticated banking, credit, and ultimately fiscal and monetary processes, will emerge quickly enough to produce a relatively balanced, efficient economy. It takes decades, for example, to evolve a Federal Reserve-type banking operation or a reasonably fair and operational tax system. The difficulty in creating a host of new and highly complex institutions from scratch is compounded by the absence of qualified personnel. Not only were the most innovative and productive farmers destroyed as a class by the early 1930s, but for decades Soviet authorities punished or suppressed anyone who demonstrated entrepreneurial instincts. Nor did the Soviet Union train a cadre of technocrats in the mysteries of monetary and macro policy. To assign Soviet officials bred in the environment of central planning the task of fine tuning the economy by manipulating the money supply and adjusting tax policies would be like assigning a railroad engineer who has never flown before the task of flying a Boeing 747. It is not impossible, but it has its risks.

An illustration of where Soviet officials with inappropriate backgrounds and training ran afoul of a very different economic environment occurred in May 1990. Seeking to reduce the government's budget deficit, Soviet planners decided to reduce agricultural subsidies that were used to hold down retail prices. One way to accomplish this was to raise retail prices. Therefore, as we saw they decided to raise the prices for bread and some other basic foodstuffs on July 1, 1990, and again on January 1, 1991. Such a decision was bound to generate protest, but in an effort to win the confidence of the people and change their secretive practices, Soviet officials decided to announce their plan in May, six weeks in advance of the planned action.[24] Inexperienced in dealing with market forces, the planners were stunned and simply unprepared when, like locusts, Soviet consumers mobbed the state stores and emptied them of what little was left, including some basic products such as groats and flour. To pay for all these goods, consumers dipped into their savings, which in turn provoked a run on the banks.[25] The result was not only a short-run depletion of money in the banks and goods in the stores, but the breakdown of the Soviet distribution system for several months. By the time the Ministry of Finance eventually decided to call in all 50- and 100-ruble notes and followed that a few months later, on April 2, 1991, with a price increase, the distribution system seemed unable to respond.

With so many institutional complexities to master, so many ideological obstacles to overcome, and so much bureaucratic opposition to break down, it was no wonder that Gorbachev soon found himself in a virtual twilight zone where neither the market, the plan, nor a combination of both worked effectively. As Pavel Bunich, the deputy chairman of the Supreme Soviet's Committee for Economic Reform, put it, "We now have neither a carrot nor a stick." Instead of enjoying the strengths of both economic systems, more often than not, the Soviet economy has been afflicted with the weaknesses of both.

The decision in 1989 to pay hard currency to peasants to increase their grain harvest was another illustration of these weaknesses. The assumption was made, probably correctly, that if the peasants knew that they would be paid with *valuta* (convertible currencies) rather than the depreciated ruble for any extra effort, they would work harder, thereby making more food available for the general population. But another assumption based on their bureaucratic interests led Soviet officials to believe that Soviet peasants could not suddenly be entrusted with large sums of *valuta*. After all, the peasants lacked knowledge and experience in spending such funds responsibly. Given the opportunity, they would probably squander those funds on speculative ventures with dishonest operators or might waste them in the purchase of frivolous consumer goods. To prevent such happenings, Soviet authorities decided not to give the peasants the actual foreign cash to which they were entitled, but to place it in special *valuta* accounts at the bank. The funds in such accounts could then be applied to the special list of goods drawn up by the authorities. The price of the goods listed in the catalogue was jacked up and a one-third mark-up charge for all transactions was added to cover the administrative cost for this extra effort. Recognizing that they were being taken, the peasants for the most part refused to participate in these efforts. As a consequence, despite a slightly higher 1989 harvest, deliveries to the state actually fell 27 million tons below plan. The experiment thereafter was downgraded and more or less forgotten.

Because of such misadventures, the move to the market was associated with the exploits of opportunists who took advantage of the shortages to charge exorbitant prices. At the same time, bureaucrats and government enterprise managers continued to provide one another with operating subsidies from the national budget for inefficient, unprofitable heavy industrial operations. Such endeavors did little to satisfy the population's clamor for more consumer goods. Instead, the growing budget subsidies continued to add to the country's budget deficit and consequent inflation while not satisfying the consumers' purchasing power.

III

As the Soviet economy and ruble continued to falter, so did confidence in Gorbachev's leadership. One after another, local leaders began to take economic as well as political matters into their own hands. In some instances this was done out of self-defense; in others there was a growing conviction that adherence to the Gorbachev way of doing things would almost certainly bring economic collapse and what eventually would become the supply-side depression. Economic secession and increasing independence admittedly would be risky, but at least it allowed for some chances of success. Just as jumping on a life raft might be risky, it was probably better than staying on board the *Titanic*.

Those who first acted out of self-defense were usually people from the relatively more prosperous and successful regions of the country. As the increase in the issuance of rubles outpaced the increase in the production of consumer goods, those with rubles began to seek out pockets of the country with relatively more goods available. Muscovites, for example, had always complained that as much as 40 percent of Moscow's retail sales were grabbed up by those from outside the city.[26] For many years, this had been taken as part of the price one paid for living in Moscow; but when economic conditions in 1989 began to deteriorate at an accelerating pace, such tolerant attitudes toward out-of-towners began to disappear.

The residents of the Baltic republics who were also better provided were among the first to react as an increasing number of outsiders found their way to the Baltic shops. As before, these outsiders along with local residents paid in rubles; but as shortages became the rule, there was less willingness to accept rubles because suppliers from outside the Baltics refused to replenish supplies for rubles. They insisted on barter. Thus, to ensure there would be enough available for local residents, and in accord with the rise of republic nationalism, authorities in the Baltic states banned the sale of high-priority products such as meat and appliances to non-residents. Before they could make a purchase, those with Russian accents were required to show their internal Soviet passports to prove they were residents of one of the Baltic republics and thus less likely to take their purchases outside the republics. Naturally this provoked charges of discrimination, especially from the Russian-speaking residents of the region.

These restrictions had economic consequences beyond the borders of the Baltic republics. The first outsiders to feel the economic pinch were the people of Leningrad, who depended heavily on the Baltic republics for much of their meat deliveries. As these supplies became more and more irregular, the Leningrad authorities in turn began to protect their residents by banning sales to those who were not legal inhabitants of the city and who could not show identity papers or ration coupons. As of January 10, 1990, people shopping in Leningrad were also required to show their internal passports, and as of December 1, 1990, actual ration coupons were demanded. This unprecedented municipal protectionism infuriated residents of the surrounding areas, who not only shopped in Leningrad but also supplied many of the goods, food in particular, that Leningraders enjoyed. Soon after, the nearby city of Novgorod imposed a similar shopping embargo on all visitors from Leningrad. At the same time, similar bans were imposed by Uzbeks on Kazakhs, and Kazakhs on Uzbeks. Before long, such protective measures were instituted all over the country. After the ill-fated May 1990 announcement of the impending July 1 price increase, even Moscow followed suit. As one of the best-supplied cities in the country, Moscow became the target of a nationwide shopping spree. Within days after the depletion of its shop counters, Moscow also insisted that shoppers show proof of residency, which in turn provoked similar restrictions by the suburbs on Moscow visitors. By December 1990, eight of the regions surrounding Moscow also in retaliation banned the delivery of milk to Moscow itself. From being one of the best-provisioned cities in the Soviet Union, Moscow sometimes found itself one of the poorest.

Normally tariff walls are designed to keep competing goods from coming in so to avoid job loss. But unlike the usual tariff protection, the goal of tariff protection in the Soviet republics has been to keep goods within their local jurisdiction from being shipped out. Little is done to discourage the delivery of goods from other jurisdictions. When Estonia raised the price of vodka sold within the region, for example, neighboring regions discovered that their shortage of vodka was more severe than ever. Speculators were buying vodka, not for drinking, but for delivery and sale to Estonia. For that reason, when Estonia announced that it planned to raise a long list of retail prices in late 1990, officials in Latvia engaged in an intense debate about the need to protect themselves with a tariff or wall around their republic to prevent the drain of desirable goods to their neighbors. Within a few months, Latvia also raised its prices.

IV

As if protests from increasingly strident local and republic governments were not unusual enough, Gorbachev and his colleagues were then confronted with another by-product of glasnost and deteriorating economic conditions—labor unrest.

During the preceding five decades, strikers could expect to be imprisoned or committed to mental institutions.[27] But as workers began to see that glasnost significantly reduced the likelihood that protesters would be punished, they started to speak out and strike when their demands went unanswered.

National agitation was a source of some of the earlier labor unrest. Workers in Armenia and Azerbaijan went on a strike to protest what they saw as the abuse of their countrymen in Nagorno-Karabakh, an area claimed by both republics but assigned to Azerbaijan for political purposes. Gradually the workers expanded the scope of the protests not only to pressure the authorities in their own republics, but where possible to pressure the government of the enemy in the neighboring republic. Armenian workers in 1988 and 1989 had withheld shipments of their own products from the rest of the Soviet Union. In 1990, railroad workers in Azerbaijan blockaded the railroads leading into Armenia, thereby preventing products from coming in or going out.

Increasingly the strike became a major weapon of ethnic conflict. Occasionally the strike would boomerang and complicate the drive for independence. When told, for example, that Estonian would soon replace Russian as the dominant language, Russian workers in Estonia's larger cities went on strike, hoping in part to provoke intervention from Moscow. Whatever the immediate goals of the strikers, these unprecedented manifestations of worker independence added to the economic destabilization of the country.

The greatest stimulus to worker unrest, however, was the impact of the faltering economy. It was not that the Soviet work force had been overindulged, but until Gorbachev, each year economic life seemed to improve, even if marginally. There had been an occasional work stoppage, usually to protest some specific complaint of managerial abuse or incompetence. But as it become clear in 1989 that the stagnation or *zastoi* of the Brezhnev era had become eclipsed by the *zastoi* II of Gorbachev, the workers began to stir in an effort to prevent deterioration in their living conditions. Some workers' grievances centered on salaries that were too low. Librarians and teachers, for example, were finally driven to demand higher wages in January 1990. Increasingly, however, it was the heavy industrial workers, such as coal miners, who went on strike, not so much for more money as for the delivery of consumer goods so they could spend the money they had already earned. Over one-half million workers in Siberia and the Ukraine walked out in July 1989 for several days, protesting their inability not only to find adequate food supplies in the shops but such basic necessities as soap. The coal they mined earned hard currency and was essential to industrial life, but all they received in exchange was one bar of soap every three months.

Responding to the miners' demands was not easy. Prime Minister Nikolai Ryzhkov had to intervene directly. However, the miners demanded more than personal involvement and promises—they wanted more consumer goods. But as the economy began to disintegrate, there were no readily available solutions. With soap in short supply all over the country, it was not merely a matter of shifting supplies around. It was necessary to rely in part on purchases from abroad. Those extra imports came at a cost: they added significantly to the Soviet Union's foreign trade long-term debt and its unpaid current bills, creating yet another obstacle to economic revitalization. Moreover, those extra imports were only a temporary help. By March 1991, conditions in the mining communities were worse than they had been two years before and about one third of the miners went out on strike again. This time, however, because their economic grievances remained unsatisfied, they broadened their demands to include a call for Gorbachev's resignation.

Like so much else that has taken place in the Gorbachev years, it is natural to ask what caused the miners to be so assertive. It turns out that there had been a series of more or less isolated minor walkouts prior to the mass strike in July 1989, but none of these incidents had been well organized or well supported. Nor did they generate much attention. However, in June 1989, when a new, freely elected Congress of the

People's Deputies convened for the first time in Moscow, these independent delegates began to speak out over issues that had never before been aired so publicly and boldly. For the first two weeks or so of the meetings, Soviet television provided live broadcasts of the sessions. Eventually Soviet authorities ordered a halt to live coverage, because while the televised sessions were being shown the economy came to a virtual halt as the general public sat fascinated by what they saw as glasnost in action. The impact of these debates was felt far beyond Moscow. When asked what moved him to agitate among his friends and lead them out on a strike, one of the leaders of the Kuzbass region of Siberia where the coal strike took place had a simple answer. After he saw the politicians complain openly about grievances never aired before, he decided he and his comrades could do the same thing in the mines.

Once emboldened, the Soviet work force took their right to strike as a serious matter. During the first five months of 1990, the number of workers on strike averaged 130,000 a day.[28] This included those who were protesting for political as well as ethnic and economic reasons. This contrasted with an average of only 15,000 workers per day during the first half of 1989, and 50,000 during the second half.[29] After a while, however, excesses began to occur. Responding to the same kind of pressures that ultimately led to the passage of the Taft Hartley Act by the U.S. Congress, the Soviet leadership also sought to limit strikes in some of the more essential Soviet industries. But these regulations, like so many others put through by Gorbachev, became less and less of a restraint. Moreover, as work conditions continued to deteriorate, many of the strikers, particularly those in the coal mines and the oil fields, began to go beyond demands for more goods in the shops. Since promises were too easily broken, they realized that it was not enough to win promises from Moscow. Commitments more often than not were disregarded. How could mine operators honor their promise to increase supplies of soap and cigarettes in the Kuzbass when there were similar shortages all over the country, including Moscow itself? No wonder the situation in the Kuzbass in July 1990 and in March 1991 was worse than it had been in July 1989, when the promises had originally been made.

Out of desperation, the miners, among others, began to call for the removal of party control over the work place and in some instances, as in Siberia, miners began to demand that control of the mines be turned over to the workers themselves. Not all miners agreed, particularly where the coal deposits were no longer as abundant as they had once been. This was demanding too much; they did not want to forsake the guarantees that came with being part of the old ministerial administrative system. They wanted their jobs protected, whether or not production rose or fell. Nevertheless, miners from both factions argued that they should be consigned a share of their output and be allowed to sell or barter their coal for consumer goods both within and outside the Soviet Union. How was it, they asked, that after so many years of producing readily exportable products, such as petroleum and coal, the oil drillers and coal miners had so little to show for their efforts? What had happened to all of those hard currency earnings? The workers demanded a share and after their strike in May 1991 won control over as much as 80 percent of the revenues from the mines.[30] But this victory for the miners came at the expense of the central government, which as a result was no longer able to count on these revenues. This further weakened the center.

V

The growing militancy of the Soviet labor movement was but one of many destructive reactions to the effort to undo the administrative planning system. Gorbachev may not have been able to create the market system that he kept pointing toward, but he did manage to undermine the five-year plans, Gosplan, Gossnab (the government supply organization that is responsible for storing, delivering, and receiving industrial output), and the ministerial prerogatives of the prevailing system.

The attraction of a switch to a market system was that when the market was fully functional, it would supposedly provide rewards of cheaper and more abundant to the populace that would more than offset the unemployment and dislocations the market also brings with it. But with the breakup of the strictly controlled Stalinist system, disruptive forces such as labor unrest were unleashed before the self-regulating processes of the market could assert themselves. In the aftermath, Soviet managers found themselves in the same kind of twilight zone mentioned earlier, uncertain as to who was in charge and what kind of an incentive system they should respond to, increasing further the uncertainties and economic disruptions.

Several examples may help to illustrate the effect of this "twilight zone" on the economy. Soviet enterprises have always sought to be as self-contained as possible, because they want to free themselves from being dependent on subcontractors. Delays in shipments by suppliers frequently resulted in penalities and the loss of bonuses for those dependent on such supplies. But no firm could be completely self-sufficient. This meant that everyone was dependent on Gosplan, Gossnab, or the ministries for their suppliers and customers, and for the issuance of the necessary requisitions.

By 1989 and 1990, this arrangement became increasingly ineffective. First, the ministries were dissolved or reorganized. Next, the suppliers began to withhold deliveries in disregard of the usual orders and requisitions. With the collapse of the ruble, managers wanted something more tangible for their goods, especially with the breakdown of food distribution. In September 1990, factory managers in the city of Sverdlovsk, for example, united to warn they would suspend deliveries on their outputs (most of it military and nuclear weaponry) unless they were provided with the promised supplies of food.[31]

The disintegration of the Soviet political system had a similar impact on the effectiveness of the planning system. The outbreak of virtual civil war between Azerbaijan and Armenia had very serious consequences for the economy, among other things. The Azeri blockade of Armenia not only prevented the inflow of goods but the outflow as well. This meant that a tractor factory in Vladimir was cut off from its sole source of tires, which came from Armenia. Given the taut and "efficient" nature of the Soviet planning system, there were no alternative sources of supply, because it would have been wasteful if there had been factories with excess capacity. The absence of redundancy has heretofore been a source of pride among Soviet planners. For example Gossnab reports that out of 7,664 products manufactured in the machine building, metallurgical, chemical, timber, construction and social sectors, 77 percent or 5,884 product lines were manufactured by only one producer.[32] That meant, however, that when the Armenian tire factory became inaccessible, there was no backup; there were no other factories to turn to. Nor was there as yet a wholesale or commodity market for the tractor factory to use. The market processes had not yet begun to take shape. As a consequence, many tractors were shipped to rural areas without tires. That had certain limitations.

A breakdown in one part of the economy almost always has secondary effects. Many of the tractors from the Vladimir tractor factory were destined for the Ukraine. But during the summer of 1990, many of the Ukrainian peasants complained: "What is the point of tractors with no tires?" And as for those tractors that did come with tires, it turned out that even they were often useless. Ukrainian officials had ignored planning orders from Moscow to deliver meat and grain to parts of the Russian Republic because it made no sense to send such commodities when all they received back was rubles that had lost their value because of inflation. In retaliation, Russian authorities withheld deliveries of diesel fuel.[33] Eventually many peasants did manage to find tractors, tires, and diesel fuel. But then because of the decline in the value of the ruble, many peasants simply refused to deliver the harvest to the state. This combination of peasant resistance and supply disruptions explains why despite what proved to be the richest crop in Soviet history, there was no bread in Moscow bakeries. This was one of the first overt manifestations of the supply-side depression that was reflected in a drop in national income that in 1990 was officially reported as a decline of about 4 percent and was double or triple that in 1991.

Paradoxically, the collapse of the macroeconomy served to stimulate private initiative at the local level. Because of the growing scarcity of consumer goods and such things as construction materials, those in need were often willing to pay increasingly large sums and even hard currency *valuta*. As a consequence, after a time more and more ordinary citizens decided that the potential gains from trading in such commodities would be worth the risks. Thus willy nilly and in spite of official efforts more and more would-be entrepreneurs have stepped in to fill the gaps between the empty state shelves and those with rubles and *valuta* to spend. Their offerings ranged from jars of caviar and cigarettes to sweaters and pantyhose. Others in more than a dozen Soviet cities created what they have imaginatively come to call "stock markets" but which were often nothing more than rudimentary wholesale markets. As of May 1991, there were 29 such exchanges throughout the Soviet Union. Instead of trading shares of yet nonexistent stock, they sold and bartered sides of beef, sacks of flour, fax machines, tons of coal, and meters of timber.

The transfer of authority from the center and Gosplan to the republics which Gorbachev agreed to in 1991 increased the opportunities for such trading. For example, given control over the coal they mined, the miners were eager to enter barter agreements for a whole range of local needs from meat to Toyotas. They found "stock markets" one of the few mechanisms available to help them arrange such swaps.

From an economist's point of view, such pockets of opportunity on a large enough scale could have the makings of real reform. Some argue that reform from the bottom up by the creation of cooperatives and privatization is the way real reform will take hold and be meaningful. However, this is not what the average Russian sees. In his eyes, those engaged in such activities are profiteers, gougers, or under the control of the Mafia. Reportedly this includes not only restaurants, retail stores, and taxicabs, but now all non-state trucking in Moscow. To top it off, the so-called privatization of state enterprises amounts to little more than illegal confiscation by senior state and party officials. They simply claim as their own what used to be public property. This explains in part the opposition to the privatization process and why there are doubts that such micro efforts will gain enough momentum to offset the accelerating collapse of the economy on a macro level.

VI

The undermining of the planning system and the collapse of the economy, combined with continuing restrictions on non-government groups, has inevitably had a negative effect on efforts to expand Soviet foreign trade and attract Western investment. Early on in the reform process it was decided to break up the long-standing monopoly of foreign trade regulated by the Ministry of Foreign Trade. In the pre-Gorbachev era, the Ministry of Foreign Trade traditionally had imposed itself between the Soviet enterprise and the foreign market. With few exceptions, this prevented direct contact between foreign buyers and sellers and Soviet sellers and buyers. When Soviet enterprises needed to import some item, they turned to a preassigned foreign trade organization set up under the Ministry of Foreign Trade, which would also act as an exporter. While the system made it possible to coordinate import and export efforts and on occasion allowed the Soviet Union to play off foreign firms wishing to sell to the Soviet Union, it also had some significant disadvantages. Because Soviet importers were not able to deal directly with their suppliers, they were denied the benefit of after-sale service and were also unable to obtain guidance as to which models would best suit their needs. Instead, the foreign trade organization usually sought to buy the cheapest model available, thereby showing how much hard currency it had saved. In contrast, the actual user usually argued for the most expensive and elaborate model available. Since from the standpoint of the ultimate user, the foreign currency being spent was essentially a free good, cost was no obstacle. Access to *valuta* and imported machinery was more a matter of political influence than economics. Thus the ministry of the chemical industry and its well-connected minister, Leonid Kostandov, accounted for 25 percent of all the machinery imported from the hard currency bloc, but only 8 percent of the Soviet Union's total industrial investment. The typical Soviet enterprise was not allowed to hold *valuta* and therefore anything that it had was provided to it by the Ministry of Finance and the Ministry of Foreign Trade. In turn, the enterprise had to forfeit anything that it earned by exporting and depositing the proceeds with the same two ministries. No wonder Soviet enterprises never seemed to be interested in expanding their exports or moderating the magnitude of their imports.

In an effort to encourage Soviet enterprise managers to behave in a more rational way, it was decided to involve them more directly in the foreign trade process, making them more accountable for their own actions. Thus, on August 19, 1986, a new set of regulations was announced which would go into effect in 1987.[34] The powers of the Ministry of Foreign Trade were reduced and the deputy minister of foreign trade, Boris Aristov, was appointed as the new minister. In the spirit of the times, the State Foreign Economic Commission, a superministry type of organization, was imposed over the Ministry of Foreign Trade. Among other things, the new State Foreign Economic Commission also assumed responsibility for the creation of joint ventures. One year later, in January 1988, the Ministry of Foreign Trade was dissolved and some of its functions combined with those of the longstanding State Committee of Foreign Economic Relations, an agency responsible for administering the Soviet foreign aid program. Together these two organizations were merged and evolved as the Ministry for Foreign Economic Relations, but with a considerably smaller bureaucratic staff.

With the powers and staff of the Ministry of Foreign Trade significantly reduced, twenty-one ministries and sixty-seven of the larger Soviet enterprises were authorized to engage in foreign trade on their own. After a while the number of enterprises able to act for themselves increased until over 14,000 could do so.[35] For the first time, the enterprise itself could negotiate directly with its foreign partners, and it became common for Western buyers and sellers to visit actual factory sites. Though economically more rational, the initial results were discouraging. Suddenly there was enormous confusion. Many Western firms began to look back longingly at the old Ministry of Foreign Trade system. Under the old system, a foreign firm at least knew where to go to discuss possible sales. The sellers simply went through the list of foreign trade organizations (FTOs) until they found one responsible for their particular product. Under the new system, some of the foreign trade organizations were reassigned directly to ministries, some to large enterprises, and some were simply dissolved. For those unfamiliar with the Soviet economic structure or without previous contacts, there was no regular source to turn to. Salesmen or buyers looking for sales or purchases in the capitalist world may turn to something such as a trade association listing, Dunn & Bradstreet, or a Chamber of Commerce listing for guidance. In a pinch there are even Yellow Pages in the phone book; but there is nothing comparable in the Soviet Union. For secrecy reasons, the Soviets even refuse to distribute phone books. American officials in the Moscow branch of the trade office of the U.S. Department of Commerce could always tell when a visitor was new to Moscow: their first request was for a Dunn & Bradstreet or a Moscow phone book.

There were disadvantages from the Soviet Union's point of view as well. Each enterprise could put forward a special plea for a special hard currency rate for its products. This was necessary because the ruble was not convertible. By 1988, there were over ten thousand different ruble hard currency ratios, a number impossible for Soviet authorities to control and offputting for foreigners to deal with. Whereas before there was excessive coordination, in 1988 there was almost none.

Many Soviet managers were ill-equipped and without the training needed to deal in the sophisticated world of foreign trade. Many succumbed to the temptation of easy credit and committed themselves to import Western goods financed by credit from those suppliers through their own Western banks. These transactions seemed safe enough for the Western banker. After all, in the past Soviet banks had traditionally guaranteed transactions undertaken by the Ministry of Foreign Trade and it was assumed that the practice would continue. Soon it became apparent, however, that the old way of doing things was very different from the new. For one thing, Soviet banks no longer guaranteed loans made by the various enterprises within the Soviet Union. In addition, just as in China when the same type of decentralization took place, and there was no one to coordinate and regulate who might borrow how much money, the Soviet Union quickly found itself with more accounts payable to foreign firms than accounts receivable.

By mid-1989, several Western companies had begun to notice that the Soviets were taking more and more time to pay their bills. Before long, even firms like Du Pont found themselves being owed as much as $16 million for deliveries of agricultural chemicals made in 1989.[36] Union Carbide was similarly affected, as were most American grain companies.[37] One important seller of U.S. grain was said at one time to be owed as much as a half billion dollars, something that had never happened before. Nor was it only Americans who found themselves being owed money. The Soviet Union fell $99 million in arrears to the Australians, $600 million to the West Germans, and $200 million to Japanese trading houses and steel companies.[38] Even New Zealand built up accounts receivable of $53 million for shipments of wool and butter. The Soviets sold some gold to pay off some of the debt and put up diamonds as collateral. In addition, they borrowed money from several Western governments such as West Germany, France, and Italy to pay off several of the companies in each country.[39] As of early October 1990, Soviet bank officials reported that they had paid off $4.5 billion in overdue bills, in part with the proceeds from those loans.[40] But later in the month debt obligations began to accumulate again, and the overdue debt reached 2.7 billion rubles

($4.8 billion), up from 2 billion rubles ($3.6 billion) owed as of midsummer 1990.[41]

To meet these payments, the Soviet Union sought yet additional funding. Before the end of the year, the Soviet Union was able to obtain $3 billion in new loans, even from previously hostile countries, such as Saudi Arabia and Kuwait.[42] But as before, these were loans—not grants—which meant that in theory at least, they would someday have to be repaid. To some officials in the State Foreign Economic Commission these loans only compounded the Soviet's economic problems, particularly since the proceeds of the loans were used either to repay old loans or to increase consumption. To these critics, at least such loans should have been used to make the Soviet Union more competitive and to enhance export potential. Instead, the Soviet Union was increasing its financial burden and complicating the eventual recovery process. Gorbachev's order in November 1990 that all Soviet enterprises earning hard currency turn over 40 percent of the proceeds to the state in order to repay these loans did not help. From the viewpoint of the managers of these enterprises, this took away much of the incentive to export at a time when some of the managers for the first time had begun to think about increasing their exports. Consequently, hard currency deposits received by the government began to shrink, not increase.

The growth in debt involved more than uncoordinated purchases by Soviet enterprises and a lack of backbone to face up to the mounting fiscal crisis. The Soviet Union discovered that it could not necessarily sustain the export earnings that it needed to meet repayment levels and debt service, which in 1991 was estimated to be 9 billion rubles. As a result of the country's political and economic turmoil, shipments of oil equipment were disrupted and Soviet oil output began to drop. Oil production was down 3 percent in 1989 from the year earlier, down 5 percent in 1990, and 9 percent in 1991. With production down, the Soviets found it necessary to reduce oil exports. Total crude oil and petroleum product exports fell 10 percent, from 205 million tons (4 million barrels a day) in 1988

to 185 million tons (3.75 million barrels a day) in 1989.[43] Petroleum exports dropped by about 14 percent in 1990, to 159
million tons. There were predictions that exports would fall by
60 percent in 1991, to 61 million tons.[44] Gorbachev warned that
unless remedial steps were taken, the Soviet Union would
become a net importer by 1993. The Iraqi invasion of Kuwait
in August 1990 pushed up prices at least for a time and boosted
Soviet export earnings somewhat. But the temporary price increases were apparently not enough to offset the growing problems the Soviet Union had in finding enough oil to satisfy most
domestic needs and export opportunities, and by extension its
unpaid creditors.

VII

The accumulation of unpaid debts and the continuing inability to convert rubles into hard currency also affected the operation of joint ventures. As with other reform measures, good
ideas became hamstrung with red tape and bureaucratic backtracking. This was vividly seen in an early interview with the
bureaucrat assigned to facilitate the development of joint ventures in the Soviet Union. In March 1987, less than a year after
the August 1986 decision of the Politburo which authorized the
creation of joint ventures, Yuri Dryomov, the newly appointed
director of the joint venture department of the Ministry of
Foreign Affairs, gave an interview in *Moscow News* in which he
criticized almost all of the joint venture proposals then being
considered.[45] Rank Xerox, one of those attacked, was later
allowed to respond, but it was easy to see why joint ventures
in the Soviet Union might feel uneasy about their status in the
Soviet Union.[46] Dryomov's attack was like the director of the
zoo confessing to his dislike of animals.

Evidently afraid that someday a new leadership less sympa-
thetic to the concept of joint ventures might assume control in
the Soviet Union, authorities like Dryomov did their best to
protect themselves against potential political charges that they
had sold out the Soviet Union at too cheap a price to foreigners.

(Such accusations indeed were ultimately made in Poland against Prime Minister Tadeusz Mazowiecki and contributed to his defeat in his race for president.)[47] Others joined Dryomov in expressing their concern that joint ventures would foist outdated technology onto the Soviet Union and treat the Soviet Union as if it were a Hong Kong.[48] The Soviet Union should have been that lucky. For that reason, proposals for the preparation of joint ventures were carefully scrutinized and the foreigner's share in any joint venture was limited to 49 percent. Moreover, virtually nothing could be done without the acquiescence of the Soviet partner. But with or without the partner's cooperation, operating conditions were seldom "user friendly." Even with the best of goodwill, operating conditions in the Soviet Union with Soviet enterprises are difficult. Offices and manufacturing space are hard to find, telephones nearly impossible to obtain, work regulations complex, and access to raw materials and manufacturing components almost always uncertain. Once up and operating, several of the Western junior partners often complained that their joint venture in fact existed only on paper and that it was actually not much more than the traditional Soviet factory operation with the U.S. partner reduced to the status of a supplier. Finally, since the ruble is not convertible, even if profits are earned, it is very difficult to repatriate them. That may explain why as late as April 1988, only thirty joint ventures had been formally registered.

In an effort to make the operating climate more attractive, some of the more antagonistic regulatory officials were removed. In addition, joint ventures were provided a two-year tax holiday, effective only after the enterprise started to earn a profit. Eventually even the restriction on 49 percent equity share for foreigners was lifted. By 1990 Gorbachev promised that should they choose to, foreigners could own 100 percent of their venture. Few exercised that option because most foreigners quickly realized that navigating through the mystery of the Soviet bureaucracy would be a near impossibility without a partner with inside connections.

Several efforts, however, did bear fruit. For example, some

joint ventures, including Dialog and the one operated by Honeywell, found a way to increase hard currency exports, and as a result they were able to make profits in rubles and dollars. By 1991, nearly 3,000 joint ventures were officially registered with the Soviet authorities. This was a fraction of the 20,000 or so joint ventures operating in China at the time, but even the 3,000 Soviet figure was deceptive. Estimates vary somewhat, but Soviet officials acknowledge that out of the 3,000 or so that had actually been registered, fewer than 1,000 joint ventures were actually operating in the Soviet Union, and most of those were service-type operations such as hotels and consulting operations. Equally important, fewer than fifty to one hundred were actually earning dollars. Almost all Soviet joint ventures so far have attracted relatively small capital investments by the foreign partner. Even more disturbing, some joint ventures have subsequently closed down, including one or two that were initially very promising.

Given the initial high expectations and the resulting limited success rates, perhaps it is not surprising that after a time a backlash of resentment toward foreigners and their joint ventures began to occur. In part, this was a consequence of the growing concern inside the Soviet Union that all too many foreigners were only interested in get-rich-quick schemes when dealing with the Soviet Union. Moreover, when the joint ventures do involve something more than service activities, the foreigners seem primarily interested in exploiting Soviet raw materials or labor. This feeling is reinforced by the fact that those few joint ventures that do go beyond providing services are almost entirely dedicated to extracting Soviet raw materials. Some Soviet critics and nationalists call this the foreigners' rape of the Soviet Union.

Yet given the obstacles and uncertainties, it is understandable why foreigners are hesitant about committing large sums to the Soviet market. A stable political climate is usually a prerequisite for meaningful foreign investment. Yet by 1989, it became all but impossible to determine who on the Soviet side had the power to enter into a joint venture agreement; the

Soviet Union, the republics, or local officials, or all of them? Should potential investors negotiate with the Soviet Ministry of Foreign Trade or the State Committee for External Economic Relations; indeed, would either organization be in existence a year from now?

Some businessmen thrive on such chaos. As they see it, because everything is collapsing, there may be great opportunities and certainly great needs. What better time is there to find customers and charge higher prices? The lure of high profits is in fact what attracts them to these situations. They stand in contrast to the more typical foreign investors who seek order and avoid anarchy. These more traditional businessmen do not have the time or the inclination to take great risks. They operate on smaller profit margins and make their money by offering better-quality goods at prices cheaper than their competitors— not by charging extra high prices or gambling that they will make enough money on those projects that succeed to offset the losses that come from the risky projects that might fail. It is also the risky projects with their high prices that anger Soviet consumers and generate complaints of exploitation and price gouging. For example, some factory enterprise managers have gone so far as to propose that all foreign competitors be excluded from the Soviet Union. They would "immediately let down an iron curtain and be separated from the rest of the world."[49] This growing hostility has been manifested by an increase in the number of foreigners in Moscow who find the tires on their cars slashed and their cars vandalized.

Such attitudes also scare away those interested in creating joint ventures. The best way to encourage a joint venture would be to take one or two of them that provide products or services that have a high priority in the Soviet Union and make them showcases. Do everything possible so that these joint ventures can earn profits and repatriate those earnings outside the Soviet Union. Instead, some Soviet and local authorities have been doing just the opposite. For example, Combustion Engineering, which was one of the first American companies to engage in a Soviet joint venture, in 1990 found that its Soviet partners refused to adhere to conventional Western managerial practices. The Soviet manager insisted on living like the conventional Soviet managerial autocrat, with big cars and expensive perquisites. Inevitably his behavior began to affect profits, and after trying but failing to put a halt to these excesses, Combustion Engineering began to recall its employees from the Soviet Union.

Even McDonald's has started to feel the squeeze. That is most discouraging because McDonald's was theoretically at least the answer to a reformer's dream. George Cohon, the executive in charge of the McDonald's operation in Canada and the initiator of the McDonald's effort in Moscow, began working on opening McDonald's in Moscow almost fifteen years before his dream actually came true. His goal was to open up twenty restaurants, at least as a first stage, and supply these outlets from a $40 million processing plant in the Moscow suburbs, which McDonald's would build for itself. The plant that opened to service the first McDonald's outlet in January 1990 was a state-of-the-art facility designed to process as much local food as possible. This way McDonald's could use its ruble revenue from the hamburger sales to pay its suppliers. Its second store would sell exclusively for dollars, which would then be used to recover the capital and operating expenses as well as profits. In effect, the McDonald's staff knew from the beginning that they would have to create their own micro economy, from the seed potatoes they brought in and helped plant to the cattle they began to watch over and nurture for special care. Through such special efforts, McDonald's was able to operate despite the disappearance of meat from the Moscow shops in 1990 and 1991 and with only occasional supply shortages such as potatoes.

From the beginning, however, the staff had to deal with what some might regard as sabotage, but was more often ineptitude. What seemed especially frustrating was that as often as not, its formal partner in the effort, the Moscow city government, turned out to be McDonald's main antagonist. In selecting the site for the processing plant, for example, the Moscow city authorities after a while found a suitable piece of land, but warned McDonald's corporate offices that construction could not begin until the corn growing in the field had been harvested. Since that would have delayed construction by about two months, the Western partner offered to pay an equivalent sum to the farmers for the crop and simply dig up the field. "You don't understand," they were told, "once planted, the crop must be harvested." In response, McDonald's offered to import an equivalent amount of corn and pay the farmers as well. "You still don't understand," they were told, and so construction had to wait sixty days. Once the processing plant was up and operating (no mean trick because for several months the Moscow city authorities insisted that they could find no sand and gravel for construction), McDonald's staff found that their trucks could not move freely outside of Moscow to their farm suppliers, because foreigners need special permits to drive beyond the Moscow city limits. They also had to demonstrate to Soviet farmers that potatoes need special tractors, not caterpillar-type tractors which compact the earth as well as the potatoes.

Further, they had to train their own processing-plant workers how to remove the bones and prepare the meat. To look at the typical meat in a Soviet shop, one would think that the Soviet farmers breed cattle without any good cuts of meat, whereas in part this is due to poorly trained butchers. Finally, McDonald's put great effort into selecting its one thousand counter clerks. One small notice in the Soviet paper brought in 27,000 applications. Some of those selected were sent to Canada and the United States for training, and they in turn returned home to teach others. This special training extended to maintaining a constant watch over the washrooms to ensure that they were kept clean and that no one stole the toilet seats or the toilet paper.

McDonald's did its job well. The Moscow branch set world records for volume and the number of customers served. Expecting 15,000 people, McDonald's found itself serving as many as 40,000 to 50,000 patrons a day. Given their experience in Soviet shops, customers had trouble believing that all the counter help were Muscovites. Some insisted that they were in fact émigrés brought in from the United States and Canada.

In addition to setting records for numbers of customers served in a day, the staff at McDonald's in Moscow has discovered that its customers have some other features that differentiate them from McDonald's customers elsewhere in the world. Despite the fact that there are twenty-seven cash registers normally open for service, Soviet customers tend to line up behind the longest queue. After years of experience, Soviet consumers have come to expect that the longest line forms in front of the counter with the most desirable goods. McDonald's had to station special ushers to reassure customers entering the restaurant that each counter position offers food of equal quality and quantity.

But with the increasing breakdown in civil order and the surge of inflation, even McDonald's is having some difficulties. With such heavy volume, it ran out of its own potatoes and had to go to Poland and Western Europe to buy some for hard currency. For a time it also had to set limits on how much a customer could purchase. Given the shortages throughout the city, some buyers tried to order "one hundred to go," and then resell them to those waiting in line. The increase in meat costs and rent hurt the most. When McDonald's opened in January 1990, its partners, the Moscow municipal authorities, charged the joint venture 2.5 rubles for a kilogram of meat. As the sales increased, the Moscow partners decided to take their profit out at the front of the transaction and raised meat prices to 7.1 rubles in May and then 14 rubles in October.[50] The Moscow authorities insisted this was what it cost them to produce the meat, although elsewhere in the country the accepted cost of producing meat was 5 rubles per kilogram. In addition, the city authorities increased the McDonald's office rent tenfold.

By late 1990, therefore, McDonald's found it necessary to double the price of its Big Macs to 6.95 rubles—and by another 50 percent shortly after the retail price rise on April 2, 1991. This meant that the price was now equivalent to almost a full day's average wage. In each case this caused the line waiting to get into the restaurant to shrink, at least for a time, from two hours to about twenty minutes; but it also meant that McDonald's could no longer count on covering its ruble costs. In response, McDonald's decided to reconsider its timetable for opening twenty stores and reportedly revised its second-round target to six over the next five years, beginning in 1990.

From the point of view of the Soviet partner, grabbing the profits at the beginning of the process rather than waiting patiently to share them at the end may make sense. As political and economic conditions deteriorated, the time horizon of the Soviet partner became shorter and shorter. There was growing pressure to take its profits out while it could. When McDonald's raised its prices so it could pay its bills to the Moscow city authorities, McDonald's then became the target of complaints that it was charging Soviet consumers five or six times more than their Western counterparts were being charged for a Big Mac in the United States.

Some critics also insisted that McDonald's was demanding that it be allowed to buy meat at a subsidized price. Although not true, these attackers insisted that McDonald's profits stemmed almost entirely from subsidies paid out of the state budget.[51] And while McDonald's executives were priding themselves on using domestically produced food supplies, their Soviet critics were complaining that McDonald's was bringing nothing into the Soviet Union except some "sauce and condiments." The implication was that McDonald's was doing nothing to help alleviate the food shortage. These critics ignored the fact that McDonald's was being paid only in rubles that were not convertible. Nor did it matter that one of McDonald's prime goals was to improve the productivity of the Soviet food processing system. Moreover, these opponents reasoned that eating Soviet food at McDonald's reduced the overall supply of food available to the Soviet public. The sense that McDonald's was doing nothing to alleviate the Soviet food crisis was compounded by rumors that McDonald's was exporting meat to Scandinavia. Though untrue, such rumors fan resentment of joint ventures and lead to charges that foreigners are once again exploiting the Soviet people. It was just such emotions that led some nationalists, like Valentin Rasputin a year earlier, to introduce legislation calling for the annulment of the joint venture law.[52]

Others, particularly within the nationalist movement, have demanded the removal of the Coca-Cola sign installed in Pushkin Square.[53] "It is an insult to one of Russia's sacred places," they insist. This xenophobia even led the city of Novgorod initially to turn down a proposal to open a special economic zone. "It would have opened the door to foreign exploitation and flooded the city with prostitutes eager to earn hard currency, the critics charged."[54] Such attitudes help explain why it has taken the Soviet authorities at least three years to approve the concept of special economic zones of the sort that have been so successful in China. Of course, Gorbachev has also been fearful that if special economic zones were opened up in the border republics, this might accelerate the move to economic independence. Finally however, in late 1990, the Russian Republic approved the concept, and the far eastern city of Nakhodka announced that it would soon set up the first special economic zone in the Soviet Union.

VIII

Much as he tried to change things, Gorbachev himself invariably reverted to the old habits of "experimenting" and "campaigning." In the pre-Gorbachev era, this meant shifting between centralization and decentralization or between ministries and *sovnarkhozy* (regional economic councils), or as Lyudmila Telen stated in *Moscow News,* "the five-year chemicalization campaign gave way to the five-year quality campaign. Brigades of communist workers gave way to brigade contracts. Gross output [*val*] gave way to normative net output. 'Make the economy economic' gave way to *uskoreniie.* The first model of cost accounting gave way to the second."[55] Most of these campaigns go back to the Khrushchev era, but the last two examples were carried out by Gorbachev and to them could also be added intensification, Gosagroprom, and Gospriemka. By trying to solve all the country's problems with one stroke, such campaigns are almost always a recipe for failure.

Some of Gorbachev's experiments such as allowing joint ventures have been daring, even heretical in terms of Marxist doctrine and Soviet traditions. But despite his initiatives, he always seems to be holding one hand behind his back, for as bold as some of his reforms have been, in almost every case he has been reluctant or unable to push that "experiment" far enough so that it could make a difference. In part this is a consequence of Gorbachev's coalition-building approach to politics. As we have seen, he invariably seeks to surround himself with representatives from the conservative political spectrum, such as Yegor Ligachev, Veniamin Yarin, and Valentin Rasputin. Eventually he ends up purging many of these conservatives; but for a time at least, he uses their implicit acquiescence to give his innovative changes the appearance that they are backed by conservatives as well as the radicals. But this comes at a price. Indeed, Gorbachev can introduce previously unprecedented reforms such as private enterprise and joint ventures, but then he ends up circumscribing the scope of their operations as a compromise with the conservatives. Private enterprise and cooperatives, for example, at first could only be opened by pensioners and students, thus having a minimal impact on the regular work force and state enterprises. Similarly, foreign partners in joint ventures were limited to a 49 percent ownership and peasants who set up their own farms could not sell the land they had leased to other private owners. Such limits made it inevitable that initially relatively few people would risk involving themselves in such ventures, thereby guaranteeing that the numbers attracted to these new opportunities would not be able to generate any significant increase in supplies. Sooner or later criticisms will be heard about the ineffectiveness of such initiatives, which always seem to precipitate increases in prices but not increases in goods.

Most likely, even an all-out reform would not have increased supplies significantly. After seventy years of bureaucratism, the

Soviet people have learned to weather the various storms of reforms that blow in from different directions. Sooner or later they pass, without making too much of a mark. Unfortunately, each failure leads only to increased cynicism, which in turn compromises other efforts in the future.

7

The Reaction Comes

In retrospect it is striking that the anti-reformers and defenders of the Stalinist status quo took so long to react to Gorbachev's perestroika in any systematic way. If implemented fully, sooner or later these reforms would affect every segment of Soviet society and, at least initially, in a disruptive way.

Since it took some time for Gorbachev to formulate his ideas, some beneficiaries of the status quo might not have realized initially how far-reaching Gorbachev's economic and political changes could be and how subversive to their way of life. Moreover, as pointed out, those ideas kept changing; on more than one occasion, Gorbachev reversed himself. Furthermore, as in the case of private property, for example, Gorbachev never seemed to overcome his commitment to socialism. Yet despite numerous ambiguities and policy reversals, it became clear by 1988 that Gorbachev was determined to shake up the status quo ideologically, politically, and economically, as well as in terms of personnel.

Hints of structural upheaval actually date from Andropov's election as general secretary, but Andropov seemed mainly interested in rooting out corruption and ineptness. Gorbachev broadened the circle of those he wanted retired to include those opposed to reform. Between the two of them, there was a wholesale turnover of personnel. By March 1987, 70 percent of the members of the Politburo, 60 percent of the *oblast* party secretaries, and 40 percent of the members of the Central Committee, who had been in power in October 1982 shortly before Brezhnev's death, had been replaced.[1]

Sooner or later there was bound to be a reaction. After all, the Soviet Union—and pre-revolutionary Russia before it—was not noted for its receptivity to evolutionary change. Russia and the Soviet Union after 1930 were among the most conservative societies in the Western world. The fact that the Soviet people put up with the Soviet system for almost seventy years with little protest and with the czarist form of government for centuries before that suggests that the people were not all that unhappy with the type of government they had. Indeed, it would seem that a good case could be made for arguing that they felt comfortable with it. The Moscow historian and outspoken proponent of reform, Yuri Afanasyev, for example argues that "Lenin's Bolshevism was preceded by a people's Bolshevism. There is no point in trying to shift the blame away from the people. . . . It was and is very characteristic of Russia to have the people at the 'bottom' harshly subordinated to the people at the 'top,' and for people generally to be subordinated to the state: such relations were formed back in the twelfth century. The eternal oppression in Russia created a reaction against it of intolerance, aggression, and hostility; and it is this oppression and the reaction to it that create cruelty and mass violence. It is true that the policies of the Bolsheviks did not derive from the will of the people, but the people participated in those policies, and took part in the mass terror."[2] As President Václav Havel put it when referring to the similar acceptance of totalitarian control in Czechoslovakia, "If I speak about a spoiled moral atmosphere, I don't refer only to our masters. . . . I am speaking about all of us. For all of us have grown used to the totalitarian system and accepted it as an immutable fact, and thereby actually helped keep it going. None of us are only its victims; we are all also responsible for it."[3]

Given this history, it is not too surprising that the conservative forces finally began to organize against perestroika and glasnost and to thwart Gorbachev's far-reaching reforms. What is surprising is the passivity with which those opposed to the reforms accepted the first two or three years of the Gorbachev reform process and the purge of their like-minded colleagues. The process of purging reform opponents and the super-annuated seemed to be so easy. After years of taking their power and prerogatives for granted, they marched off to collect their pensions with no perceptible complaint. True, unlike the Stalin era, the purged officeholders were not sent off to camps, exile, or death; but the scope of the upheaval, at least in terms of the percentage of fired ministers and *oblast* leaders, brought back memories of the 1930s purges.

Gorbachev did not manage to suppress all opposition to his reform efforts. Some of the newly appointed conservatives would in time emerge to claim a conservative or anti-reform mantle. But often as not with time they too would be purged. Some of these latterday victims, such as Ligachev, would make more of a fuss not only about their treatment but also about their ideological opposition, but in the early years very few if any of those fired from office moved to criticize perestroika or glasnost overtly. There seemed to be general agreement that the Soviet Union could not continue to function as it had during what almost everyone came to agree were the "stagnation years" of the Brezhnev era. As one of his hosts told Gorbachev on a visit to Latvia in February 1987, "Life 'stank' in the Brezhnev regime."[4] Moreover, as long as they were lacking in clear and detailed definitions, glasnost and perestroika were essentially non-threatening concepts. During my visit to the Soviet Union in those early Gorbachev years, there was nary a discouraging word. Nearly all levels of society appeared to welcome the prospect of change.

Gorbachev's purging efforts were also facilitated by the general perception that those being purged deserved it. The fact that economic and political conditions had fallen to such a low point was not solely Brezhnev's fault. An unusually large number of long-serving officeholders bore a share of the blame for that decline as well or had benefited from it. Consequently, the few protests about Gorbachev and his scary ideas were submerged by the louder public outcry over past incompetence and arrogance.

Nevertheless, throughout most of the first two years of Gorbachev's administration, there were mutterings and unsigned letters in the press as well as on-the-job obstruction. Those aggrieved included large numbers of workers as well as party and government bureaucrats. Their complaints were variously ideological, personal, and practical. Some feared a sell-out of socialism by Gorbachev and/or a surrender to the United States and its materialistic ways. Others worried about a collapse of the center and a growth of ethnic turmoil. There were also protests that reforms, including Gorbachev's, always fall on the backs of the workers. In particular, there were mutterings about the crackdown on the sale of vodka and the drop in wage bonuses resulting from the more rigid quality standards imposed by Gospriemka.

Even though complaints about Gorbachev and his reforms were disorganized and often at cross purposes, their rumblings reached Gorbachev, evoking at times some disquiet. On occasion his concerns were heightened by the receipt of actual physical threats against him and his family.[5] Periodically he sought help in dealing with this opposition from those whom he considered to be his natural constituency, the press and the intellectual community. In an off-the-record meeting on June 19, 1986, Gorbachev complained that the country's bureaucrats were particularly resistant to change.[6] After all, it was "the apparat that broke Khrushchev's neck," and Gorbachev feared that his opponents might now use the apparat to "break the neck of the new leadership."[7] On more than one occasion, he threatened to resign if he did not get his way. One of his earliest threats was made prior to the January 1987 meeting of the Plenary of the Central Committee, when he demanded approval of procedural changes.[8] The threat was repeated several times thereafter, including a session of the Congress of the People's Deputies in December 1990 when Gennady Yanayev, Gorbachev's nominee for vice president, was initially rejected.[9]

Given that for seven decades it had been illegal to organize anything like formal opposition to the Soviet leadership, the absence of an organized opposition to Gorbachev, particularly from anti-reform conservatives, was perhaps not so surprising. Those supporting the status quo presumably adhered to the idea that in a communist country, there should be no organized opposition. For them to organize, even in a time of glasnost, would be equivalent to committing an anti-social if not an illegal act. When members of the National Rifle Association, normally one of the staunchest law-and-order organizations in the United States, ultimately decided to disobey a 1991 California law banning the possession of most semi-automatic weapons, their hesitancy about defying the law reflected similar ambiguities.[10]

Nevertheless, as noted earlier, some of Gorbachev's early policies, especially the callous way in which he treated the labor force, brought a quick end to his honeymoon and lost him goodwill that he would need later. Particularly upsetting for the workers was Gorbachev's crackdown on the sale of vodka.[11] For most workers, the fact that such a policy might bring better health or a happier marriage was not as important as their bottle, which was the only way they could escape from Soviet reality. Lines would form two hours before the two o'clock opening of liquor stores. That did not bother the alcoholics; they had nothing else to do. But it was a bother for those who wanted an occasional bottle of vodka or wine to celebrate some anniversary. Initially their resentment was deflected into humor. After standing in line for two hours, one drunk complained to the other, "This wait is due to the fact that Gorbachev is a teetotaller." "Shsh!" responded his partner. "Imagine what would happen if Gorbachev were celibate!"

Gorbachev was fully aware of such criticisms.[12] He acknowledged publicly that his critics referred to him scornfully not as the *Generalnie Secretar* (General Secretary of the Communist Party) but as the *Mineralnie Secretar* (Mineral Water Secretary).[13] Even though by late 1988 Gorbachev began to relax controls on the sale of vodka, the workers became more alienated and labor productivity continued to fall. Thereafter the workers met almost all of Gorbachev's initiatives with resistance and cynicism.

Installing inspectors from Gospriemka in all Soviet factories in 1987 only seemed to confirm Gorbachev's supposedly anti-labor bias. Initially at least, these inspectors took their work very seriously. On average they rejected from 7 to 30 percent of the typical engineering factory's production, causing a drop in industrial output and reducing the bonuses of wages of managers and workers.[14] When instead of spending money on building new factory capacity, Gorbachev moved to institute second and third shifts in many existing factories, a logical byproduct of the intensification campaign associated with the machine-tool industry, it further antagonized the workers.[15] What was not explained, however, was how workers would be enticed to leave their daytime shifts. No wage supplements were anticipated and no infrastructure was provided to service night-time workers who complained that at the end of their shifts, there was no transportation available to take them and no restaurants open to feed them.[16] In addition, working the night shift disrupted family life. As one Soviet worker complained at the time, "Why is it that every time there is a new reform initiative, it is always the workers who are asked to make the first sacrifices?" Eventually this discontent precipitated strike threats, strikes, and the formation of both radical and reactionary labor groupings. The radicals sought more worker control over their unions and working conditions; the reactionaries sought a return to the older order and control. Both groups were clearly opposed to any kind of extra work.

Not surprisingly, similar efforts to revitalize the bureaucracy met similar resistance. Any change in leadership is potentially unsettling to the party apparatus. New leaders usually bring with them new conceptions and initiatives, sometimes for the better, sometimes for the worse. Moreover, the more serious the existing situation, the more extensive the resulting bureaucratic upheaval. Yet just like their counterparts in the non-communist world, Soviet *apparatchiks* have also learned to protect themselves from such upheavals. In some cases that means falling back on friends, shifting jobs, or verbally agreeing with the reforms, but in fact stonewalling in the realistic expectation that sooner or later the current boy wonder or brainstorm will pass just like those before them. In that way the infrastructure in the apparatus, particularly the bureaucracy, survives all such changes. There have been of course major discontinuities such as the 1917 Revolution and the Stalinist purges, but the durability of the Russian *chinovnik* (the czarist equivalent of the *apparatchik*) is impressive and reassuring to those who believe that bureaucracies somehow never die.

Nonetheless, attempting to learn from the failure of Khrushchev's reforms, Gorbachev insisted that his effort would be more extensive and far-reaching. Khrushchev's mistake was that he was not ambitious enough; Gorbachev by contrast sought to encompass all aspects of Soviet life, supposedly making his reforms irreversible.[17] That certainly seemed ominous, and Gorbachev did little to comfort his intended targets. Equally unsettling, Gorbachev began to target not just individuals in bureaucratic strongholds like Gosplan, the ministries, and ultimately the Central Committee of the Party, but he threatened the remaining bureaucrats' continued access to special privileges.[18] To many defenders of the party elite, that was the cruelest cut of all. Yegor Ligachev charged that criticism of special treatment for the party faithful was undeserved. He explained, "The Party worker has one privilege—to be at the front, to fight for the Party's policies and to serve his people with faith and truth. Believe me, he has no other privileges."[19] (That was not a widely shared view.) And as for pay, Ligachev argued that Communist Party workers receive a wage equal to the national average. "It transpires that contrary to the widely held view, party workers rank 26th in the country as regards pay—the average pay of a party worker is 216 rubles per month."[20] For that matter, Ligachev insisted that criticism of most party workers was even unjustified during the Brezhnev period. Defending himself before the 19th All Union Communist Party Conference, Ligachev reminded his fellow delegates that " 'during the years of stagnation—I lived and worked in Siberia, a harsh land but a truly wonderful one. People often ask me what I was doing at the time. I answer with pride: I was building socialism. There were millions like me.' Applause."[21]

Because it seemed to epitomize the bureaucracy's resistance to his efforts, Gorbachev seemed particularly distressed about what became known at the time as the Chabanov affair. A. I. Chabanov was a party member in good standing, a director of the Research Institute of the Ministry of Electrical Engineering in the Ukrainian city of Cherkassy.[22] His research institute had developed a new type of machine-tool and control system that according to Gorbachev was shown overseas and was ordered by foreign and Soviet customers. However, the Cherkassy factory of the Ministry of Electrical Engineering steadfastly refused to produce this new equipment. In July 1985, when most of the senior managers were on vacation, Chabanov was appointed acting manager of the factory. He proceeded immediately to produce his new designs. Upon their return from vacation the regular management reported Chabanov's unauthorized acts to the ministry and regional party committee. Chabanov was accused of padding his reports and misappropriating state funds.[23] Ministry officials thereupon relieved Chabanov of his duties and set up a special investigation.

Learning of the miscarriage of justice, officials in the party's Central Committee and the procurator general intervened to protect Chabanov. Although he was absolved of all criminal intent, the local party *apparatchiks* nonetheless proceeded with their effort to expel Chabanov from his Communist Party cell. Moreover, when some of his supporters wrote to complain to Moscow authorities about the continuing abuse of justice, the letters were confiscated in the Cherkassy post office and never reached their intended destination. Ultimately justice was done and Chabanov remained in the party, but similar resistance to bureaucratic revamping led Gorbachev to postpone a meeting of the Central Committee three times because of the refusal of its rulemaking bodies to make the changes he requested. With good reason he warned in February 1987 that "the next two or three years will be the most difficult."[24] However, Gorbachev or his associates were to warn almost every year that "the next two or three years" would be the hardest.

II

Finally in 1988, the anti-reformers became emboldened enough to make their grievances explicit. On March 13, 1988, the day before Gorbachev's scheduled departure for Yugoslavia and while his ideological ally, Alexander Yakovlev, was in Mongolia, a 4,500-word "letter" entitled "I Cannot Renounce Principles" appeared on page 3 of the newspaper *Sovetskaia Rossiia,* ostensibly the official government paper of the Russian Republic. While claiming support for Gorbachev's policies of perestroika, it was in fact a blistering, hate-filled attack on almost everything Gorbachev stood for.

Its author was Nina Andreyeva, a chemist in the Leningrad Technology Institute. According to a reliable report, the published letter had the imprint of her husband, Vladimir Klushin, an instructor of Marxism-Leninism and a party ideologue.[25] Although Andreyeva insists the words were entirely hers, Ligachev and the editors linked to him may also have had a hand not only in its publication but also its content.[26] Giuletto Chiesa, then the Moscow correspondent for the Italian paper *L'Unità,* reported that he saw a draft of the article before it was published.[27] He says that of the original eighteen pages, only five emerged substantially as they were sent in. The rest were either omitted or heavily edited. Andreyeva does acknowledge that she sent a copy of the letter to Ligachev after it had been rejected by several other national papers in September 1987.[28]

Whether or not he had anything to do with the article's content or its publication, there is substantial evidence that Ligachev did everything he could to publicize its content after it had been published. On March 14, the day after the appearance of Andreyeva's manifesto, Ligachev convened an unauthorized meeting of the leading middle-of-the-road and conservative newspaper editors to impress upon them the significance of the Andreyeva letter.[29] He intentionally excluded invitations to the liberal editors of *Moscow News* and *Ogonyek.* Simultaneously the Tass News Agency alerted its subscribers to Andreyeva's article and notified them that they might want to consider reprinting it. This led to the republication of the letter in at least forty-three regional papers, including many military publications.[30] It was also printed in the conservative East German anti-perestroika party paper, *Neues Deutschland,* and discussed on Leningrad television. While Gorbachev was in Yugoslavia, Andreyeva's letter and its implications became the focus of a widening circle of special Communist Party meetings convened throughout the Soviet Union.

For those supporting perestroika and Gorbachev, the Andreyeva manifesto was a frightening throwback to the era of repression. Andreyeva criticized what she viewed as a growing disavowal of the past, particularly of the Stalinist years, as well as the recent growth of multi-party freedom, tolerance for religion, emigration, sexual promiscuity, and criticism of the army and the army draft. As she saw it, there was entirely too much "verbiage about 'terrorism' [criticism of anti-reformers], 'the people's political servility,' 'uninspired social vegetation,' 'spiritual slavery,' 'unusual fear' and 'dominance by boors in power' " to explain the spiritual, social, political, and economic "emptiness" of the country since the Bolshevik Revolution. For those who believe in the uniqueness of "the Russian soul," such self-flagellation was too much. No wonder her students had begun to express "nihilistic sentiments" and lose their "political bearings."

She rejected charges that Stalin was responsible for the advent of fascism or Hitler or the assassination of Trotsky or Kirov. Instead of attacking Stalin, the Soviet people should praise him for defending the Soviet Union from Hitler and bringing industrialization, collectivization, and the cultural revolution to the Soviet Union. Was this fair to those who gave their lives for the Soviet Union in World War II and had worked so hard to industrialize the country, she asked. Such criticisms were making the Soviet people question the value of their own lives. How disgraceful it was when students of university age had the audacity to ask army heroes from World War II not about the great accomplishments of the Soviet Army but "about the political repressions within the army." After all, Czar Peter the Great, like Stalin, also had "personal qualities" that were "disturbing." Yet today Peter is praised as the one who made Russia "a great European power."

Those criticizing the Soviet past were newly ascendant "left wing liberals," she charged, who have "cosmopolitan tendencies" (a code word used by Stalin when he attacked the Jews) and encourage "refuseniks" (Jews). They "kowtow . . . to the 'democratic' charms of contemporary capitalism . . . its real and supposed achievements." What, Andreyeva asked, has happened to "the class struggle-[and] the leading role of the proletariat?" Don't the workers "oppose world capitalism" any more? What about the millions in the world who are "dying of starvation, epidemics and military adventures by imperialists?"

Even more astounding than the tone and content of the Andreyeva manifesto was the lack of response to it, particularly among Soviet intellectuals. With few exceptions, almost everyone assumed that the party line had been reversed and that a new course had been set over which reformers had little influence. As one of my Soviet friends put it, "I had been nervous about how far the reform process had gone. Sooner or later I knew there would be a reaction and a halt. When I learned of the Andreyeva letter, I assumed that this was it and I accepted the consequences. The reform process had been exciting while it lasted."

The fact that her letter had appeared in a major newspaper like *Sovetskaia Rossiia* (which until April 1986 when the conservative Valentin Chikin took over as editor had been one of the more outspoken papers in favor of reform) and had the undoubted sanction of Yegor Ligachev, the number-two man in the Politburo, was proof enough.[31] Virtually no one responded to her. The exception was a thoughtful but relatively unnoticed critique in *Moscow News.*[32] In addition several papers, including a major paper in Belorussia, refused to reprint the Andreyeva declaration, despite some high-level pressure.[33] But the willingness to accept the abortion of the reform process, and the paucity of protests in support of reform, suggest just how frail Gorbachev's reforms were and how shallow their roots had been.

For three weeks there was also no official reaction. Finally, after his return from Yugoslavia and amidst considerable lobbying, including yet another threat to resign, Gorbachev was able to craft an authoritative response.[34] His intellectual comrade in arms in the Politburo and the official responsible for ideology, Alexander Yakovlev, was assigned to prepare the answer. According to Roy Medvedev, Gorbachev convened a meeting of the Politburo during the last week of March, probably March 30, to force a showdown.[35] By coincidence, Ligachev had left for a trip to Vologda.[36] Yakovlev's strong reply was then delivered to *Pravda* and other editors in Moscow were told to publish the article over the weekend. But nothing appeared, which only increased the sense of doom and panic among many of the reformers.[37] Determined to force the issue, Gorbachev apparently convened another meeting of the Politburo, and this time warned that unless there was a vote of confidence for a continuation of the reform process and a reprimand for *Sovietskaia Rossiia,* Gorbachev would resign.[38] With that Yakovlev's response was finally published on April 5, 1988, in *Pravda* as "Principles of Perestroika: The Revolutionary Nature of Thinking and Acting."[39] While acknowledging the need for discussion, Yakovlev warned that Andreyeva's letter was not constructive. It attempted to set one group against another, and in its continued defense of Stalin, it sought to build on his arbitrary methods and stifle all criticism just as Stalin had. Furthermore, Yakovlev insisted, attacks on Stalin did not invalidate or blaspheme the sacrifices of the Soviet people. "The lives of the Party, War, and Labor veterans were not in vain." Nevertheless, he argued, those sacrifices did not mean that there were no abuses.

In the end, Gorbachev and Yakovlev prevailed. Reportedly

the Politburo voted to reprimand Chikin, the editor of *Sovet-skaia Rossiia,* and *Sovetskaia Rossiia* duly reprinted the *Pravda* article on April 6.[40] The Politburo also reprimanded Ligachev for convening the editors' meeting the day after the publication of the Andreyeva letter.[41] Yeltsin, who was out of the Politburo by then, asserted that in the aftermath, Gorbachev and Ligachev stopped speaking to each other.[42] Nonetheless, the confrontation demonstrated that despite three years of glasnost and democratization most of the country's intellectuals were still easily intimidated. Democracy and due process were still fragile transplants.

It could be argued that Ligachev and Andreyeva acted prematurely. Gorbachev was able in 1988 to deflect their efforts to halt the reform process. Moreover, after the showdown Gorbachev moved to undercut Ligachev's power, and two years later, at the 28th Congress of the Communist Party, he forced Ligachev into retirement. Perhaps if Ligachev and Andreyeva had waited another year or two, particularly as economic and political conditions continued to deteriorate, they might have been able to muster more support. The accelerating discontent openly expressed just a year or so later in large part reflects the bold assertiveness shown by the anti-reformers in late 1990. Nonetheless, the timing of Andreyeva's statement defined the position of a heretofore unfocused opposition to the reform process. It had taken almost three years from the day that Gorbachev had assumed power; but once articulated, the Andreyeva effort rallied others. When asked why it took so long, several of my Soviet friends have explained that it was not only the reluctance of these anti-reformers to challenge Soviet authority (loyal, disciplined party members always obeyed the party general secretary), but that these traditionalists tend to be less articulate than the liberal intelligentsia and reformers. Those opposed to Gorbachev and his reforms tended to be "strong and silent" types, not used to verbalizing their feelings. Moreover, they usually avoided contact with foreigners, particularly those from the West. Nor were they always in agreement about their concerns. But Andreyeva's going public provided encouragement and stimulus to others.

Subsequently, Andreyeva continued to protest, and eventually she took the lead in organizing *Edinstvo* (Unity), an association of like-minded supporters.[43] *Edinstvo*'s impact has been difficult to judge, but many of its stands and members are also those of *Soiuz* (Union), a caucus of hard-liners in the Supreme Soviet and the Congress of People's Deputies that was formed in February 1990. They were able to muster 561 votes at the fourth session of the Congress of People's Deputies in December 1990. They were blamed by the supporters of reform for Shevardnadze's resignation and Gorbachev's retreat from his advocacy of the reform process.

As the members of *Soiuz* grew in numbers and shrillness, as glasnost seemed to turn into anarchy, and as perestroika brought more bad economic news each day, Gorbachev found himself deferring more and more to the hard-liners' point of view. By December 1990, Gorbachev had in effect isolated himself from some of his longtime fellow reformers and close associates such as Alexander Yakovlev and Eduard Shevardnadze, and had aligned himself instead more and more closely with traditional party functionaries. His selection of Gennady Yanayev as vice president of the Soviet Union reflected that shift. Only a few months earlier while chairman of the Soviet Trade Union movement, Yanayev actually sought to generate opposition among the workers to Gorbachev's economic reforms. He warned of price increases, mass unemployment, and bankruptcies if the perestroika process were not halted. Even after his election as vice president, Yanayev identified himself as a supporter of the *Soiuz* faction.[44]

Gorbachev's shift did not pass unnoticed among his onetime opponents. After Shevardnadze's resignation, Yegor Ligachev in an "I told you so" interview trumpeted that "many of Gorbachev's proposals seem realistic to me now: on the structure and executive authority, on the strengthening of law and order and on improving management and economic ties. . . . I once had an argument with Gorbachev—a little less than two years ago. He declared that the main danger stems from the conservative forces. This is wrong."[45]

III

Theoretically, Gorbachev should have welcomed the overt manifestation of a conservative opposition. That was presumably what democratization and glasnost were all about. Gorbachev in fact had actively sought grass-roots involvement and the questioning of the government processes from both the left and the right—reformers and anti-reformers. The expectation was that such involvement would uncover and expose the malfeasance of those working against Gorbachev's reform efforts. That was true when the criticism came from those supporting glasnost and perestroika. But as the anti-reformers became more articulate, they began to use the same opportunities to attack not only the reforms, but the reformers. This disoriented at least some of the reformers, who saw it not as legitimate criticism but as ingratitude and disloyalty.

Even someone like Eduard Shevardnadze, who probably had as much exposure to the ways of Western democracies as anyone in the reform group around Gorbachev, apparently had trouble understanding just what a true democratic process entails. In his dramatic December 1990 speech announcing his unexpected resignation as minister of foreign affairs, most of his focus was on warning about an impending dictatorship and Gorbachev's turn away from reform. Shevardnadze also complained bitterly, however, about the criticisms that were being made of him and Gorbachev. As he saw it, government officials in a democracy must be treated with respect. After all, they were not just hired hands. "Because many people think that the ministers who sit there or the members of the government or the President or someone else are hired, they [the critics] can do what they want with them. I think that is impermissible." Why had no one defended him, Shevardnadze demanded to know. "Not one person could be found, including the person in the chair [Gorbachev] who was willing to reply and say simply that this was dishonorable, that this is not the way, not how things are done in civilized states [sic]. Why is no one rebuffing them?" he asked.[46]

As we noted earlier, democratization and glasnost can be a prickly, even painful process. It is likely to spawn not only "right thinking" but "wrong thinking," even deviant groups such as *Pamyat* or Memory. *Pamyat* is a perfect example of what so concerned Shevardnadze. This organization dates back to 1979, when several preservationists joined together in an effort to protect historical buildings and monuments.[47] Initially, it was a non-partisan organization linked to the non-controversial All Russian Society for the Preservation of Historical and Cultural Monuments (VOOPIK). In late 1987, a rump group led by Dmitri Vasiliyev, a charismatic but controversial part-time actor and essayist, managed to seize control of the Moscow branch of VOOPIK.[48]

With *Pamyat* as his forum, Vasiliyev and his associates urgently sought to broadcast the message that Russia was in trouble because its leaders had fallen under the spell of a Masonic Zionist plot. As proof, they cited the fact that the Masons use six-pointed stars and that Lenin supposedly had a Jewish grandfather. If further proof were needed, they also discovered that Lenin had three copies of the *Protocols of the Elders of Zion* in his library.[49] (This was the faked 1890s French essay contrived to show that the Jews were bent on taking over the world.) Even more to the point, they noted that Marx was a Jew and Stalin had fallen under the influence of Leon Trotsky and Lazar Kaganovich, both Jews. Trotsky, *Pamyat* insists, was responsible for the first purges of the peasants and Kaganovich for the destruction of so much of what was old Moscow. Kaganovich supposedly constructed the Moscow street network in the form of the six-pointed star of David. Several true believers noted that the *Protocols of the Elders of Zion* had predicted that someone someday would do just that. Moreover, Kaganovich designed the Moscow subway system so that "all the principal transfer stations are located under party and government institutions. This, insists Vasiliyev, made it easy to blow up all the government organizations and their documents.[50]

Pamyat also demanded a change in the design of the monument to the Soviet victory in World War II that was being built outside Moscow on Poklonnaia Hill. While others in the Soviet Union were upset by what they saw as a wasteful expenditure of millions of rubles and the desecration of an environmentally important site, *Pamyat* supporters were incensed by what they insisted were the use of Masonic and Zionist symbols in the monument.[51] Last but not least, they added their voices to those critics of Stalin who insist that flooding on the site selected by Stalin for what was to have been the world's largest skyscraper was God's wrath for tearing down the Church of Christ the Savior. Several splinter groups that spun off from the original founders, each professing its own unique version of the truth, have taken even more outlandish stands. In the most extreme wing of *Pamyat* there are some who are opposed to anything Western, including Christianity. For that reason they also criticize Solzhenitsyn and see the conversion of Kievan Rus (the ninth-century original precursor of the modern Russian empire) to Christianity as a Zionist plot.[52] After all, Jesus was a Jew.

If *Pamyat* had restricted itself merely to espousing these ideas, it might not be much of a threat, but its members also believe in action. Activists wear black shirts and frequently express themselves by beating up those they regard as opponents.[53] When one of their members was on trial, they disrupted court proceedings, and they have also disrupted public and private meetings. Because it was videotaped and subsequently shown on Soviet television, the *Pamyat* raid on the liberal Soviet Writers' Club on January 18, 1990, was seen as a particularly dangerous manifestation of fascism. Members of *Pamyat* broke into the meeting, roughed up a few members, and warned that they would return with machine guns. After a rather stormy and occasionally disrupted trial, the leader of the attack,

Konstantin Smirnov-Ostashvili, was found guilty and sentenced to jail.

So far, however, *Pamyat*'s threat appears to be more symbolic than actual. Its members can mount demonstrations and call for pogroms; their threats have probably done as much to precipitate the emigration of Soviet Jews as the breakdown of the country's economy and the social disorganization. But *Pamyat* has been unable to win any significant support at the ballot box. Its candidates have done poorly in elections. Rumors that they have friends in high places (Ligachev was viewed as a supporter and Yeltsin when he was head of the party in Moscow met with them), and that *Pamyat* is a creation of the KGB, just as its predecessor the Black Hundreds was a puppet of the czarist secret police, are hard to verify. The emergence of such deviant forces is probably a source of embarrassment for Gorbachev, especially in his dealings with Western leaders, but it is an unavoidable product of glasnost.

IV

Given the way ordinary workers have been exploited under communism, it might have been expected that Soviet workers would have been in the forefront of the reform movement. In the Brezhnev years, some dissidents in fact did try unsuccessfully to establish their own independent unions and demand better working and living conditions.[54] In fact in 1989, almost half the country's coal miners struck and eventually organized their own independent unions dedicated to promoting economic reform. But offsetting these examples of support for reform which were not always necessarily sought by Gorbachev were efforts by other worker groups to halt the whole process. Some of these efforts were devious maneuvers by anti-Gorbachev bureaucrats and economic administrators to embarrass Gorbachev and ultimately abort his efforts. Others reflected honest fears among workers about the real possibility of unemployment, further exploitation, and economic impoverishment.

The official trade union movement was notorious for its adherence to the party line and willingness to tolerate working and living conditions that would provoke strikes in most other societies. Thus, it was not surprising that in the more relaxed political conditions evolving out of glasnost and democratization, some members of the official labor movement became emboldened enough to create their own labor movement. What was surprising, however, was that several of these efforts were so opposed to change. One of the most influential groups, the United Russian Workers Front, was closely identified with a charismatic rolling-mill operator from the Nizhnii Tagil metallurgical combine, Veniamin Yarin.[55] As one of the few workers elected to the new Council of People's Deputies, Yarin captured the country's attention with his early outspokenness and willingness to criticize the Soviet economic system and its leadership.[56] There are rumors that Yarin's group (he is co-chairman) is a front for the apparatus.[57] He has denied that. Nevertheless, he has been highly critical of Gorbachev's efforts to switch the Soviet economy to a market orientation and the resulting income inequalities that the market is likely to bring. He has warned, properly so, that sooner or later there will be proposals to legalize private property and then who knows, capitalism may be right around the corner. He was also distressed that in an open election, worker candidates have fared worse than candidates who are white-collar workers and intellectuals. In the pre-Gorbachev years, workers did not have to subject themselves to such competition and thus were assured a sizable number of seats. Consequently Yarin demanded that candidates for the Supreme Soviet be elected in their work place—not place of residence.[58] If it had been adopted, this arrangement would have guaranteed that candidates picked by the labor movement would dominate legislative bodies.

For a time Yarin's movement seemed to generate considerable enthusiasm and support. The leaders of the anti-reform coalition had been looking for some way to broaden their base among the general population. Going back in history, they first decided to take a page from the nineteenth-century *narodnik* effort and began their organizing efforts by attempting to reach out to peasants in the countryside. The peasants have always been romanticized by Russian intellectuals, and it was assumed that if the peasants could be mobilized by the intellectuals, the rest of the population would follow. However, the twentieth-century effort was not much more successful than its historical antecedent. The peasants essentially refused to involve themselves in the political struggle. Eventually Yarin and his allies came to realize that they could generate more opposition to the reform movement by concentrating their organizational efforts among Soviet workers, where political awareness and discontent were more acute. By capitalizing on the discontent of the industrial workers, there were serious concerns that Yarin might evolve as a leader of a semi-Fascist labor coalition. These fears were dissipated at least temporarily several months later, in March 1990, when Gorbachev co-opted Yarin and installed him as a member of the cabinet-like Presidential Council. At that point, Yarin seemed to sublimate his energies into more conventional channels. Temporarily at least, the United Workers Front dropped off the front pages.

V

Yarin's failure with the peasants notwithstanding, by 1990 political unrest also began to appear in the countryside. Opposed to any diminution in their authority, a large group of collective and state farm managers on October 6, 1990, organized themselves into what they called the USSR Peasant Union. The USSR Peasant Union opposes efforts to set up private and family farms. Led by Vasily Starodubtsev, a collective farm director from the Tula region, and encouraged by Yegor Ligachev, the USSR Peasant Union, despite its name, is made up primarily of collective and state farm managers and ministry officials who are determined to maintain the status quo.[59] They point out that 25 percent of the country's state and collective farms are unprofitable.[60] In their eyes, breaking up these collectives and converting them into private farms where the peasants would be left to fend for themselves would, they argue, cause enormous hardship for the members. To the farm managers, and other members in the USSR Peasant Union, this would be a step backward and "deeply reactionary."[61] Given that the large collective farms generally were unprofitable, Ligachev assumed that smaller farms would be equally unprofitable. Without support from the larger collective or state farms, how would the peasant or the family farms support themselves? Would they too go hungry? For a believing communist like Ligachev, this was heresy. This was not, he insisted, what he had stood for as a communist all these years.[62] To Ligachev, the solution was not to turn state and collective farms into private and family farms, but to increase the national funds allocated to agriculture.[63] That was only fair, Ligachev argued, because it would partially compensate for the "billions of rubles" which the state in the 1930s took from the peasants "through low fixed prices for agricultural produce in order to create a socialist industry."[64]

Similar sentiments were expressed by other members of the USSR Peasant Union. In fact, however, the governing principle for most of them, particularly the farm directors and other former members of the Gosagroprom apparat who dominate the USSR Peasant Union, was their fear that a breakup of the collective and state farms would mean an end to their prerogatives and power. Nikolai Petrakov, for a time Gorbachev's chief economic adviser, referred to these farm directors as "the red landowners."[65] Their reaction was not too different from the way Russian landowners responded when Czar Alexander II announced his intention to emancipate the serfs in 1861.

VI

Although they were fewer in number, Soviet managers also began to organize in order to press their views. The deconstruction of the central planning process and the growing disregard of orders issued by Gosplan began to cause chaos among those dependent on Gosplan for the supply of manufacturing components. In July 1990, for example, managers of fifty leading Soviet engineering factories petitioned the government to reinstitute the central supply and planning system for raw materials.[66] Production in 1991 would be jeopardized, they warned, without a return of power to Gossnab and Gosplan. Less than six months later, in December, 3,500 managers joined the 50. Together they criticized not only the breakdown at the all-union level, but also the growing anarchy at the republic and *oblast* level.[67] They wanted a return to central dictate for the delivery of supplies and "guarantees of managerial rights," as well as the reinstitution of discipline in the work place. From their perspective, the switch to the market was not working. Even if it were, most state entities would not benefit because they were not equipped to seek out customers or respond quickly to customer needs. Many of them were purposely designed to handle massive projects with an emphasis on long-term production runs rather than on flexibility and change.[68] The Uralmash combine in Sverdlovsk with 45,000 employees in one location, for example, was well suited to mass-produce machine tools, products that required infrequent model changes. Without millions of dollars in foreign currency to modernize their facilities, Uralmash officials insisted they would be unable to attain the production flexibility that is necessary to be competitive in world markets.

Perestroika, therefore, has created heretofore unprecedented problems for managers of state factories. In addition, the cut in the Soviet military budget had a devastating impact on almost all Soviet military producers. According to the deputy director of the Uralmash plant, orders for tanks and other weapon parts fell by one third from 1988 to 1990.[69] Moreover, with the breakup of the Council of Mutual Economic Assistance in January 1991, the longstanding and obedient purchasers of Soviet industrial equipment located in Eastern Europe were no longer obligatory customers of Uralmash. They are now free to look elsewhere, and since they have to pay for their purchases in hard currency, they look first to the West rather than the East.

On top of everything else, some of the best and most enterprising Soviet engineers and managers have set off on their own or have joined up with cooperatives where the pay is higher and the room for creativity is greater. To those brought up in the central planning tradition, this is heresy. It hurts even more when engineers in these new cooperatives devote themselves to making consumer goods such as pots and pans rather than space missiles. To an economist, this makes sense if the salary for making pots and pans is higher than it would be for making space missiles. Presumably this shows that society places a higher value on consumer goods. Engineers, particularly in the Soviet Union, have trouble understanding how making such trivial products is not a misuse of engineering talent.[70] In their eyes, it would make so much more sense to bring back central planning where orders are obeyed, machine tools have priority, deliveries are assured, and chaos is a description of capitalism, not communism.

VII

Elements in the military and the KGB also made similar but obviously more threatening complaints about the viability of perestroika. This opposition was expressed by Vladimir Kryuchkov, the chairman of the KGB, in a speech to the Fourth Congress of the USSR People's Deputies.[71] In a throwback almost to the days of Stalin, Kryuchkov launched an all-out assault on the changes wrought in Soviet domestic and foreign policy under Gorbachev. He is not a "witch-hunter," he insisted; he is only seeking to weed out the criminal, dishonest, subversive, secessionists, and those bent on foreign infiltration and espionage. The only ones who have benefited from the move to the market, he asserted, are the speculators and black marketeers. These members of the mafia have bribed and bought up the government and the police. Today, the rich are those who thrive on unearned incomes. In the meantime, crime and pornography have become major forces in our society. Is this what we aspire to? he asked. What happened to socialist morality, to Russian dignity?

Kryuchkov is especially concerned about the breakdown of a unified Soviet Union and the growth of ethnic tensions and divisiveness. The different nationalist and splinter groups as well as those who criticize existing government structures are of particular concern. How can the KGB be blamed for insisting on law and order and instituting violent measures when there are already "over 20 nationalistic politicized associations in the country which have paramilitary units or armed detachments of guerrillas?" Yet there is a campaign to discredit not these secessionists, but "the army, the procuracy, state security bodies [the KGB], and the Soviet militia [police]."

He also attributed the breakdown in the Soviet economy to both open and covert conspiracies. "KGB organs have recently uncovered cases of people causing serious damage to our financial system," he said ominously. "One can observe unjustified losses of foreign currency in the carrying out of foreign economic activity. These are particularly palpable on the oil and oil products export market. Note this: In 1989, 127 million tons of oil were sold at the then comparatively low prices. This year [1990] when prices rose considerably, exports fell to 101 million tons. In 1991 it is planned to supply 61 million tons in the foreign market."[72] Coming from someone else in a different context, this would simply be an interesting piece of news. But following a comment which points out that "in a number of places, procuracy bodies [the attorney general] have initiated criminal proceedings," the paragraph on the drop in exports suggests that there is something deeper at work here.

The implication of foreign as well as domestic conspiracy was heightened when Kryuchkov went on to warn that rubles were being smuggled out of the Soviet Union. He estimated there were as many as 12 billion rubles in Switzerland alone that could be used to undermine the Soviet economy. More than that, "a number of our foreign partners" were committing economic sabotage, and some foreigners were attempting "to inflict economic damage on our country."[73] Food exporters were delivering "impure and sometimes infested grain as well as some that is radioactive or mixed with chemical additives."

(This is a particularly sensitive matter in the Soviet Union because of its experience with food contamination after Chernobyl.) According to his calculations, 40 percent of the Soviet Union's imported grain was weed-infested and 10 percent was substandard.

Conditions were not much better in industry. Used equipment was being exported to the Soviet Union instead of new, and some of the foreign equipment was "ecologically dirty." In addition, some of the Soviet Union's best minds and technicians, Kryuchkov complains, were being lured outside the country to work for the Soviet Union's rivals. At the same time, outsiders were seeking "to foist questionable ideas and plans" on the Soviet Union as it tried to solve its problems.

Kryuchkov was not the only one to call for heightened vigilance against economic crimes and foreign economic intrigue. Valentin Pavlov, who replaced Nikolai Ryzhkov as prime minister, justified his January 23, 1991, currency reform by asserting that it "was not a matter of confiscation but a matter of protection."[74] His reform invalidated all fifty- and one hundred-ruble notes in circulation and allowed the redemption of no more than an amount equal to one's monthly wage or at most 1,000 rubles. Pavlov claimed, however, that the victims of the monetary reform were not Soviet citizens but Western bankers and "ultraradicals" determined to "get rid of uncooperative political figures" like "President Gorbachev," who "has begun to step on someone's toes."[75] These alleged Western manipulators were charged with putting up $7.8 billion to buy 140 billion rubles.[76] Such accusations seem highly fanciful. Anyone putting up that much money to buy that many rubles even at the then highly favorable but illegal exchange rate of 18 rubles to the dollar must have a serious personality flaw. Yet apparently some investors did put up some money for that purpose.[77] Presumably they were attracted by the favorable rate of exchange, which was far superior even to the tourist rate of 6 rubles to the dollar. According to the KGB, the originator of the plot was Colin Gibbins, an Englishman who was the head of the Dove Trading Company. Nonetheless, it is hard to see what foreigners could buy with 140 billion rubles. The same question puzzled Pavlov, who still accepted the KGB's accusation at face value. "Such an influx of money would be tantamount to a financial catastrophe."[78] In his eyes this was part of a "financial war" that had been declared against the Soviet Union.

To hard-liners like Kryuchkov and Pavlov, perestroika by opening the door to Western capitalists had exposed the Soviet Union to the evils of capitalism, allowed foreigners more opportunities to undermine the Soviet economy, and in addition provided Soviet enemies with access to the Soviet Union's most vital military installations and secrets. To the extent capitalism gains a foothold in the Soviet Union, socialism dies. How can we in the KGB, Kryuchkov asked, be anything but alarmed when perestroika stands for almost everything those who defend the Soviet Union have always opposed? In Kryuchkov's words, "Do all the negative features and vices of the capitalist market really have to become an automatic part of our life?"[79]

VIII

Senior military officers have come to share many of these same views. Prior to 1989, such feelings were muted. Gorbachev appeared to be very much in control of the military. After the military leadership embarrassed itself by failing to detect the young West German, Mathias Rust, as he flew in a rented Cessna Skyhawk from Finland into Red Square on National Border Guard Day, May 28, 1987, Gorbachev shook up the military command, making very clear that he was in charge. He then ordered the withdrawal of Soviet troops from Afghanistan by February 15, 1989, and made far-reaching arms agreements with the United States at the expense of the military. Soviet troops had to withdraw from Eastern Europe as East Germany became absorbed into West Germany and as the other countries of Eastern Europe renounced their adherence to communism.

It mattered little that Gorbachev, as well as Shevardnadze, was as surprised as anyone at the speed of the collapse of the Communist regimes of Eastern Europe and the unification of

Germany. Evidence suggests that Gorbachev's actions in East Germany were done in the hope of nudging the East German leadership under Erich Honecker to liberalize some of its hardline positions in order to ward off an explosive reaction and violence. In other words, Gorbachev sought the same kind of change in East Germany that he had overseen in the USSR, under the assumption that the pattern would be the same. He expected that the East German and other East European Communist parties would remain in control and change would come gradually. Gorbachev miscalculated. The peoples of Eastern Europe, sensing their opportunity, decided to break with the communist system completely. It had been imposed on them from the outside by the Soviet Union; now that the Soviet Union was undergoing its own transformation, the peoples of Eastern Europe guessed correctly that 1989 was the year to escape and change. Whether stunned or not, Gorbachev acquiesced. For that he received the Nobel Prize and the world's applause. But for the anti-reformers inside the Soviet Union, especially among the military, these concessions amounted to an enormous sacrifice and the breaching of Soviet security.

Thus, by 1989 there was a marked turn in military attitudes. From a Soviet military officer's point of view, the world had been turned upside down. Instead of praise, critics now attacked the army for its behavior in Afghanistan. Mothers demanded an end to the draft as the more open media reported there had been 15,000 non-combat deaths among army draftees over a five-year period. Partly in response to the deaths and partly due to growing ethnic tensions, the number of deserters totaled 4,300 in 1990, and 35,000 young men failed to answer the draft call.[80] The situation was particularly alarming in some of the non-Russian republics. Monuments to the victory in World War II were defaced or torn down. In the Baltic republics, threats were made to cut off supplies of food, water, heat, and energy to Soviet Army bases.[81] In the Chita *oblast* in East Siberia, civilian authorities decided not to feed or clothe the army out of regional stocks.[82] Other areas declared that there was not enough housing to relocate officers and their families being reassigned from Eastern Europe. Just among the elite missile troops, ten thousand lacked housing in late 1990.[83] To make matters even worse, delegates to the Congress of People's Deputies complained that non-Russian nationalists in some of the Baltic states had thrown stones at "little children of Soviet officers, causing them serious injuries." Others were charged with throwing Molotov cocktails at weapons depots or raping the wives of Russian officers.[84] Such accusations seemingly were exaggerated in order to justify the creation of Committees for National Salvation in all three of the Baltic republics. These committees were shadowy front groups made up of hard-line communists, military officers, and Russians. Reacting to the confusion and chaos which they in large part had generated, they then demanded the use of military force to restore law and order and prevent the restoration of "bourgeois" regimes.

Undeniably, Soviet troops felt unappreciated. Even in Moscow, some acknowledged openly that when they could avoid it, they no longer wore their military uniforms in public for fear of being insulted. By early 1990, there was a growing sense that the Soviet Union had squandered all the gains it had made in World War II. With Gorbachev and Shevardnadze's acquiescence, Germany had been reunited and the Soviet Union had committed itself to withdraw within five years all its military forces from their positions in Eastern Europe. Indeed, in the case of Hungary and Czechoslovakia, the Soviets had promised to withdraw before the end of 1991. Many in the Soviet military saw this as a sell-out by Gorbachev and other civilians to the United States.

In addition, a growing number of military officers suspected that in exchange for supporting Gorbachev's domestic politics, the United States had maneuvered the Soviet Union into supporting U.S. policy in the Persian Gulf. They saw themselves in the uncomfortable position of backing U.S. imperialist oil policy in the Middle East and turning their back on their previous allies in countries such as Iraq.[85] They also feared that the Soviet Union might agree to send its troops to the area and find itself bogged down again in another war.[86]

Against this backdrop, several once timid military officers began to express their frustration publicly. Many joined *Soiuz,* the conservative anti-reform faction within the Congress of People's Deputies. Two of the more outspoken critics of Gorbachev, Lieutenant Colonel Viktor Alksnis and Colonel Nikolai Petrushenko, decided to escalate their demands and pressured for the resignations of Vadim Bakatin, a liberal reformer who was then serving as the minister of the interior, and Eduard Shevardnadze. Both men subsequently resigned, with Shevardnadze complaining openly that no one had defended him when the two colonels boasted that they had toppled Bakatin and warned that Shevardnadze would be next.[87]

In such a climate, there was reason to believe rumors of a coup attempt when two elite regiments of Soviet paratroops suddenly appeared in Red Square in early September 1990 dressed in their battle gear. Subsequent explanations that the troops were on their way to pick potatoes (in their flak jackets) or rehearsing for the November 7 Revolution Day Parade two months hence were laughable.[88]

Indications of the tensions between Gorbachev and the military were revealed at Gorbachev's meeting on November 13, 1990, with one thousand military personnel.[89] Accounts reported that Gorbachev was heckled and booed as he tried to address their complaints.[90] This confrontation was followed a few days later by another meeting between Gorbachev and military personnel who had been elected as delegates to various parliamentary or national and republic Supreme Soviets. Apparently it was at such a meeting that Colonel Alksnis challenged Gorbachev head on and warned him that he had only thirty days to impose order or face a vote of no confidence. According to Alksnis, Gorbachev had already lost the support of the army, which might well adapt its own operating procedures.[91] Reportedly that evening Gorbachev succumbed and drafted a new plan to impose stringent presidential controls.

Certainly not all Soviet military personnel hold similar views. Some junior ranking officers have formed a union called Shield *(Shchit)* and work within the liberal Interregional Group of

Deputies in the Congress of People's Deputies to press for the sort of reforms that so upset their superiors. But increasingly these supporters of reform find themselves on the defensive. Reflecting the growing climate of distress and bitterness, two military officers aligned with the more reformist Interregional Deputies were ordered out of the proceedings of the military delegation to the Congress of People's Deputies because of accusations that the Interregional Group was being financed by the CIA. Dissent in the army can be hazardous.[92]

X

The anti-Western and chauvinistic views of the anti-reformers in many ways bear a strong resemblance to the attitudes of the Slavophiles and nationalists of the nineteenth century, just as today's reformers have much in common with the nineteenth-century westernizers. Concern for the communal life of the peasants, fears that the Soviet Union will become westernized, or even a "marionette of Western Zionism"—all views expressed at the 1990 Congress of the Russian Writers' Union—are themes similar to warnings heard a century earlier.[93] The cast is different, but the sentiments are much the same. As one delegate put it when attacking Alexander Yakovlev, Eduard Shevardnadze, and Mikhail Gorbachev, "Some people may be even worse than the Jews."[94]

Of course not everything is an echo of the past. Certainly the central planning versus market debate is a Soviet, not a prerevolutionary matter. But the complaints that Gorbachev and other reformers are spending too much time in the West and, as Kryuchkov of the KGB insisted, foisting too many alien concepts on the country are old refrains. As proof that the reformers are too taken with their foreign admirers, they published the mayor of Moscow Gavril Popov's itinerary. It shows him roaming from Western Europe to the United States to Japan, and Sergei Stankevich, the vice mayor, traveling from India to Mexico to Guatemala to Greece to the United States to France to Poland to Sweden to Japan. This, their critics say,

is evidence of their Western orientation and lack of commitment to the Russian tradition and soul.[95]

As the reform process began to falter, Gorbachev found
himself facing increasing polarization within the country. The
reformers looking to the West for inspiration stressed the
1986–88 Gorbachev emphasis on democratization, pluralism,
and move to the market. The bureaucrats and military officers
who found their prerogatives threatened by such reforms were
joined by those primarily concerned about the increasing
anarchy and empty shelves in their daily lives. To save the
empire and himself, Gorbachev began to turn away from his
earlier aspirations. He found himself moving ever closer to
those who looked to the past and inward. Besides, the reformers
had had a chance and failed. It was their policies which led to
the 4 percent drop in national income in 1990 and an anticipated drop exceeding 10 percent in 1991. They had been unable
to put food on the shelves or quiet ethnic discontent. Discredited, they began to lose popular support. By December 1990,
the Interregional Group of reformers shrank from 330 supporters early in the month to 229 in late December.[95] As described
by the army hard-liner Colonel Petrushenko, "the struggle is
now caught between the two camps we have in this country: the
democrats and the patriots. The democrats have had their day.
We, the patriots, will now dictate the future direction of the
country. We are people who do not rush off to the United States
to read lectures or open foreign bank accounts. We stay at home
and think through our plans for the future of a great Russia."[96]
Caught between these increasingly divergent views, Gorbachev
found himself agreeing to a series of successive compromises
that ultimately satisfied neither him nor his various opponents
and led him in mid-1991 to move back at least partly to the
reformist fold.

8

Where Does the Soviet Union Go from Here?

As first perestroika and then glasnost failed to produce the reforms Gorbachev was seeking, and as pressure from the public and the military industrial complex could no longer be ignored, Gorbachev switched course. Like a ship's captain who unexpectedly finds himself in a hurricane, Gorbachev first headed to the port side. When the wind shifted, he abruptly reversed course and headed to starboard. But none of these shifts has helped stabilize his ship. In the meantime, more and more of his passengers have become seasick. Similarly, the impact of Gorbachev's indecisiveness on the economy and the Soviet political system has generated more confusion than meaningful action. Amidst the turmoil, Supreme Soviets in the country have become more and more like debating rather than legislative bodies. After a time, no one seemed to be complying with orders from the center. Gorbachev even tried issuing orders demanding compliance with his earlier orders, but these were ignored as well.

For those of us living outside the Soviet Union it is hard to appreciate just how disorienting the Gorbachev years with all their course reversals in industry, agriculture, administration, and legislative and economic advisers have been. Earlier we saw how on taking over as general secretary, Gorbachev's industrial strategy initially emphasized the machine-tool industry, intensification, *uskoreniie* (acceleration), discipline, superministries, Gospriemka, and a 1986 crackdown on private trade. Reversing course the following year, he legalized cooperatives and private trade, reduced the role of central planning, and enacted the Enterprise Law, with the goal of generating more initiative from factory managers. He also encouraged joint ventures formed with partners from the capitalist world.[1]

The pattern in agriculture was similar. At the 27th Communist Party Congress in February 1986, there was some initial discussion about allowing individuals and families to sign contracts with the state and *kolkhoz* farms. That was considered to be a move toward semi-independence. The following year, in June 1987, the Central Committee Plenum issued a decree authorizing long-term leases in agriculture of up to ten to fifteen years.[2] But when finally forced to act, Gorbachev backed away from the idea of private property and the right to buy and sell it. Similarly, after initially attacking and dissolving the Ministry of Agriculture, he created Gosagroprom in its stead, only to close down Gosagroprom and reconstitute the Ministry of Agriculture in 1991.

In the political sphere, Gorbachev also undercut the role of the Communist Party. Political change was a principal theme of the Central Committee Plenum in January 1987, and of the 19th Communist Party Conference in June 1988. In addition, of course, there were ongoing changes. An early Gorbachev objective was to reduce the role of the Secretariat. While there were still secretaries, the Secretariat seldom met as a body. The Politburo also was subjected to a somewhat similar diminution in function as Gorbachev gradually appointed officials of secondary rank to it.[3] From March 1990 to December 1990, he shifted his attention to a newly created and non-party-based governmental organ called the Presidential Council, which was joined and then superseded by a Federation Council, made up at least in principle of the presidents of the different republics. Gorbachev's intent was to involve the heads of the different republics in his decisions in the expectation that as participants in the process, the republic presidents would then feel committed to implementing the decrees in their home republics. This, Gorbachev thought, would be a good way of increasing compliance with the orders he was issuing. But Gorbachev almost immediately ran into trouble with this Federation Council. Some of the presidents of the more independent republics refused to acknowledge the Council's mandate. Those who did participate had to spend much of their time in Moscow and not in their own republics, which was certain to reduce their power and effectiveness at home.

Discontented with the Federation Council, Gorbachev decided in March 1991 on yet another innovation. As economic and political life became more chaotic, he decided to create a Security Council reporting directly to the president. Its most important members were the heads of the KGB, army, and police. It symbolized Gorbachev's increasing emphasis on law, order, and restraint.

In the process of creating and dissolving these various organizations, Gorbachev kept accumulating more and more powers for himself in his non-party post as president. But formal and effective power are not the same. By late 1990, Gorbachev evidently concluded that to attain the effective power he sought, he would have to switch course again. After having built up his governmental powers and weakened the Communist Party, he decided that he needed the party after all. Thus by March 1991 he reversed himself one more time and began to emphasize his role as general secretary over that as president.

Gorbachev evidenced the same inconsistency when dealing with the Soviet Union's legislative institutions. He seemed to be in a continual search for new and effective ways of drawing up and implementing legislation. However, more often than not, like the administrative bodies he created, the legislative bodies seemed to lack a workable set of operating procedures that might make possible the achievement of concrete measures. It was almost as if Gorbachev had decided that what mattered was novelty, not practical procedures.

In 1988, for example, he created an entirely new entity—the

Congress of People's Deputies. One third of its members were appointed to their seats by special-interest groups; they were primarily associated with the Communist Party. The remaining two thirds had to run in elections, many of which were closely contested. This enhanced the standing of those delegates whose ability to win an election gave them an increased sense of their responsibilities and importance. Unlike those delegates who were elected by the people, Gorbachev never subjected himself to a public election. He was elected to the post of president not by the general public, but by the Congress of People's Deputies. For that matter he was allocated his seat as delegate to the Congress of People's Deputies by the Communist Party and therefore did not have to risk a competitive race in the public at large as did Boris Yeltsin. This was one of Gorbachev's most significant miscalculations. As a consequence, Gorbachev and the public have never had the sense that he was acting with a popular mandate from the people. That undoubtedly has limited his effectiveness.

The Congress of People's Deputies was superimposed over the existing two houses of the Supreme Soviet, but it was unclear why yet another legislative body was needed. Members of the Supreme Soviet were then elected from the Congress of People's Deputies. But given their overlapping nature, it was never clear precisely what the function was of these continually changing bodies. Nor was it clear how the expanding functions of the soviets (councils) in the municipalities and the republics were to be integrated. Each adopted powers claimed by other echelons in the legislative chain. Moreover, in a two-year period, from 1988 to 1990, Gorbachev pushed through at least one hundred constitutional amendments in the process of creating and destroying bodies like the Presidential Council.[4] His constant creation of new bodies and continuing constitutional amendments intensified the confusion.

The newness of suddenly having real legislative power compounded the confusion of governing. In the pre-Gorbachev years, there was no meaningful legislative process. Thus there were few administrators who had any real experiences with the operation of legislative bodies. For example, there was nothing equivalent to Roberts's Rules of Order. It was not surprising then that amidst great expectations, most of the legislative bodies in the Soviet Union, especially at the local level, evolved into little more than debating societies, if that.

Most Soviet legislative groups were not even clear as to their basic responsibilities. In established democracies, for example, the most important task of the legislature is to determine taxes and authorize funds for expenditures. In this way, the representatives of the people prevent undue exploitation of the public and restrain power abuses by the leadership. The suddenness with which the Soviet people found themselves with meaningful legislative power gave them little time or understanding of the significance of the power to tax and spend. This was illustrated at the Fourth Session of the Congress of People's Deputies, which met in December 1990. Waiting until the day after the Congress adjourned, Gorbachev then issued an *ukaz* (order or decree) announcing that he as president had decided to impose a 5 percent sales tax on the Soviet people.* Even worse, no one from the Congress of People's Deputies protested the usurpation of what should have been their prerogative.

I

Gorbachev's shifts in structures, strategies, and solutions were paralleled by his shifts in economic advisers. As the country's economy began to falter, he reacted like the owner of a losing National Football League team who keeps changing coaches. As we saw, initially Gorbachev relied primarily on the advice of Abel Aganbegyan.[5] But in less than three years Aganbegyan had become the target of more and more criticism.[6] In addition, Aganbegyan found himself under attack for

*See p. 222. Recognizing how ill-equipped these new legislative groups are to handle their newly granted authority, American organizations like the National Democratic Institute for International Affairs and the Project on Strengthening Democratic Institutions of Harvard University have been conducting on-site workshops on such essential matters as budgets, taxes, privatization, and governmental interaction.

what were viewed as inflammatory statements about the Armenian right to retain Nagorno-Karabakh. The Azeris were incensed that the Armenian public seemed to take Aganbegyan's statement as a sign that the Soviet leadership supported a reexamination of Nagorno-Karabakh's status as a part of Azerbaijan.

In looking for a successor to Aganbegyan, Gorbachev selected Leonid Abalkin. Abalkin was not only the director of the Institute of Economics of the Academy of Sciences, which he had headed since 1986, but he was the assistant to Aganbegyan in the scientific section of the Commission on Management.[7] Abalkin, a man of dour and unruffable countenance, was regarded as honest, earnest, and courageous. He was one of the first to criticize publicly Gorbachev's increasing grasp for power. At the 19th Party Conference in late June 1988, he stunned the nation by complaining on television that the general secretary of the Communist Party should not simultaneously sit as a senior executive of the national government. He urged voting against a proposal of Gorbachev's whereby the general secretary automatically became the head of the Supreme Soviet: "To combine in one person the function of party First Secretary and Chairman of the Supreme Soviet raises serious questions; it will be a vote of confidence, not a choice for many options."[8] He also expressed his doubts as to whether the Soviet Union could have a democratic life as long as there was only one legal political party.

Gorbachev did not respond kindly to Abalkin's criticism. As Gorbachev saw it, Abalkin "reeked of economic determinism" and lacked faith in the communist system.[9] But as happened so often in those early heady days of Gorbachev reform efforts, instead of punishing his critics, he eventually drew them closer. Several months later, in the summer of 1989, Abalkin was nominated by Gorbachev to become a deputy prime minister of the country and made chairman of a State Commission on Economic Reform.[10]

Although Abalkin had little formal training in Western economic theory, in 1986 he became a frequent visitor to the West.

Conversations with him indicated important gaps in his understanding of what was involved in moving to a market economy, but there was little doubt about his earnestness and his determination to tackle Soviet economic problems. He came to realize, for example, that the amalgamation of Soviet factories into massive vertical entities had economic disadvantages. Even though large-scale operations, what the Soviets called *gigantimania,* were considered to be a strength unique to Soviet socialism, many Soviet economists, Abalkin among them, began to understand that such a system was poorly suited for any kind of competition in domestic and world markets. There was in fact little to distinguish Soviet enterprises from the classical capitalist monopolies. Consequently Abalkin became convinced that if there was to be any internally generated pressure working to push down prices, Soviet enterprises would have to be broken up and made to compete with one another. Only in that way would the Soviet consumer, not the enterprise manager, reap the gains of economic reform, and only in that way would the Soviet Union become competitive in world markets.

As imperfect as it may be, Abalkin looked to the United States for guidance in addressing these problems. On a visit to the United States in 1988 and in a subsequent discussion with U.S. businessmen, he learned about U.S. antitrust procedures. Concluding that this would also be useful for the Soviet Union, he instructed one of his assistants to ask me to provide them with reading materials about American antitrust law. As I delivered several legal and economic textbooks to them, I warned that antitrust laws were designed specifically for the American legal and economic systems, and cautioned that they may be inappropriate in the Soviet context. There was a good chance they could even be counterproductive. Undaunted, Abalkin and his staff insisted that a transplant of the antitrust system or at least major segments of it was just what the Soviet Union needed.

Such incidents reflected Abalkin's conviction that he and his colleagues could take the best of both worlds. At a December 1988 meeting in Luxembourg, Abalkin was challenged to specify his definition of socialism. How could the Soviet Union retain socialism while moving more and more toward a market system? What, if anything, did he want to retain from socialism? Taking a lead from Deng Xiaoping, Abalkin replied, "We don't care what color the cat is as long as it catches mice." But he added an important condition, one whose absence has bothered socialist idealists. "And by the way this cat should not steal sausage, nor attack children."

Unlike his predecessors, Abalkin concluded that the Soviet economy must carry out a systematic overhaul rather than piecemeal adjustments. Using his mandate, he gathered together a team of highly motivated economists and administrative specialists. In a style more typical of Washington than Moscow, they worked ten- and sometimes twelve-hour days in an effort to design a coherent operational plan that could be put into effect in 1990 or at the latest by 1991.

It would have been much simpler if Abalkin and his staff could have drawn on a previously prepared transition plan that had already been successfully adopted by some other country. Unfortunately, in mid-1989 no such plans existed, and no country, including China and Hungary, had managed to evolve successfully from a centrally planned to a market system. There had been some partial successes, such as China's decollectivization. More typically, such reform efforts have been piecemeal and characterized by failure. There seemed to be nothing suitable for Soviet use. Thus the Abalkin commission had to start virtually from scratch.

While there was no coherent or already tested plan, there was no lack of advice about what to do. Suggestions came from both within and outside the Soviet Union. As Anatoly Lukyanov, the chairman of the Supreme Soviet, put it: "Reforming the economy is like making love in public. It is not so much the embarrassment, but all the advice you get." In the summer of 1989, Soviet economists and officials were subjected to a parade of visiting Western economists and businessmen, each one presenting his own instant cure. My prescription was presented to over one hundred Soviet economists and officials at a June 1989 lecture in Spasso House in Moscow. At the time I thought my proposal might be too controversial for a Soviet audience. It included provision for price reform (price flexibility), monetary reform, convertibility of the ruble, abolition of the industrial ministries, the privatization and breakup of state enterprises and of state and collective farms, freedom of entry for family farmers, private and cooperative stores and factories as well as joint ventures, including some that could be owned 100 percent by foreigners. There would also be a series of safety-net provisions to sustain the poorer members of society. The switch to price flexibility would make possible a reduction or near elimination of food subsidies. When combined with the continuing cuts in military expenditures, this would help bring the national budget into balance. A more nearly balanced budget along with the monetary reform would stem the outpouring of newly printed rubles, which in turn would reduce inflationary pressures. A few months later, on January 1, 1990, many elements of this plan would be incorporated into what in Poland came to be known as the shock-therapy strategy. For that matter, many of the same features would come to form a common core of the various plans that would subsequently be considered and presented to Gorbachev as part of a sequentially phased-in plan. The difference was that in my plan, all these changes were to be introduced simultaneously.

Other foreign specialists urged the adoption of programs stressing a switch to a gold standard or the increased use of input/output techniques or supply-side methods. Some insisted that help would only come when the Soviet Union came to accept the theories of monetary economists and focused the bulk of its efforts on regulating the flow of the money supply.

In the race against economic disintegration, Abalkin unveiled his own plan in October 1989, a mere four months after his appointment as deputy prime minister.[11] His reforms were to be introduced in four stages. The first stage, which was to begin in 1990, would lead off with an increase in wholesale prices, to be followed in 1991 by the relaxation of some retail price controls, especially on luxury goods. Prices on basic goods such as bread and children's clothing would be subjected to continued control for the immediate future, while prices on an intermediate category could be negotiated between buyers and sellers. Various new property forms would also be legalized. Under the proposal, private individuals and business groups could rent or lease state property. In addition, state-owned assets would be offered for sale in order to soak up some of the 300 billion excess rubles that were in circulation. There were still no provisions, however, for the private ownership of land or a monetary reform. To finance these various activities, the banking system would be reorganized to make it more responsive to the credit needs of private as well as state enterprises. Eventually stock, money, and financial exchanges would be established. There would also be auctions where foreign currencies and industrial products would be bought and sold. Other measures included provision for wage reform and the creation of a labor market. Most important of all, unprofitable enterprises which found it impossible to rehabilitate themselves would be forced to declare bankruptcy or turn over their operations to non-state owners. This reform along with a reform of the tax system would be part of a major effort to reduce and eventually eliminate the national budget deficit. What was unexplained, however, was how retail prices on basic goods could be kept unchanged and the budget deficit reduced at the same time. A good portion of the deficit is a consequence of the subsidies provided to prevent retail prices from rising.

The second stage in 1991 and 1992 involved introducing and establishing more retail price flexibility, which in turn was to be accompanied by an indexing system for wages designed to protect the workers. At the same time, the process of denationalizing state industry would continue. Toward the same end, unprofitable *sovkhozy* and *kolkhozy* would be broken up and the land turned over to cooperatives, families, or individuals by the end of 1991. The effort to increase competition and ensure anti-monopoly policies would be a main feature of the third stage, which would run from 1993 to 1995. By the end of the period, individuals as well as enterprises would be allowed to convert their rubles into Western currencies. The final stage, running from 1996 to 2000, would perfect the different reforms, create market equilibrium, and raise the standard of living.

Abalkin's plan was discussed at a November 1989 conference of Soviet economists and then passed on to Prime Minister Nikolai Ryzhkov, who in turn submitted it to the Congress of People's Deputies where it was debated. Some critics, including Aganbegyan and Nikolai Petrakov, asserted that the plan was too cautious. Conservatives led by the then minister of finance and subsequent prime minister Valentin Pavlov complained that on the contrary, the plan was too radical and would increase inflation and the role of the black market. Abalkin, sensing that the conservative voices were stronger than he had anticipated, warned that there was "a danger of creeping back into the old ways of the centralized economy."[12] An indication of the difficulty of implementing some of these reforms can be seen in the defeat of a 1989 proposal to increase prices of beer, tobacco, and other luxury products in the Supreme Soviet.[13]

By the time Prime Minister Ryzhkov submitted a reworked version of Abalkin's reform proposals to the Congress of People's Deputies a few weeks later, in December 1989, some of its more market-oriented features had been altered. While Ryzhkov continued to support the eventual introduction of a new tax system and a reform of wholesale and eventually retail prices, as well as a restructuring of the banking and finance system, he backed away from other critical elements of the plan.[14] He opposed the effort to close unprofitable factories and farms and set up a free market for labor. His plan called for a much more cautious approach to price reform. As he put it, "If contrary to objective reasons we should try to introduce full fledged market relations by 1991, it will bring us a serious social economic upheaval, a new stage of galloping inflation, falling production, mass unemployment and aggravated social tensions."[15] Most important, he showed almost no willingness to reduce the role of central planning. In fact, he offered a near complete five-year plan for 1991–95 with traditional specifications as to production, distribution, and consumption levels.

Ryzhkov's insistence on a much-watered-down version of the Abalkin plan dismayed many of the more outspoken reformers, who regarded this plan as a step backward. Their hopes were renewed, however, with the rather unanticipated announcement in January 1990 that Gorbachev had decided to shift course again and bring in a new economic adviser, Nikolai Petrakov.[16] Of all the senior Soviet economists, Petrakov seemed to have one of the clearest understandings of what a switch to the market entails and how the different parts of an economic system interrelate. Commenting on the Abalkin plan, for example, Petrakov noted a bit unfairly perhaps that "the people who put together this program do not understand what a market is."[17] Some American Sovietologists predicted that Petrakov's more market-oriented ideas would lead to a significant market reform and by the year 2000 might produce a Soviet economy with a strong resemblance to Sweden. Indeed, for at least a few weeks in March and April Gorbachev seemed committed to the implementation of a more radical Petrakov version of the Abalkin plan, which was to be presented for public discussion before May 1, 1990. But like a bridegroom who could not quite make up his mind whether he wanted to get married or not and kept postponing the date, Gorbachev postponed the implementation of each economic reform. He not only put off consideration of a Petrakov variant, he also put off voting on the revised Abalkin plan. He decided he needed another six months to reconsider the whole effort.[18]

In the midst of all the discussions, Gorbachev and the Council of Ministers somewhat unexpectedly on May 22, 1990, announced that they did plan after all to move ahead with a comprehensive five-year reform that would lead to a "regulated market economy."[19] What exactly that somewhat contradictory phrase meant was unclear; but as an indication of its seriousness, the government announced that it intended to raise prices on some basic products such as bread and utility costs by as much as threefold on July 1, 1990, and then again on other food products on January 1, 1991. To the economists, such a step was long overdue. The price increases would help to restore equilibrium to the market and reduce the budget deficit. But most of the price increases would only be a onetime event. Only 15 percent of the prices used by the consumers would be determined by market forces.[20] The bulk of the country's prices were still to be set by government planners. Supporters of market reform warned that such a step was not enough. This was not like the shock therapy of higher prices and simultaneous adoption of market processes introduced on January 1, 1990, by the Poles. Instead, as accurately noted by Pavel Bunich and Oleg Bogomolov, two of the Soviet Union's more thoughtful economists, this was "shock without the therapy."[21]

Reformers complained that these latest proposals were as usual a case of too little, too late. At the same time those opposed to reform warned that even if this version of the plan had been a bit more carefully thought out and designed to be applied over a longer period of time, it involved price increases that imposed a major burden on the poor.

The debate as to whether this reform was far-reaching enough or too far-reaching quickly became irrelevant. Warned that prices would double and triple within five weeks, Soviet consumers withdrew millions of rubles from their savings bank accounts, descended on Soviet shops, and bought up what few goods had been overlooked by earlier hoarders. It was of little consolation that wages would be increased 15 percent to help pay for the price hikes, especially since the retail prices were to rise an average of 43 percent.[22] In a few days' time, shop shelves were emptied out. Out of political necessity, the government backed off and canceled the price increases and other reform measures.[23]

As mentioned earlier, this announcement by Soviet officials about future price hikes not only brought about the collapse of the Soviet distribution system, it also triggered hyperinflation. Whereas prices on the collective farm markets were growing at a rate of 23 percent a year during the first six months of 1990, by July the rate increased to 33 percent and in September to 45 percent; by October 1990, it exceeded 50 percent, by March 1991, almost 70 percent and then in April there was the three-fold price hike on state retail prices.[24]

Yet while one reform plan lay dying and prices were multi-plying, a different group embarked on another effort. Following what had become a pattern, Gorbachev decided in midsummer to commission another study of reform, with a reporting dead-line of September 1. The charge to this new group was to pick and choose a number of different plans that had already been proposed. Composed of several of the country's leading econo-mists, this latest group was headed by Abel Aganbegyan. The reemergence of Aganbegyan as adviser to Gorbachev after hav-ing been blamed by many for Gorbachev's initially faulty strat-egy was a surprise not only to Soviet economists but to Aganbe-gyan himself. According to an article in *Izvestiia,* Aganbegyan first learned about his appointment from an announcement in the press.[25]

II

On August 2, 1990, while Aganbegyan was completing his work, Gorbachev decided to join with Yeltsin to see if they could agree on a common approach.[26] Given their ongoing feud, the news was greeted with great anticipation. Finally it looked like there might be a willingness to confront and deal directly with the country's accelerating economic problems. The expec-tation was that this new joint effort would build on a 400-day comprehensive reform proposal that had been prepared for Yeltsin by two younger economists, A. Mikhailin of the Insti-tute of the Government Committee on Prices (Goskomtsen) and M. Zadornov of the Institute of Economics.[27] Their initial draft then had been reworked by G. Yavlinsky, a Yeltsin ad-viser who had also served for a time as deputy chairman of the Council of Ministers of the RSFSR (the Russian Republic).

To head up the new working group assigned to refine the Yavlinsky draft, Gorbachev turned to yet another economist, Stanislav Shatalin, a modest but highly respected scholar. Strikingly candid, Shatalin first met Gorbachev in October 1989 at a conference organized by Gorbachev to discuss the Abalkin economic reform.[28] Impressed by Shatalin's insights, Gorbachev appointed him to membership in the Presidential Council when it was created in March 1990.

Shatalin and his group hammered out their ideas in a government guest house outside of Moscow in late August 1990. Both Gorbachev and Yeltsin contributed personally to the debate. The resulting document came to be called the Shatalin Five Hundred Day Plan, and seemed to offer hope that it would embody the combined efforts of the two major political leaders, Mikhail Gorbachev and Boris Yeltsin. Presented to the Federation Council (the heads of the fifteen republics plus Gorbachev and Ryzhkov) and the President's Council on August 30 and August 31, 1990, Gorbachev seemed to signal his all-out support for this new and in many ways radical document.[29]

During the first one hundred days of the Shatalin outline, which some assumed would begin the following month, on October 1, there would be a massive sale of state property. The proceeds from this sale would serve to reduce the state budget deficit and also reduce the supply of excess currency that prevented any meaningful price reform. While collective and state farms would not be dismantled, land reform would be introduced which would authorize peasants to set up their own farms and to drop out of collective farms. The banking structure would also be decentralized and opened to private participants. In a further effort to reduce the budget deficit, Shatalin called for a 75 percent drop in Soviet foreign aid as well as a reduction of 10 percent in the military budget and 20 percent in the KGB budget.

The second phase thereafter would last one hundred and fifty days. With the money supply reduced, the government would end its control over prices on non-staple consumer goods, which would be determined by market forces. An effort would be made to privatize one half of the country's small shops and restaurants, and most ministries would be abolished. A wage index system to provide some protection to workers would be introduced and steps would be taken to make the ruble convertible.

During the next one hundred and fifty days, efforts would continue to privatize state enterprises, including those in construction as well as heavy industry. More prices would be decontrolled, but prices for food, oil, gas, and drugs would remain subject to state control. A safety net would be expanded, and rationing of basic goods at low prices and an income supplement to the poor would be provided.

In the last one hundred days, a modern and flexible banking, currency, and tax program would be introduced. The privatization process would also continue. Government reserve commodities would be released and sold to put downward pressure on prices, and the government would use its expenditures to sustain employment.

On paper, the difference between the Shatalin and Ryzhkov-Abalkin variations did not seem to be that great. To some, it seemed more like a difference in nuance and political sponsorship. Both plans contained such features as the marketization of the Soviet economy and the privatization of state industry, a reduction of state subsidies, and a balancing of the budget. The main difference was timing. Shatalin's plan had a fixed five hundred-day timetable. Shatalin acknowledged in an informal discussion, however, that the days in his plan were more like days in the Bible's chapter of Genesis.[30]

The Ryzhkov-Abalkin plan was not as specific. In contrast to the five hundred days of the Shatalin plan, the Ryzhkov-Abalkin plan would require about five years. Moreover, the Ryzhkov-Abalkin plan would retain control at the center along with most of the existing ministry bureaucracies. As prime minister and as a graduate of the military industrial complex, Ryzhkov was much more opposed to delegating power to the republics. In contrast, Shatalin would give the republics the power to tax. The republics in turn would pay a form of dues to the national government. They would also have the authority to own their own natural resources within their boundaries and claim a share of the gold and hard currency originating from trade activities. And they could set their own timetable for the privatization of land and industrial price flexibility.

Perhaps the biggest difference concerned pricing policy. The Shatalin plan provided for the growing influence of the market on prices. Prices on basic commodities, however, would remain set until almost the end of the five hundred days. As Shatalin put it, his first goal was to stabilize the economy; only after that would there be the complete restructuring sought by the more radical reformers. By contrast, the Ryzhkov-Abalkin approach sought to reduce the budget deficit and the size of the food subsidies which aggravate that deficit by raising food prices on basic goods as quickly as possible. But these prices would be set by state authorities, not necessarily by market forces. Only much later, in 1992, would there be price decontrol. This explains their ill-fated announcement on May 22, 1990, about the intended threefold price increases on bread as of July 1 and January 1, 1991. But ill-fated or not, to some extent the Ryzhkov-Abalkin price policy remained more appealing to many economists. Even though they planned to ease the way to higher prices by raising wages at the same time, at least Ryzhkov and Abalkin were prepared to raise prices. Shatalin would have held them fixed, at least on basic products, for some time. Yet because Ryzhkov and Abalkin would continue to determine prices by government edict rather than by market forces, neither program fully met the criteria set by most Western economists as necessary for changing the economy.

In the end, all the efforts of the Shatalin Commission were for naught. Reverting to habit, Gorbachev backed away from his commitment to the Shatalin plan just as he had backed away from the Ryzhkov-Abalkin plan. On September 4, 1990, he decided to refer the whole effort to still another commission again headed by Aganbegyan. This latest commission was asked to integrate the Shatalin plan with the Ryzhkov-Abalkin plan. While nothing was definitive, from most appearances it seemed that Gorbachev might ultimately agree to back the Shatalin variant.

Given the continual turnover in economic advisers, it was

apparent that Gorbachev was having trouble finding economists whose advice he trusted. Reflecting his frustration, Gorbachev told a joke on himself. It seems that there was a summit
meeting with François Mitterrand, George Bush, and Mikhail
Gorbachev. During the discussion, Mitterrand complained that
he was having a serious problem. "I have ten mistresses; one is
untrue, and I don't know which." Bush interjected, "You think
you have a problem. I have ten advisers. One is a KGB agent,
and I don't know which." To which Gorbachev interjected,
"You think you have a problem. I have ten advisers. One says
he's an economist, and I don't know which."

In the midst of all this indecision, Yeltsin decided to present
the Shatalin plan to the Supreme Soviet of the Russian Republic, which then proceeded to adopt it. He criticized Gorbachev
for his procrastination and indecision. To Yeltsin, amalgamat-
ing the Shatalin and the Ryzhkov-Abalkin plans was impossible. In Yeltsin's words, "It was like mating a snake and a
hedgehog."[31]

III

This welter of proposals and counterproposals began to wear
not only on the leadership, but also on the general public, all
of whom were rapidly running out of patience. Responding to
these conflicting pressures, Gorbachev in mid-September once
again shifted his position. Based on his meeting with Yeltsin
and his support for Shatalin in his Presidential Council, it
appeared to most observers that Gorbachev had finally opted
for a unified plan which Shatalin said was 99 percent his.[32] But
threats from Ryzhkov that he might resign caused Gorbachev
to reconsider.[33] Unable to make up his mind, he announced on
September 17, 1990, that he would call a nationwide referendum to vote on accepting the concept of private property and
market-type reforms.[34]

Gorbachev's mid-September surprise call for a referendum
seems to have marked a critical turning point in his thinking.
In addition to his fear that Ryzhkov might resign, he also was

influenced by the growing anxiety among the more conservative elements of society—particularly managers of large state enterprises, party officials, the military, and the KGB, and the military industrial complex in general—about the impact of perestroika and glasnost.* The threat of budget cuts on military expenditures and staffing and the increase in power of the republics at the center's expense roused these conservative elements into action. They were also firmly convinced that Gorbachev and Shevardnadze had gone too far in agreeing to a reduction in Soviet conventional and nuclear weapons. As seen earlier, these anxieties sparked them into a series of overt actions, including the dispatch of troops to Red Square. While there was no coup as such, Gorbachev came to realize that he and his reforms were in real danger. He probably feared that if he himself did not slow or reverse some of the reforms, somebody else would.

As a minimum, Gorbachev concluded that he could not support the Shatalin plan. To have done so would have effectively destroyed the economic control of the USSR. By denying the center its authority to tax, for example, power would have shifted to the republics at the expense of the union. For that reason, on October 16, 1990, he announced that he had decided to postpone further market reform, in effect abandoning the Shatalin plan, which in the meantime had more and more become the Yeltsin plan.

In the October variation, Gorbachev withdrew his support for allowing farmers to opt out of collective and state farms. Instead, each republic could set aside land that was presently unused so that farmers could set up individual farms. That decision may also explain why nothing more was heard from Gorbachev about his call for a nationwide referendum on private land. He also retreated on price reform and the decision to allow enterprises to operate without subsidies. Republic

---

*Reports about Gorbachev's fear that Ryzhkov might resign may have been overstated. Before the end of 1990, Gorbachev himself would in effect fire Ryzhkov by eliminating the job of premier. In its place Gorbachev created the post of prime minister and appointed the finance minister, Valentin Pavlov, to that post.

rights would be curbed and their powers defined by "an interregional economic committee." In the end, Gorbachev decided to increase his authority as president. This way he could decide to act unilaterally without the need to consult with the Congress of People's Deputies and the Supreme Soviet. He obtained for himself the power to issue presidential decrees, or *ukazy,* the same word used to describe similar powers of the pre-revolutionary czars. On paper, at least, Gorbachev had managed to accumulate for himself more power than Stalin.

IV

It may well have been inevitable that sooner or later Gorbachev's odyssey and search for appropriate reforms would lead him away from the market that had attracted him a few years earlier. As Gorbachev moved back and forth from one comprehensive reform to another, he became more and more uncertain about subjecting the Soviet Union to the type of shock therapy such reforms would inevitably necessitate. He also concluded that unless reined in, the reform process would ultimately shrink his powers and those of the Soviet Union over central economic control, thus reducing the Soviet Union to an ineffective economic entity.

But while his enthusiasm may have waned, Gorbachev has not abandoned all interest in the market processes, particularly if it seems like the politically expedient thing to do. Thus in June 1991, Gorbachev seemed to edge back in among the proponents of market reform. By implication at least he seemed to show support for what was presented as a new set of proposals called the Grand Bargain. This was cobbled together by Gregory Yavlinsky and a group from Harvard but was in fact resurrected from the recently abandoned Shatalin 500-day plan.

Yet no matter how much difficulty Gorbachev seems to have committing himself to the actual implementation of a comprehensive plan of economic reform and as flawed as it was, the reissuance and semi-confiscation of 50- and 100-ruble notes in January 1991 was at least a step in the right direction, as was the related decision to raise prices in April 1991. Yet in both instances it was a case of lost opportunities. Unlike earlier efforts at reform, the public by early 1991 seemed almost resigned to some kind of market-type move. But because both reforms were so poorly conceived, Gorbachev lost a golden opportunity. The monetary reform should have been more progressive in nature, so those with lower incomes would have been allowed to reclaim more of their savings and those with higher incomes would have ended up with a smaller fraction. At the same time, the monetary reforms should also have been applied to savings accounts. Moreover, the monetary reforms should have coincided with not only a far-reaching price reform, but a move to liberalize private trade and decentralize and break up state enterprises. Instead, the price reform was taken in isolation from other measures. The prices of only 30 percent of the goods affected would be set by something approximating supply and demand conditions. The rest would continue to be set by central planning authorities. Most inexplicable of all, the authorities did nothing to increase the supply of goods. Everyone expected that on April 2 there would at least be goods, although at sharply higher prices, in the shops. However, the increased revenues from the price hikes were not passed through to the producers; they were sent instead to the national budget to reduce the amount being spent on price subsidies and the budget deficit. Thus while some customers might have been deterred by the higher prices, the suppliers were largely unaffected. Consequently, most shops remained as empty as before. Once more, a golden opportunity had been lost.

Most likely there will be other proposals, other committees, and other policy reversals in the future; but the failure of past reforms and the continuing deterioration of the Soviet economy seem to have created enormous confusion in Soviet society. Gorbachev's efforts emerge as noble but ultimately futile.

9

Epilogue

In many ways it was too good to be true. Mikhail Gorbachev's struggle to bring a better life to his people was a valiant initiative. However, even if Gorbachev had adopted a more rational and coherent policy, it is unlikely that he would have succeeded. The Soviet population, especially those in the Russian Republic who had lived for sixty years in a Stalinist system, were too resistant to evolutionary change. For that reason, the odds are that no one else would have done much better.

Historians will probably come to regard Gorbachev as a tragic figure. If he had only resigned when he was ahead! Had he quit in mid-1990, his role as the liberator of Eastern Europe and Afghanistan, the essential partner in nuclear and conventional weapons disarmament, the resolver of the Cold War, and the exponent of perestroika, glasnost, and democratization in the Soviet Union would have ensured his place as one of the major leaders of the twentieth century. Gorbachev should have learned from Deng Xiaoping's mistake. History will treat Deng very differently from the way it would have done if he had only retired before he sent troops into Tiananmen Square. Instead, Gorbachev fell into the same trap in January 1991 when he ordered paratroops into Lithuania and six other republics to repress ethnic demands for independence.

The use of tanks in Vilnius in some ways parallels the use of tanks in Tiananmen Square. Though the crackdown was not as severe, it will shadow Gorbachev's image even if he might make amends politically or revitalize the economy in the future. The Vilnius incident also reminded the world that this was not the first time Gorbachev had either ordered the use of violence or been associated with its use. Since December 1986 he has been directly or indirectly involved with military and police repression and crackdowns in Kazakhstan in 1986, Georgia in April 1989, Azerbaijan in January 1990, and continuing violence in Armenia. The violence in Vilnius, however, not only occurred on the heels of the warning about the country's imminent move to dictatorship by Eduard Shevardnadze, until then one of the two or three people closest to Gorbachev, but in the presence of journalists from almost all of the major Western television networks and newspapers. No Western press representatives were present at the earlier repressions, which as a consequence had little impact on Western consciousness.

The return to the hard line, not only by Gorbachev but by most of his new appointees, reinforces the conviction of those who from the beginning questioned his sincerity and the meaningfulness of the whole reform process. Some Western observers have always insisted that his whole effort was an attempt to lull the West, obtain our secrets and cash, and leave us disadvantaged relative to the Soviet Union. These attitudes in many ways mirror similar suspicions by Soviet hard-liners. The KGB likewise views the West's positive response to Gorbachev's reforms as a masterful snare and diversion. Ronald Reagan and George Bush attempted to do with smiles exactly what Reagan had been doing earlier in his "evil empire" phase. To the KGB, the United States should not be trusted in either guise.

There is no way of knowing Gorbachev's real motivation, but my own instinct is that Gorbachev's reforms were a sincere effort to improve day-to-day economic and political life in the Soviet Union.* That does not mean he sought a Western-style

*When I made such an assertion in a Moscow lecture in May 1991, I was challenged by at least three members of the audience who questioned whether Gorbachev ever sincerely wanted to help the Soviet people.

democracy or was a proponent of free enterprise. On the contrary, in a revealing speech on November 28, 1990, to a group of intellectuals, Gorbachev reiterated his "profound convictions" as a socialist—in the Soviet, not the West European context.[1] Although he insisted he has "always supported the market and still does," there is reason to question what he means by the market. For example, while he has affirmed over and over again that he is "in favor of the market," he goes on to add that "I do not accept, for example, private ownership of land—do with me what you will. I do not accept it."[2] He added, "private ownership with the right to sell land—that I do not accept. That incidentally is the tradition of the rural community." As a product of that rural community, he reflects its views.

Another peculiarity of the Gorbachev approach is that while he probably brought more change to the Soviet Union than anyone since Stalin, Gorbachev did not always accept new ideas or ideological change willingly. Almost always he showed some initial resistance. For example, initially he opposed private and cooperative trade, press freedoms, more autonomy for republics, emigration, joint ventures, and the end of the monopoly of the Communist Party. Eventually these would all become the hallmarks of perestroika.

Nevertheless, Gorbachev's most admirable trait was that he was willing to listen and learn. Moreover, he seemed determined, at least in the early stage of his administration, to push his reforms forward, not backward. Without articulating it, or perhaps not even being aware of the comparisons, Gorbachev seemed determined to avoid policies that might encumber the country's future as his predecessors had done. As mentioned earlier, Stalin and those before and after him, in their efforts to modernize the country, had adopted methods that served to hinder future, self-sustaining growth. The irony is that despite his best efforts, by late 1990 Gorbachev nonetheless began to fall back into the old pattern. By discrediting the reform process, he had provoked opponents of reform to action. As a consequence, he has made future reform difficult not only for himself, should he survive, but for his successors. The tragedy is that inside the Soviet Union Gorbachev has given reform a bad name.

I

Gorbachev probably did not realize what he was getting himself into. Reducing the role of central planning and political control seemed so sensible and rational. It is worth repeating Gorbachev's explanation of how he and Shevardnadze reached such a decision. "We spoke simple words. . . . We stated that we could not go on living as we were."[3]

Since he needed their advice and skills, Gorbachev's initial strategy was to seek the support of the intelligentsia. But as almost always happens with intellectuals, once involved, many begin to add to the agenda. Sometimes it suited Gorbachev, but more and more often it did not. Finding themselves stymied, many members of the intelligentsia then began to divert their energies to subordinate jurisdictions, such as the various republics, cities, and even neighborhoods. Not surprisingly, the agenda in these subjurisdictions began to clash with the center. With time the struggle grew to include not only conflicting claims over property ownership, but over taxes, the issuance of money, banks, culture, freedom of the press, political reform, and even military and foreign policy. Compounding the problem was the fact that Gorbachev's economic reforms were not working, or at least had not improved living or economic conditions. On the contrary, conditions began to deteriorate, as reflected by the failing state enterprises and empty shops. There was reason to question whether Gorbachev really knew what he was doing. His continual course alterations did nothing to reassure the skeptics.

The increasing weakness at the center added to the assertiveness of the republics. From a strict economic point of view, political and economic independence may not make sense for the various republics, especially the smaller ones, but many of them concluded that they had less to lose than by being tied to an ineffective union. The Soviet economic situation was deteriorating at an accelerating rate.[4] Would they be any worse off on their own?

Once the non-Russian peoples in the outlying republics began to sense that they might be able to take advantage of political pluralism or secession, some probably would have refused to continue as part of the Soviet Union even if the prospects for economic improvement had been excellent. Having been denied the chance to express their sovereignty for at least four decades, these nationalists would not be denied. Nevertheless, if a reformed Soviet economy had been able to show a potential for economic development comparable with Western Europe, the pressure for political and economic independence within the Soviet Union may have been considerably less strident. The contrast with Western Europe, where forces of nationalism used to be especially urgent, is instructive. There seems little doubt that the prospect of increased prosperity that comes with membership in the Common Market as much as anything accounts for the eagerness of West European nations to participate in the EEC, even if it means surrendering some sovereignty to the larger body.

The growing political disintegration accompanied with and precipitated by increased economic anarchy have combined to create a new form of economic depression. As we noted in Chapter 1, heretofore the cause of almost all Western depressions and recessions has been a lack of demand. Factories close down and workers are fired because there are no orders. Corporations worry that they too may face bankruptcy if their customers cannot pay their bills. Keynesian economics with its use of government spending to prime the economic pump is an attempt to remedy such problems.

In the preceding chapters we have seen why the situation in the USSR under Gorbachev is very different. Instead of inadequate demand, the Soviet crisis is due to a breakdown in supply. Gosplan's ability to allocate and move goods through the production process has been weakened not only by a political decision to diminish its powers, but by the growing inflation.

Factories and farms have been ordered to ship their output, but have refused because they have been unwilling to accept payment in rubles. They would rather engage in barter. But since barter is inefficient, that only has served to cause further economic confusion. More and more factories have found themselves without the inputs they need to sustain manufacturing operations. And as we reported, more and more factories like the tire producer in Armenia that is still willing to ship to the tractor factory in Vladimir have sometimes been precluded from doing so by political turmoil.

It is this disruption of supply, then, that characterizes the Soviet Union's current problems. One factory after another finds itself without the needed inputs. And given the Soviet practice of preventing manufacturing duplication, there are usually no substitute sources of supply. Thus the tractor factory in Vladimir had nowhere else to turn when its Armenian producer was unable to supply it with tires. This break in the chain of supply disrupts not only factory production but retail sales. Then, frustrated by the empty shelves, workers pay even less attention to their formal work assignments and turn increasingly to strikes to demand improved conditions. That, however, disrupts the supply process even more. It also leads to poor maintenance. Gas pipelines explode, oil pipelines leak, and trains crash. It is the combination of such factors, the collapse of Gosplan, the inflation, ethnic separatism, and single-source manufacturing, that has caused the breakdown that led to the 10–15 percent drop in Soviet GNP in early 1991, a drop that can best be described as a supply side depression. What is particularly worrisome about this type of economic crisis is that once under way, it is unclear whether there are any easy or purely economic cures. Once such economic deconstruction becomes widespread enough, there is a real danger that more and more factories will be affected until the economy finds itself in a free fall.

II

After over six years of enormous effort, time seems to have run out for Gorbachev. Perhaps if he had had more time for trial and error, he might have come up with a better strategy of reform and produced some positive success. Almost any sign of economic success would have helped. Until 1989, production of heavy industrial products, life expectancy, and housing construction all increased; but that brief episode was not enough, particularly when almost everything else seemed to deteriorate. Perhaps if he had concentrated on some short-run successes, particularly increasing production of food and consumer goods, he could have demonstrated he was moving on the right track. It would have given him credibility when he promised better days ahead. But after repeated warnings that the next two years would be the hardest, particularly when that was said every succeeding year, and with little tangible results, the public lost faith. By early 1991, Gorbachev was receiving support from 10 percent or less in Soviet public opinion polls.[5]

Gorbachev was handicapped by his lack of a comprehensive approach. Every few months, he would come up with some new brainstorm, trumpeted as a panacea for economic reform. But increasingly his efforts appeared ad hoc, and often contradictory. By the time he found an adviser like Abalkin, who understood the need for a more systematic approach, it was too late. By 1989, the hard-liners and anti-reformers, always a preponderant part of the population, had aroused themselves and actively began to organize and oppose the reform process.

Some warned from the beginning that by organizing and agitating for even faster political and economic change, the intelligentsia and reformers were running an enormous risk. At a September 1988 meeting in the Moscow headquarters of the Central Committee of the Communist Party, I was told that while the liberal reformers could make a lot of noise, they lacked the necessary deep-rooted support among most of the Soviet people for their cause. By agitating and trying to put more pressure on Gorbachev, these liberal efforts would prove counterproductive. As these officials saw it, agitation by reformers would probably have little impact on Gorbachev, but it would provoke the anti-reformers who, once mobilized, would draw the larger numbers of the disgruntled to their cause. Those caught in the middle might side with the reformers initially, but the Central Committee members warned against being misled by the 1989 victory of reformers and anticommunist non-party candidates. Once economic conditions began to deteriorate, the general public would withdraw into passivity or gravitate to the anti-reformers—particularly if there was any growth of disorder *(besporiadok)*—a long-running nightmare of the vast majority of the Soviet people. This erosion of popular support was revealed in the drop-off of votes in the spring election of 1990, and in the shrinkage in the size of the Interregional Group and the Congress of People's Deputies from 330 at the start of December 1990 to 229 later in the month.

The greater success with glasnost than with perestroika guaranteed that the combination probably would not work. Glasnost combined with the lack of economic results meant that sooner or later there would be protests about the reform's failures. If Gorbachev had the power to stifle dissent effectively, or if he could have relied on the American occupation army as the Germans and Japanese did when their systems were reformed, he might have had more success. There are those who point to Taiwan, Singapore, and South Korea as other societies that stifled political protests while successfully implementing economic change. Such an approach is not the only way, and clearly it is not a positive one, but it highlights how daunting the challenge Gorbachev set for himself by trying to combine simultaneous evolutionary economic and political change.

III

As he came to realize how unsuccessful his efforts had been, Gorbachev seemed to have been persuaded by his early conservative critics that unless he reversed course, the Soviet Union was in danger of deconstruction. The turning point appears to have occurred in the fall of 1990, after the unexplained military moves in Red Square and the increasingly strident attacks on Shevardnadze, Yakovlev, Bakatin, and Gorbachev himself. After having shown initial support for the Shatalin Five Hundred Day Plan, and a far-reaching revamping of the economic system, Gorbachev reversed himself and gradually began to retreat. If he did not initiate the crackdown in Lithuania, at least he tolerated it. And by acquiescing as the specious Committee for National Salvation began to issue calls for the sending in of Soviet troops, Gorbachev adopted policies little different from those used by Brezhnev to suppress the Prague Spring in 1968 or Khrushchev who squelched the Hungarian reform effort in 1956 or Stalin who used the same methods to take over the Baltic states after the Nazi-Soviet Pact.

It may have been, as Gorbachev insisted, that he could find no other way to hold the country together. Unresolved, of course, is whether or not it makes sense to hold it together. Moreover, it is possible that Gorbachev decided to reinstitute the powers of a dictator to prevent someone less benevolent from doing so at his own expense. For Soviet liberals as well as Western governments, the dilemma is whether or not the Soviet Union is better off supporting Gorbachev as he moves to pre-empt a dictator from taking power while he himself takes on the trappings of a dictatorship. At least the earlier Gorbachev did show he favored some of the institutions that democracy brings with it. Further, he has insisted that he is not interested in dictatorship; he only wants the power to hold the nation to-gether. He has noted that if he really wanted to be a dictator, he would never have embarked on glasnost or democratization or perestroika in the first place.[6] As he put it, once elected as general secretary in March 1985, he inherited vast powers. "A General Secretary of the Communist Party of the Soviet Union's Central Committee was a dictator who knew no equal in the world at the time. No one possessed more power. No one, do you understand? So why then did I need to undertake all of this?"[7] Nonetheless, his reassertion of some of those all-encompassing powers may be another instance where the means becomes confused with the ends. Like the Sorcerer's Apprentice, Gorbachev set in motion forces he cannot control. In a sorrowful drama, he ended up acting not as the savior, but as the terminator of so many of the positive changes he himself had sought to introduce.

IV

Like Moses, Gorbachev will probably not be the one to bring his people to the promised land. Perestroika and glasnost were too much to ask the Soviet people to take in one gulp. Yet while the resurgence of the conservatives is likely to be painful, ultimately it may be short-lived. Sooner or later other reformers will rise to power and reinstitute reforms much as Gorbachev resurrected some of the reforms originally instituted by Khrushchev. With Boris Yeltsin's acquience for example, Gorbachev reached a truce of sorts in April 1991 with nine of the fifteen republics. To do this, Gorbachev had to agree to yield taxing authority and the possession of the land and its underground riches to the republics. If effective this could mean an end to the center as an economic force. One thing is clear: each succeeding reformer, Yeltsin included, may be able to move the effort along, but it is not to be assumed that any time soon the reform process will be completed.

Beginning with the Chinese reforms, economists have come to realize the need to devote more attention to examining the transition process from one economic system to another. Until recently, almost no one had addressed the question in any serious way.[8] But with the 1990 study *The Road to a Free Economy* by Janos Kornai, and the nine or ten plans prepared in the Soviet Union, as well as the involvement of the World Bank, the International Monetary Fund, economists such as Jeffrey Sachs in Poland, and the example of Poland's reforms, future reformers may have a series of road maps and "how-to" manuals to refer to.[9]

A number of reforms are prerequisites for successful transition. They need not all come at once, but they must come at some point. Price flexibility is necessary to keep supply and demand in balance and eliminate state subsidies. The monetary overhang must also be eliminated, preferably with a monetary reform that is more far-reaching and fairer than the misconceived reform of January 1991. Subsidies and unprofitable factories and farms must be curbed and a hard budget constraint instituted. These steps, along with a resumption of budget cuts on military expenditures, are necessary to reduce the budget deficit so that the outpouring of money from the government can be brought to a halt. A key priority is the creation of a wholesale market and banks. There must be freedom of entry for anyone, Soviet or foreign, who wants to set up their own business. Equally important, Soviet industries and shops must be privatized and the larger entities broken up to encourage competition, which should keep inflation in check. In the same spirit, the collective and state farms must be broken up and the peasants allowed to reorganize themselves into any farming arrangement they want. It may be private, family, cooperative, or even state farms, but the only way to ensure that there is real choice is first to remove the neo- or red landlords in charge of the *sovkhozy* and *kolkhozy*. Only then will the peasants risk moves such as increasing agricultural productivity that otherwise would be sure to invite retribution. There should also be an ease of exit for enterprises that cannot make money, including bankruptcy or sale to other private or public entities.

Given the uncertain feelings Gorbachev and other senior party and government officials have for the market and private property, it may well be that widespread growth of private commercial and industrial activity will only come when the economy collapses and the state withers away. Then out of economic necessity even desperation as well as opportunity for large profits, individuals and groups, including those that previously had no use for markets, find themselves opening up private businesses throughout the Soviet Union. Without the state to interfere or implement far-reaching reforms, individuals seem to step forward and respond as others have done all over the world. That after all rather than central control and guidance is probably the best way to induce reform. Yet there is still a need for the state. If nothing else, the state will have to provide a safety net for the unemployed, the elderly, and the disadvantaged.

To carry out these reforms takes enormous political courage as well as tolerance from a restive public. Because of his dismal record, it is unlikely Gorbachev will regain his credibility and generate enough support. Indeed, if anything, he has discredited the reform effort. As he looks back at his futile efforts and the sorry results they have produced, Gorbachev may well see himself as a modern King Lear. To his people, however, he may more appropriately resemble Hamlet, a man unable to make up his mind about which reform to adopt. The danger, however, is that he may end up like Macbeth.

For those of us in the United States, Gorbachev more closely resembles former President Richard Nixon. Like Nixon, Gorbachev is decisive and insightful when it comes to foreign policy. Both of their problems, however, stemmed from their inability to deal with domestic affairs. Indecisive and wrong-headed decisions characterize both leaders. Moreover, both did their best to undercut any potential rivals. Neither man helped prime well-equipped successors. For the Soviet Union, this has especially serious implications. Given the disdain the Soviet people now have for the reform process, the growing assertiveness of the republics, and the absence of any logical or able successor, it is likely to require considerable time before a new leader can be found who will be able to generate enough support for a resumed reform effort.

Probably the most damning criticism of Gorbachev that historians will make is that he discredited the very instruments—cooperatives, joint ventures, family farming, and price flexibility—that must ultimately be well established in order to reform the system. Rather than returning to the totalitarian instruments of the past, such as calling in the KGB to supervise all forms of economic activity, including foreign investors, perhaps the noblest thing Gorbachev could do would be to announce the introduction of a package of measures similar to those just discussed and then resign.

It would be wrong to be too critical of Gorbachev. At least he tried. Yet it is hard to disregard his mistakes and the sad state which the Soviet Union now finds itself in after more than six years of Gorbachev's administration. My Soviet friends express their disappointment with Gorbachev's accomplishments, particularly his economic failures, with a joke:

A man goes into a bar.

"I'll have a pitcher of beer," he orders.

"That will be a ruble," responds the bartender.

"A ruble? I was just here a few months ago and it was only fifty kopecks."

"But now we have glasnost. You have to pay fifty kopecks for glasnost."

"Okay, I like glasnost, here is my ruble."

Bending over, the bartender takes the ruble and hands the customer 50 kopecks change.

"But I thought you just said that I had to pay fifty kopecks extra for glasnost."

"Yes, I did—but we don't have any beer."

For now, some have even begun to complain that there is even a shrinkage of glasnost.

AUGUST 26, 1991

Except for the Prologue, this entire account was written before the events set in motion by the coup of August 19, 1991. I find very little, however, that I would change. One exception is the preceding paragraph. Despite Gorbachev's efforts to curb what he saw as the excesses of glasnost in the weeks before the coup, in the end glasnost reasserted itself. This as much as anything guaranteed the eventual defeat of the coup.

Predicting what will happen next is not easy. Change is

occurring so rapidly that institutions that seemed invulnerable for seventy years or more have disappeared within hours after the coup. Who could imagine that the Communist Party would be outlawed in several of the republics or that *Pravda* would be closed down?

The conventional wisdom is that the coup failed. Yet historians will probably judge that on the contrary the coup succeeded far more effectively than anyone could have anticipated—but just opposite to what the conspirators had intended. Their goal was to tighten discipline, reinforce control from the center, and stop secession. After the coup failed, however, communist and totalitarian icons suddenly became legitimate, even priority, targets of attack. The failure of the coup and the desire for retribution put the KGB, the army, and the Party bureaucrats on the defensive so that no one group dared stop the dismantling of the Communist Party and the sealing of the Communist Party headquarters, the revamping of venerable institutions like Tass, and the secession of almost all the western republics.

The big unknown is what will happen after the euphoria of defeating the coup passes. It is hard to see how Gorbachev can regain his former power. That, by the way, is another victory for the conspirators. It is also hard to see how even Boris Yeltsin, the hero of the hour, or anyone else can solve the enormous problems that lie ahead. The Soviet people have a new sense of pride, but that in itself is unlikely to hold together a union that is coming undone. The new Soviet leaders will not only have to cure an economy trapped in a supply-side depression, they will have to do it while once integral parts of the country assert their independence. Already the Ukraine, for example, has acted to prevent its grain from moving to Russia and has established its own border and customs posts whose function is not to keep goods from moving into the Ukraine, but to keep Ukrainian products, especially grain, from moving out.

Gorbachev's reforms have changed the Soviet Union in ways he never intended. The country cannot be put back together the way it was before March 1985. Most observers would agree that that is a positive development. Still, Gorbachev's economic failures have so tainted the process that they have made economic recovery and transition even more difficult than they needed to be. With one economic system dismantled and with no substitute yet in sight the challenge of economic reform for Gorbachev's successors is as daunting as it was for Gorbachev himself—in some ways even more so.

Notes

1   A HERO ABROAD, A FAILURE AT HOME

1. *The Washington Post,* May 26, 1990, p. A18.
2. *The Financial Times,* September 4, 1990, p. 1; *Dialog,* no. 10, 1990.
3. *The New York Times,* October 31, 1990, p. A25.
4. *Los Angeles Times,* June 27, 1990, p. 1.
5. A similar call was made in December 1990. *The New York Times,* December 18, 1990, p. 6.
6. *Pravda,* February 2, 1991, p. 2.
7. *Argumenty i fakti,* June 2, 1990, p. 3.
8. *Sovset,* Radio Free Europe/Radio Liberty (cited hereafter as RFE/RL) daily report, no. 143, July 27, 1990, p. 29.
9. *Pravda,* July 5, 1990, p. 4.

2   THE PRE-GORBACHEV ERA—TRYING TO MODERNIZE —AN OLD STORY

1. See Alexander Gerschenkron, *Economic Backwardness in Historical Perspective* (Cambridge, Mass.: Belknap Press, Harvard University Press, 1962), p. 18.
2. Ibid., p. 147; Vasilii Seliunin, "Istoki," *Novyi mir* (May 1988), pp. 180–182.
3. Abel Aganbegyan, *The Economic Challenge of Perestroika* (Bloomington, Ind.: Indiana University Press, 1988), p. 50.
4. Marshall I. Goldman, *Gorbachev's Challenge: Economic Reform in the Age of High Technology* (New York: W. W. Norton, 1987), p. 86.
5. *Pravda,* November 20, 1962, p. 4.
6. Fyodor Dostoevsky, *The Brothers Karamazov* (New York: The Modern Library, Random House, 1950), pp. 306–307, 299, 300.
7. *The New York Times,* November 11, 1989, p. 27.
8. *The New York Times,* January 27, 1991, p. 9.
9. Vladimir G. Treml and John Hardt, eds., *Soviet Economic Statistics* (Durham, N.C.: Duke University Press, 1972).

10. Gerschenkron, p. 250.
11. *The New York Times,* April 24, 1990, p. A7; Victor Belkin, "Market and Non-Market Systems: Limits to Macro Economic Comparisons," economic paper prepared for the American Enterprise Institute, April 19, 1990, p. 15.
12. Belkin, op. cit., pp. 3, 4.
13. John W. Kiser III, *Communist Entrepreneurs: Unknown Innovators in the Global Economy* (New York: Franklin Watts, 1989), p. 195.
14. *Argumenty i fakti,* no. 20, May 19, 1990, p. 6.
15. Ed Hewett, *The New York Times Book Review,* July 10, 1983, p. 28; Jan Vanous, *The New York Times,* November 19, 1982, p. A34.
16. *Time* magazine, October 22, 1990, p. 82, an excerpt from Oleg Gordievsky and Christopher Andrew, *The KGB—The Inside Story* (New York: HarperCollins, 1990).
17. Hewett, op. cit.
18. Frank Durgin, *ACES Bulletin,* vol. XXVI, no. 2–3, (Summer/Fall 1984), p. 99.

3 PATCH AND PROCRASTINATION
—IF IT'S BROKE, DON'T FIX IT

1. Doris Cornelsen, "Economic Development in the German Democratic Republic," in *The Economics of Eastern Europe and Their Foreign Economic Relations,* ed. Philip Joseph (Brussels: NATO, 1987), p. 42.
2. Conversation with Yuri Shiryaev, the director of the International Institute of Economic Problems and the Council of Mutual Economic Assistance, in Moscow, January 1986.
3. *The New York Times,* March 20, 1989, p. D4.
4. Marshall I. Goldman, "Soviet perceptions of Chinese economic reforms," *Journal of International Affairs,* vol. 39, no. 2 (Winter 1988), p. 41.
5. Fyodor Burlatskii, *Literaturnaia gazeta,* June 11, 1986, p. 14.
6. Alec Nove, *An Economic History of the USSR* (London: Penguin Books, 1989), p. 160.
7. See Abel Aganbegyan, *Trud,* October 17, 1981, p. 2, and Marshall I. Goldman, *USSR in Crisis: The Failure of an Economic System* (New York: W.W. Norton, 1983), p. 170.
8. Mark Frankland, *The Sixth Continent—Mikhail Gorbachev in the Soviet Union* (New York: Harper & Row, 1987), pp. 16–18; Dusko Doder and Louise Branson, *Gorbachev: Heretic in the Kremlin* (New York: Viking/Penguin, 1990), p. 65.
9. Arkady N. Shevchenko, *Breaking with Moscow* (New York: Alfred A. Knopf, 1985), p. 304.
10. Abel Aganbegyan, *Inside Perestroika: The Future of the Soviet Economy* (New York: Harper & Row, 1989), p. 150.
11. *The Washington Post,* August 3, 1983, p. 1.
12. *Moscow News,* no. 25, 1990, p. 13: Shevchenko, p. 236.

4 MIKHAIL SERGEEVICH GORBACHEV GOES TO MOSCOW
—A LEARNER'S PROGRESS

1. Alexander Rahr, RFE/RL, RL 102/85, March 29, 1985, and Zhores A. Medvedev, *Gorbachev* (New York: W. W. Norton, 1986), pp. 29, 72.
2. This may not be so unique. Jimmy Carter, after all, rose from Plains, Georgia, to a similar position in the U.S. government.

3. Much of the material that follows comes from Gail Sheehy, "The Man Who Changed the World," *Vanity Fair* (February 1990), and from Doder and Branson's *Gorbachev: Heretic in the Kremlin.* The authors of both studies report that they visited Privolnoe and the regional capital Stavropol. Another important source is Medvedev's *Gorbachev.*

4. Sheehy, pp. 115–117; Medvedev, p. 22.

5. *Pravda,* December 1, 1990, p. 4.

6. Ibid.

7. Sheehy, p. 119.

8. Doder and Branson, p. 7; Sheehy, p. 121.

9. Medvedev, p. 32.

10. Andrew Mithta, *"An Emigré Reports: Fridrikh Neznansky on Mikhail Gorbachev 1950–1958"* (Falls Church, Va.: Delphic Associates, Inc., October 1985), p. 24.

11. Medvedev, p. 33; Sheehy, p. 122.

12. Sheehy, p. 180.

13. Medvedev, pp. 46, 47.

14. Medvedev, p. 49; Doder and Branson, p. 33.

15. Doder and Branson, p. 33; Medvedev, p. 49.

16. Medvedev, p. 50.

17. Ibid., p. 55.

18. Ibid., p. 72.

19. Ibid., p. 59.

20. Sheehy, p. 187.

21. Medvedev, p. 88.

22. Doder and Branson, p. 37.

23. Ibid.; Medvedev, p. 83.

24. Rahr, RFE/RL, RL102/85, March 29, 1985, p. 7, and Doder and Branson, p. 20.

25. *Rabochaia tribuna,* July 18, 1990, p. 1; *The Financial Times,* December 7, 1990, p. 20.

26. *Pravda,* December 1, 1990, p. 4.

27. Sheehy, p. 187.

28. Doder and Branson, p. 42.

29. Medvedev, p. 116–118.

30. Ibid.

31. Rahr, RFE/RL, RL 102/85, p. 8; *Kommunist,* no. 5 (March 1985), p. 6; *Current Digest of the Soviet Press,* May 15, 1985, p. 4.

32. *Pravda,* February 21, 1985, p. 2; March 12, 1985, p. 1; March 22, 1985, p. 1; *Izvestiia,* April 12, 1985, p. 1.

33. *The New York Times,* June 17, 1985, p. A7.

34. *Pravda,* December 12, 1984, p. 2.

35. *Pravda,* December 1, 1990, p. 4.

36. Ibid.

37. The Joint Economic Committee of the Congress of the United States, *Allocation of Resources in the Soviet Union and China—1985, Hearing before the Subcommittee on Economic Resources, Competitiveness and Security Economics* (Washington, D.C.: U.S. Government Printing Office, March 19, 1986), p. 110.

38. Personal conversation with Tatiana Zaslavskaia; Alec Nove, "Interests and Self-Interest," *Times Literary Supplement,* May 4–10, 1990, p. 466.

39. *Financial Times,* July 28, 1987, p. 2; personal conversation with Abel Aganbegyan.

40. Aganbegyan, 1989, p. 147.

41. Aganbegyan, 1988, p. 105.

42. Ibid., pp. 106, 221.

43. Robert E. Leggett, "Soviet Investment Policy: The Key to Gorbachev's Program

for Revitalizing the Soviet Economy," in *Gorbachev's Economic Plans*. The Joint Economic Committee, Congress of the United States (Washington, D.C.: U.S. Government Printing Office, November 23, 1987), vol. I, p. 240.
44. *Literaturnaia gazeta,* February 18, 1987, p. 13.
45. Abel Aganbegyan, *The Guardian,* January 26, 1987.
46. *Foreign Broadcast Information Service Daily Report: Soviet Union* (cited hereafter as *FBIS*), March 17, 1987, p. S1, from the *Le Figaro,* March 10, 1987, p. 3.
47. *Pravda,* December 12, 1984, and February 20, 1985.
48. *Pravda,* March 12, 1985, p. 1; April 4, 1985, p. 1; April 12, 1985, p. 1; May 17, 1985, p. 1; June 6, 1985, p. 3; and July 12, 1985, p. 1.
49. *Ekonomicheskaia gazeta,* no. 49 (December 1983), p. 15; no. 15 (April 1984), p. 6.
50. Abel Aganbegyan, "Na novom etape ekonomicheskogo stroitel'stva," *EKO,* no. 8, 1985, p. 3; "Strategiya uskoreniia sotsial'no ekonomicheskogo rezvitiia," *Problemii mira i sotsializma,* no. 9, 1985, p. 13; RFE/RL, October 9, 1985, pp. 338–385; *Pravda,* June 12, 1985, p. 3; Aganbegyan, 1988, p. 93.
51. RFE/RL, RL 338/85, October 9, 1985, p. 3.
52. Aganbegyan, 1988, p. 105.
53. *Pravda,* November 16, 1986, p. 6. See also *FBIS,* November 25, 1986, p. R4; December 31, 1986, p. 51; February 18, 1987, p. R11.
54. Personal conversation with Aganbegyan.
55. Goldman, 1987, p. 76; *Ekonomicheskaia gazeta,* no. 33 (August 1985), p. 1.
56. *Izvestiia,* July 29, 1985, p. 2.
57. For similar proposed but abandoned reforms, see *Ekonomicheskaia gazeta,* no. 31 (July 1983), p. 5.
58. *Izvestiia,* July 26, 1985, p. 2; *Pravda,* March 10, 1986, p. 2.

5   MID-COURSE CORRECTION

1. *FBIS,* January 28, 1987, p. R3.
2. See, for example, *Sotsialisticheskaia industriia,* January 5, 1988, pp. 2–3, and Leggett, "Soviet Investment Policy."
3. *FBIS,* July 26, 1989, p. 62.
4. Vasilii Seliunin, "Glubokaia reforma ili pevanshbiurokratri?" *Znamiia* (July 1988), pp. 156–158; *Sotsialisticheskaia industriia,* January 5, 1988, p. 23. Also see *FBIS,* July 29, 1989, p. 7, stenographic record.
5. *Sotsialisticheskaia industriia,* October 30, 1988, p. 2.
6. *Pravda,* December 10, 1990, p. 1.
7. *FBIS,* July 30, 1986, pp. R4–5.
8. Personal report of a senior Soviet economist, Ray Rayatskas, January 15, 1988.
9. *Krasnaia zvezda,* July 30, 1986, p. 1.
10. *L'Humanité,* February 8, 1986, p. 1; RFE/RL RL 78/87, February 16, 1987, p. 1.
12. *Vremia* and *Novosti* TV, July 30, 1986, and *FBIS,* August 15, 1986, p. R44.
13. *FBIS,* July 30, 1986, p. R7.
14. *FBIS,* August 4, 1986, p. R13.
15. *FBIS,* August 4, 1986, p. R14.
16. *FBIS,* January 28, 1987, p. R17.
17. *Pravda,* February 15, 1987, p. 2; *Moscow News,* no. 8, 1987, p. 8.
18. *The Federalist Papers* (New York: New American Library of World Literature, 1986), p. 322.

19. *FBIS,* September 18, 1986, p. R16; RFE/RL, RL 474/87, November 18, 1987, p. 2.
20. *FBIS,* September 18, 1986, p. R16.
21. *FBIS,* September 19, 1986, p. R19.
22. Radio Liberty Research, RL 347/87, August 28, 1987, p. 10.
23. *Pravda,* February 6, 1987, pp. 2–3.
24. *Moscow News,* no. 24, 1987, p. 9.
25. *FBIS,* February 27, 1987, pp. R5–6.
26. Ibid., p. R6.
27. Ibid.
28. Andrei Sakharov, *Memoirs* (New York: Alfred A. Knopf, 1990), pp. 614–16.
29. For differing views, see Franklyn Holzman, "Politics and Guesswork: CIA and DIA Estimates of Soviet Military Spending," *International Security,* vol. 14, no. 2, p. 10. For another point of view, see Eduard Shevardnadze, *Pravda,* July 15, 1990, p. 2.
30. Anders Aslund, *Gorbachev's Struggle for Economic Reform* (Ithaca, N.Y.: Cornell University Press, 1989), p. 61.
31. *The New York Times,* October 2, 1990, p. A 3; *The Wall Street Journal,* October 8, 1990, p. A9.
32. *Pravitel'stvennii vestnik,* no. 19, 1989, p. 10; *Beijing Review,* June 23, 1986, p. 4; *Far Eastern Economic Review,* July 18, 1985, p. 93.
33. *FBIS,* September 26, 1989, p. 37.
34. Doder and Branson, p. 42; *Vremia,* Central Television, April 6, 1989; *FBIS,* March 17, 1989, p. 70.
35. *Izvestiia,* January 9, 1990, p. 2; *FBIS,* January 17, 1987, p. 77.
36. *Moscow News,* no. 1, 1988, pp. 8–9; no. 30, 1988, pp. 1, 8–9.
37. *Ekonomika i zhizn',* no. 30 (June 1990), p. 5.
38. Note the similarity to fears expressed in December 1990 by Vladimir Kryuchkov, the head of the KGB. See Chapter 7.
39. *Foreign Trade* (September 1982), p. 18.
40. *FBIS,* December 30, 1987, pp. 63, 65; Pavel S. Smirnov, "USSR State Enterprises and Amalgamations," *US-SU Trade and Economic Council Magazine,* vol. 12, no. 2, 1987, p. 11; Richard E. Ericson, "The New Enterprise Law," *The Harriman Institute Forum,* vol. 1, no. 2 (February 1988), p. 1.
41. Alexis de Tocqueville, *The Old Regime and the French Revolution* (New York: Doubleday Anchor, 1955), p. 177.
42. *The New York Times,* August 30, 1987, p. 4; *The Washington Post,* November 18, 1987, p. A 27; *The New York Times,* November 19, 1987, p. A 7; *FBIS,* February 19, 1987, p. R12; Soviet East European Report, RFE/RL, RFE no. 8, December 10, 1987, p. 2.
43. *Pravda,* August 11, 1988, p. 2.
44. *Implementation of the Helsinki Accords, Hearing Before the Commission on Security and Cooperation in Europe, Glasnost: The Soviet Policy of Openness.* (Washington, D.C.: U.S. Government Printing Office, March 4, 1987), p. 27.

6 THE EFFORT COLLAPSES

1. *The New York Times,* October 28, 1988, p. 1; November 31, 1988, p. A1; *Pravda,* October 28, 1988, p. 4.
2. Tsentral'noe Statisticheskoe Upravlenie SSSR, *Narodnoe khoziastvo,* 1985 g; *Moscow Finansy i Statistiki,* 1986, p. 559.

3. *The Boston Globe,* November 2, 1988, p. 3.
4. *The Wall Street Journal,* November 2, 1988, p. A17.
5. Igor Birman, *Secret Incomes of the Soviet State Budget,* (The Hague: Martinus Nijhoff, 1981); Judy Shelton, *The Coming Soviet Crash,* (New York: The Free Press, 1984).
6. *The New York Times,* August 28, 1988, p. 85.
7. *The New York Times,* April 24, 1990, p. A 14; *Moscow News,* no. 32, 1990, p. 3; *Pravda,* December 30, 1989, p. 2; *Business in the USSR,* no. 8 (January 1991), p. 31.
8. Personal conversation with Revold Entov of the Institute of World Economics and International Relations, who served on one such commission, July 18, 1990, in Cambridge, Mass.
9. *Ekonomicheskaia gazeta,* no. 44, 1989, p. 6.
10. *Ekonomicheskaia gazeta,* no. 1, 1989, p. 10; *Literaturnaia gazeta* (January 1989), no. 3, p. 11.
11. *Narodnoe khoziastvo,* 1988, pp. 624–625.
12. *Narodnoe khoziastvo,* 1984, p. 573; 1988, p. 624; FBIS, June 18, 1991, p. 25.
13. *Ekonomika i zhizn',* no. 25 (June 1980), p. 7; *Pravda,* June 9, 1989, p. 2; *The Wall Street Journal,* August 7, 1989, p. A 15; *FBIS,* August 7, 1989, p. 60; *Pravitel'stennii vestnik,* no. 18, 1989, p. 6; *FBIS,* July 27, 1990, p. 50; September 26, 1989, p. 85.
14. *Sovset,* October 15, 1990. p. 43; *FBIS,* September 26, 1989, p. 49; May 29, 1990, p. 77.
15. *The New York Times,* March 15, 1990, p. 20; *Moscow News,* no. 22, 1990, p. 4.
16. *Pravda,* October 20, 1990, pp. 1–2.
17. *Sotsialisticheskaia industria,* April 6, 1989, p. 1.
18. E. Gaidar, "Trudnyi vybor," *Kommunist,* no. 2, 1990, p. 25.
19. *Rabochaia tribuna,* November 29, 1990, p. 1.
20. *Robitnycha gazeta,* September 9, 1990, p. 2; March 23, 1991, p. 1.
21. *Pravda,* January 28, 1990, p. 2; *Narodnoe khoziastvo,* 1988, p. 77.
22. *Izvestiia,* June 12, 1990, p. 1.
23. *The Washington Post,* September 13, 1990, p. A 31.
24. Discussion with Andrei Orlov, vice chairman of the Abalkin Commission on Economic Reform, July 5, 1990.
25. *Ekonomika i zhizn',* no. 29 (July 1990), p. 10.
26. *Izvestiia,* August 24, 1989, p. 1.
27. Kevin Klose, *Russia and the Russians: Inside the Closed Society* (New York: W. W. Norton, 1984), p. 53.
28. *Ekonomika i zhizn',* no. 21 (May 1990), p. 4.
29. *Izvestiia,* TsK KPSS, no. 5 (304) (May 1990), pp. 131, 132.
30. *The Financial Times,* October 19, 1990, p. 1; May 11, 1991, p. VIII. *Sovset,* October 22, 1990, p. 8.
31. *The Financial Times,* September 8, 1990, p. 4.
32. Philip Hanson, *RFE/RL Reports,* "The Dimensions of the Monopoly Problem," April 12, 1991, p. 12. See also Alexander Yakovlev, "Monopolizm v ekonomike SSSR i Faktory ego o buslovlivaiushchie," *Vestnik Statistiki,* vol. I, 1991, p. 4; Stanislav Skopolsky, "Mighty Monopolies," *Business in the USSR,* January 1991, pp. 64–65.
33. *The New York Times,* October 22, 1991, p. A6; conversation with the mayor of Kiev, September 22, 1990, at Harvard University.
34. Aslund, p. 137.
35. *The Economist,* May 19, 1990, p. 76.
36. *The New York Times,* April 14, 1990, p. 29.

37. *The Economist,* April 19, 1990, p. 75.
38. *The Wall Street Journal,* May 18, 1990, p. A 6; *The Economist,* May 19, 1990, p. 75; *The Asian Wall Street Journal,* May 21, 1990, p. 6.
39. *The Wall Street Journal,* September 20, 1990, p. A 10.
40. *The Wall Street Journal,* October 10, 1990, p. A 14.
41. *The Wall Street Journal,* September 4, 1990, p. 19; *Reuters Dispatch,* October 29, 1990.
42. *The New York Times,* December 1, 1990, p. 8.
43. *Vneshnaia ekonomicheskaia sviazi SSSR,* 1989, Moscow Publishers, Financy i Statistika, 1990, p. 73.
44. Conversation with Ivan Ivanov, deputy chairman of the Committee on Foreign Economic Relations, November 16, 1990; *Pravda,* February 11, 1991, p. 1.
45. *Pravda,* August 16, 1986, p. 1; *Moscow News,* no. 11, 1987, p. 7.
46. *Moscow News,* no. 16, 1987, p. 6.
47. *The New York Times,* November 27, 1990, p. A14.
48. *Moscow News,* no. 34, 1987, p. 7.
49. *FBIS,* December 10, 1990, p. 43.
50. *Commersant,* October 8, 1990, p. 8.
51. *Ekonomika i zhizn',* January 1991, No. 2, p. 13.
52. *Izvestiia,* June 3, 1989, p. 3.
53. *Moscow News,* no. 7, 1990, p. 4.
54. *Moscow News,* no. 31, 1990, p. 9.
55. *Moscow News,* no. 31, 1990, p. 9.

7 THE REACTION COMES

1. *The Washington Post,* March 8, 1987, p. B2.
2. *The New York Review of Books,* January 31, 1991, p. 38.
3. *The New York Times,* January 2, 1990, p. A13.
4. *FBIS,* February 19, 1987, p. R6.
5. *The New York Times,* December 22, 1986, p. A12.
6. *Pravda,* February 15, 1987, p. 1; *The New York Times,* December 22, 1986, p. 10.
7. *The New York Times,* December 22, 1986, p. 10.
8. *Moscow News,* no. 8, 1987, p. 8; Hedrick Smith, *The New Russians* (New York: Random House, 1990), p. 136.
9. For other occasions, see Doder and Branson, pp. 194, 309, 312, 341, 390, and 417.
10. *The New York Times,* January 2, 1991, p. A12.
11. *Pravda,* July 27, 1986, p. 1.
12. *Pravda,* June 7, 1986, p. 4; *FBIS,* July 30, 1986, p. R3.
13. *The New York Times,* December 22, 1986, p. 10.
14. *Moscow News,* no. 8, 1987, p. 8.
15. *FBIS,* February 27, 1987, p. R11.
16. Ibid.
17. Ibid., p. R4.
18. *The New York Times,* December 22, 1986, p. 10.
19. *Pravda,* July 2, 1988, p. 11; *FBIS,* July 5, 1988, p. 104. The last sentence in the quotation was omitted from the version that appeared in *Pravda.*
20. *FBIS,* July 5, 1988, p. 103. That was then the average monthly wage.
21. *Pravda,* July 2, 1988, p. 11.
22. *Pravda,* June 7, 1986, pp. 3–4.
23. Ibid.
24. *FBIS,* February 19, 1987, p. R5.

25. RFE/RL, RL 243/88, June 5, 1988, p. 1.
26. Hedrick Smith, p. 135.
27. RFE/RL, RL 215/88, May 26, 1988, p. 2.
28. Ibid.
29. Hedrick Smith, p. 135; Doder and Branson, p. 306. Viktor Nikonov, a former member of the Politburo, claims that he, not Ligachev, was the one who pressured other newspapers to reprint Andreyevna's letter. *Sovset,* RFE/RL, January 21, 1991, p. 12; *Selskaia molodezh,* no. 12, 1990, pp. 22–28.
30. Doder and Branson, p. 307.
31. *The New York Times,* April 6, 1988, p. A5.
32. Alexander Levikov, "Struggling and Believing," *Moscow News,* no. 13, 1988, p. 3.
33. *Moscow News,* no. 17, 1988, p. 8; no. 18, 1988, p. 16.
34. Doder and Branson, p. 306; Hedrick Smith, p. 136. Both authors seem to rely on Roy Medvedev for this information. *FBIS,* May 3, 1989, p. 31—speech by Roy Medvedev at the Congress of People's Deputies.
35. *The New York Times,* April 14, 1988, p. A22; Doder and Branson, p. 306; Hedrick Smith, p. 136.
36. Doder and Branson, p. 309.
37. Hedrick Smith, pp. 135–136.
38. *The New York Times,* April 14, 1988, p. A22; RFE/RL, RL, February 15, 1988; May 29, 1988; Doder and Branson, p. 306; Hedrick Smith, p. 136.
39. *Pravda,* April 5, 1988, p. 2.
40. RFE/RL, RL 158/88, April 8, 1988, p. 7; *Sovetskaia Rossiia,* April 6, 1988, p. 2.
41. *The New York Times,* April 14, 1988, p. A22.
42. *La Republica,* January 7, 1989, p. 7; *FBIS,* January 12, 1989, p. 59.
43. *Moscow News,* no. 33, 1988, p. 2; *Molodaia gvardiia,* no. 7, 1989; *FBIS,* November 7, 1988, p. 72.
44. *Sovset,* RFE/RL, RL daily report, no. 243, January 2, 1991.
45. *Moscow News,* no. 51, 1990, p. 1.
46. *The New York Times,* December 21, 1990, p. A7.
47. *The New York Times,* May 24, 1987, p. 10; Hedrick Smith, p. 406.
48. RFE/RL, RL 342/87, August 26, 1987, p. 5.
49. Walter Laquer, "Glasnost's Ghosts," *The New Republic,* August 3, 1987, p. 13; Hedrick Smith, p. 405.
50. *Komsomolskaia pravda,* May 22, 1987, p. 4.
51. Ibid.
52. RFE/RL, RL 342/87, August 26, 1987, p. 9.
53. Hedrick Smith, pp. 406–408.
54. Klose, p. 29.
55. *Trud,* October 5, 1989, p. 2.
56. *FBIS,* July 5, 1988, p. 25.
57. Ibid.
58. Ibid.
59. *Izvestiia,* October 19, 1990, p. 1; *CPE Agricultural Report of Centrally Planned Economic Branch ATAD-ERS Department of Agriculture,* 1301 New York Avenue NW, Washington, D.C., vol. 3, no. 6 (November/December 1990), p. 51.
60. *Literaturnaia Rossiia,* December 11, 1990, p. 4.
61. *Moscow News,* no. 45, 1989, p. 7.
62. *Izvestiia,* January 9, 1990, p. 2; *Pravda,* February 9, 1989, p. 2; August 6, 1988, p. 2.
63. *Pravda,* February 9, 1989, p. 2; July 5, 1990, p. 2.
64. *Pravda,* July 5, 1990, p. 2.
65. *The Financial Times,* January 26, 1991, p. 8.

66. *Rabochaia tribuna,* July 18, 1990, p. 1; *The Financial Times,* July 20, 1990, p. 2.
67. *The Financial Times,* December 7, 1990, p. 20; *FBIS,* December 7, 1990, p. 40; December 10, 1990, p. 43; *Pravda,* December 10, 1990, p. 1.
68. *The New York Times,* January 6, 1991, p. 8.
69. Ibid.
70. Discussion with Anatoly Kisolev, director of the M. V. Khrunichev Machine Tool Factory, manufacturers of the Burian space satellite, November 14, 1990.
71. *The New York Times,* December 23, 1990, p. 1; *FBIS,* December 24, 1990, p. 28. See also *Pravda,* December 13, 1990, p. 1.
72. *FBIS,* December 24, 1990, p. 31.
73. *FBIS,* December 13, 1990, p. 49.
74. *Trud,* February 12, 1991, p. 1.
75. *Trud,* January 23, 1991, p. 1.
76. *Izvestiia,* January 25, 1991, p. 4.
77. *The Journal of Commerce,* February 19, 1991, p. 1.
78. *Trud,* February 19, 1991, p. 1.
79. *FBIS,* December 24, 1990, p. 31; June 27, 1991, p. 24. He hints that even Gorbachev may be under the CIA's influence.
80. *The New York Times,* December 7, 1990, p. A14; *Sovset,* December 3, 1990, p. 4; from Soviet television of November 29, 1990.
81. *FBIS,* December 27, 1990, p. 20.
82. *Pravda,* November 19, 1990, p. 3.
83. *Krasnaia zvezda,* November 19, 1990, p. 1; *FBIS,* November 28, 1990, p. 71.
84. *FBIS,* December 27, 1990, p. 20.
85. *Literaturnaia Rossiia,* December 11, 1990, no. 45, p. 18.
86. *FBIS,* December 27, 1990, p. 26.
87. *The New York Times,* December 21, 1990, p. 1.
88. *Komsomolskaia pravda,* November 28, 1990, p. 2.
89. *The New York Times,* November 24, 1990, p. 6.
90. *RFE/RL,* Soviet/EE Report, Vol. 3, No. 11, December 10, 1990, p. 1.
91. *The Financial Times,* January 21, 1991, p. 8; *Business Week,* February 11, 1991, p. 41; Soviet/East European Report, RFE/RL Research Institute, vol. III, no. 16, January 15, 1991, pp. 1, 2.
92. *Komsomolskaia pravda,* December 18, 1990, p. 1; *FBIS,* December 21, 1990, p. 36.
93. *The Washington Post,* December 28, 1990, p. A23.
94. *Commersant,* December 24, 1990, p. 15.
95. *Commersant,* December 17, 1990, p. 13; *The Wall Street Journal,* December 26, 1990, p. 4.
96. *The Washington Post,* December 28, 1990, p. A23.

8   WHERE DOES THE SOVIET UNION GO FROM HERE?

1. Aslund, p. 140.
2. Ibid., p. 100.
3. *Sovset,* RFE/RL daily report, no. 154, August 6, 1989, p. 4.
4. *Moscow News,* no. 49, 1990, p. 3.
5. Aganbegyan, 1989, pp. 101–102.
6. Boris Rumer, " 'The Abalkinization' of the Soviet Economic Reform," *Problems of Communism* (January/February 1990), p. 76.
7. Aganbegyan, 1989, p. 102.
8. *Pravda,* June 30, 1988, pp. 3–4.
9. Ibid.

10. *Ekonomicheskaia gazeta,* no. 27, July 1989, p. 1.
11. *Ekonomicheskaia gazeta,* no. 43 (October 1989), pp. 4–7.
12. *The Financial Times,* November 14, 1989, p. 2.
13. *The Wall Street Journal,* November 14, 1989, p. A19.
14. *The Wall Street Journal,* December 17, 1989, p. A17.
15. *The New York Times,* December 20, 1989, p. A18.
16. *International Herald Tribune,* March 20, 1990, p. 3.
17. *The Boston Globe,* May 25, 1990, p. 2.
18. *The New York Times,* April 22, 1990, p. 12.
19. *The New York Times,* May 23, 1990, p. A1; *The Boston Globe,* May 23, 1990, p. 1.
20. *The New York Times,* May 24, 1990, p. A8.
21. *The New York Times,* May 25, 1990, p. A8; *The Financial Times,* May 31, 1990, p. 2.
22. *The Boston Globe,* May 24, 1990, p. 16; *The Financial Times,* June 4, 1990, p. 1.
23. *The New York Times,* May 26, 1990, p. 2; May 27, 1990, p. 10; *The Wall Street Journal,* June 14, 1990, p. A11; July 20, 1990, p. A8.
24. *Rabochaia tribuna,* November 29, 1990, p. 1; March 23, 1991, p. 1.
25. *Izvestiia,* July 24, 1990, p. 2.
26. *The Washington Post,* September 13, 1990, p. A31.
27. *Argumenty i fakti,* no. 33, 1990.
28. *The Sunday Times,* (London), September 16, 1990, p. 20.
29. *Business in the USSR* (November 1990), p. 19.
30. *Izvestiia,* September 4, 1990, p. 1.
31. *The Wall Street Journal,* October 26, 1990, p. A12.
32. Ibid.
33. *The Boston Globe,* September 12, 1990, p. 2.
34. *Pravda,* September 18, 1990, p. 1.

EPILOGUE

1. *Pravda,* December 1, 1990, p. 4.
2. Ibid.
3. *Pravda,* December 1, 1991, p. 4.
4. *The Financial Times,* March 11, 1991, p. 16.
5. *The Wall Street Journal,* March 11, 1991, p. A9.
6. *Pravda,* December 1, 1990, p. 4.
7. Ibid.
8. One exception is Egon Neuberger, "Central Planning and Its Legacy," RAND Corporation, Santa Monica, Calif., December 1966, p. 6.
9. Janos Kornai, *The Road to a Free Economy* (New York: W. W. Norton, 1990); International Monetary Fund, the World Bank, Organization for Economic Cooperation and Development, and European Bank for Reconstruction and Development, *The Economy of the USSR: Summary and Recommendations,* (Washington, D.C.: World Bank, 1991); Jeffrey Sachs and David Lipton, "Poland's Economic Reforms," *Foreign Affairs,* (Summer 1990), p. 47.

Index

Abalkin, Leonid, 208–14, 217–20, 230
" 'Abalkinization' of the Soviet Economic
    Reform, The" (Rumer), 245*n*
Abalkin plan, 210–14, 218–20
    Ryzhkov's reworking of, 213–14, 218–20
Academy of Sciences, Soviet, 48
    Economic Commission of the Scientific
        Center of, 90
acceleration, *see uskoreniie*
Afanasyev, Yuri, 173
Afghanistan, Soviet withdrawal from, 108,
    197, 198
Aftomatika-Nauka-Tekhnika
    (Automation-Science-Technology;
    ANT), 113–14
Aganbegyan, Abel, 85–90, 96–98, 213,
    237*n*–40*n*, 245*n*
    critics of, 96, 207–8, 216
    machine-tool industry and, 86–89, 97
    reemergence of, 216, 219
agriculture:
    in China, 50, 59, 115, 125
    in Hungary, 58
agriculture, Soviet:
    anti-reform efforts and, 191–92
    decline in output of, 63
    Gorbachev's background and work in, 70,
        71, 73–75, 77–80, 83
    Gosagroprom and, 73, 89–90, 170, 192,
        204
    see also collectivization, collective farms;
        state farms
Agriculture Ministry, Soviet, 204
Air Force, Soviet, 66
alcoholism, 50, 64, 81–82
alcohol sales, crackdown on, 81–82, 135,
    137–38, 175, 176–77
Alexander II, Czar of Russia, 192

Aliyev, Geydar, 67
Alksnis, Viktor, 200
*Allocation of Resources in the Soviet Union
    and China—1985* (Joint Economic
    Committee of the Congress), 239*n*
All Russian Society for the Preservation of
    Historical and Cultural Monuments
    (VOOPIK), 187
All Union Communist Party, *see* Communist
    Party, Soviet
Andrew, Christopher, 238*n*
Andreyeva, Nina, 180–85, 244*n*
Andropov, Yuri, 42, 52, 64–67, 69, 80–81,
    99, 172
    death of, 80
    Geneva talks and, 51, 66, 84, 108
    Gorbachev compared with, 65–67, 81, 84,
        85
    Gorbachev denied information by, 97–98,
        129
    as Gorbachev's mentor, 65, 77, 78, 80, 100,
        106
    industrial production figures under, 91
anti-reform reaction, 172–202, 221
    Andreyeva and, 180–85, 244*n*
    bureaucracy and, 177–80, 202
    KGB and, 194–97, 201
    managers and, 191–94
    military and, 197–202
    Pamyat and, 112, 187–89
    peasants and, 191–92
    workers and, 185, 189–91
anti-Semitism, 112, 182, 187–89
antitrust laws, 209
Arbatov, Georgii, 16–17, 85
Argumenty i fakti, 40
Aristov, Boris, 157
Armenia, 149, 153–54, 225, 229

arms talks, U.S.-Soviet, 51, 66, 67, 84,
    108–10, 197
Army, Soviet, 18, 21, 24, 34
Aslund, Anders, 241n, 242n, 245n
Australia, 159
Azerbaijan, 149, 153–54, 225

Baltic states, 121–24, 147, 148
    anti-militarism in, 198, 199
banks, banking, 92, 143–44, 159, 217, 218,
    234
    Abalkin plan and, 212, 213
Belkin, Victor, 46–47, 238n
Belorussia, 24, 183
Bendix Corporation, 117
Bergson, Abram, 47
Berliner, Joseph, 143
Berlin Wall, 57, 62
    tearing down of, 16, 17
Birman, Igor, 129–30, 242n
Bogomolov, Oleg, 215
Boulding, Kenneth, 143
Branson, Louise, 238n, 239n, 241n, 243n,
    244n
bread prices, 19, 144, 212, 214
Breaking with Moscow (Shevchenko), 238n
Brezhnev, Leonid, 19, 42, 63–64, 81n, 83, 99,
    126, 232
    agricultural policy and, 78, 80
    death of, 80
    industrial production figures under, 9
    Kulakov and, 74n
Brothers Karamazov, The (Dostoyevsky), 39,
    237n
budget, Soviet, deficit in, 129–37, 144, 146,
    212, 217, 219
Bulgaria, 45
Bunich, Pavel, 145, 215
bureaucracy, Chinese, 60, 61
bureaucracy, Soviet, 56, 61, 68, 73, 98–99
    anti-reform efforts and, 177–80, 202
Burlatskii, Fyodor, 85, 238n
Bush, George, 108, 220, 225
    Washington summit (1990) and, 17, 19, 22

capitalism, 18, 53, 75, 190
Carter, Jimmy, 238n
Ceauşescu, Nikolae, 45
Central Asia, Central Asians, 113n
Central Committee, 20, 53, 74, 81, 95, 101,
    108, 175, 230–31
    Agricultural Department of, 74, 77–80
    Plenum of (June 1987), 204
    purges of, 100, 173
Central Intelligence Agency (CIA), 46–47,
    84, 107, 130, 201
central planning, Hungarian, 58
central planning, Soviet, 46, 50, 89, 95,
    142–43
    anti-reform efforts and, 192–93
    Enterprise Law and, 118–20, 204
    managers' dependence on, 76
    in 1950s, 35, 36–37
    in 1970s and 1980s, 35

Stalin and, 33–34, 35, 42
    undermining of, 152–56
    see also five-year plans
"Central Planning and Its Legacy"
    (Neuberger), 246n
Chabanov, A. I., 179
Chabanov affair, 179
change, 38–40
    aversion to, 38–39
    top down, 38
    see also reforms, Gorbachev; reforms,
        pre-Gorbachev era
checks and balances, 40–42, 102–6
Chernenko, Konstantin, 42, 67, 80–81, 82,
    84, 99
    industrial production figures under, 91
Chernobyl, 100, 196
chicken deaths anecdote, 38
Chiesa, Giuletto, 180
Chikin, Valentin, 182, 184
China, People's Republic of:
    agriculture in, 50, 59, 115, 125
    Cultural Revolution in, 41, 115
    economic reforms in, 56, 58–63, 89, 95,
        114, 115, 125, 210, 233
    Soviet Union compared with, 41–42, 50,
        61, 114, 115, 125, 159, 224–25
Chita *oblast,* 198
Christianity, 188
Churbanov, Yuri, 63
Churchill, Sir Winston, 15, 18
CIA (Central Intelligence Agency), 46–47,
    84, 107, 130, 201
CMEA (Council of Mutual Economic
    Assistance), 56–57, 193
coalition building, 111–12, 170
coal miners strike, 150–52
Cohon, George, 165
Cold War, 92
    end of, 15, 107–10
collectivization, collective farms, 37, 42, 50,
    62, 70, 115, 116, 215–16
    anti-reform efforts and, 191–92
    breaking up of, 211, 212, 217, 221, 234
    contract system and, 74
    Stalin and, 33, 34, 35
Combustion Engineering, 164–65
Coming Soviet Crash, The (Shelton), 242n
Commerce Department, U.S., 158
Committees for National Salvation, 199, 232
Common Market (European Economic
    Community; EEC), 26, 57, 228
Communist Entrepreneurs (Kiser), 238n
Communist Party, Russian, 24–25
Communist Party, Soviet:
    Gorbachev's joining of, 71
    Gorbachev's weakening of, 204–5
    Russian membership in, 24–25
    22nd Party Congress of, 73
    27th Party Congress of, 100, 204
    28th Party Congress of, 20, 23–24, 27, 112,
        184
    see also Central Committee; Politburo;
        Secretariat; Supreme Soviet

Communist Party, Stavropol, 74, 75
Communist Party, Ukranian, 45, 101
competition, 209, 212
Congress, U.S., 108, 109
  Joint Economic Committee of, 239n, 240n
Congress of People's Deputies, 150–51,
    175–76, 185, 199, 200, 213, 222
  creation of, 206
  Fourth Session of, 207
  Interregional Group of Deputies in,
    200–201, 202, 231
Congress of the Russian Writers' Union, 201
conservatism, of Soviet regime, 38–39, 42,
    105, 173–86, 221; *see also* anti-reform
    reaction
Constitution, Soviet, Article 6 of, 21
consumer goods, 47, 59, 89, 136–39, 194, 217
  distribution of, 88, 144–45
  Soviet imports of, 133, 134, 135, 138, 150
  Soviet shortage of, 68, 113, 144, 146, 150,
    152, 155
  strikes and, 150, 152
consumers, Soviet, 43, 47, 76
contract system, 74
cooperatives, 58, 111–16, 194, 204
Cornelsen, Doris, 238n
corruption:
  in China, 60
  glasnost and, 100, 101
  in Soviet Union, 18, 50, 63, 64, 80, 81,
    113, 114, 115, 172
Council of Mutual Economic Assistance
    (CMEA), 56–57, 193
Council of People's Deputies, 190
credit, 159, 212
Cultural Revolution, 41, 115
currency reform, 196–97, 211, 213, 217, 218
Czechoslovakia, 122, 173, 199

Daniloff, Nicholas, 106
debt, Soviet foreign, 159–60
decision making, 91–92
  Federation Council and, 204–5
  in Hungary, 58
  Western techniques for, 55–56
  see also central planning, Soviet
democracy, 40, 83, 103–6
  lawyers for the defense in, 41
democratic centralism, 24, 99–100
Deng Xiaoping, 60–62, 95, 96, 115, 210, 224
depression, economic, 28, 35, 120, 154–55,
    229
Dershowitz, Alan, 41
Dialog (joint venture), 18, 163
diesel fuel, 154
"Dimensions of the Monopoly Problem, The"
    (Hanson), 242n
discipline, 81, 96, 98, 103, 105, 124–25, 204
disorder, possibility of, 38–39
dissent, dissidents, 39–40, 189
  repression of, 43–45, 65, 106–7
Doder, Dusko, 238n, 239n, 241n, 243n,
    244n
dollar, U.S., 47

Dostoyevsky, Fyodor, 39, 237n
Dryomov, Yuri, 161–62
Du Pont, 159
Durgin, Frank, 238n

Eastern Europe, 15, 43, 123, 197–99
  Soviet troop withdrawals in, 197
  see also specific countries
*Economic Backwardness in Historical
    Perspective* (Gerschenkron), 237n,
    238n
Economic Challenge of Perestroika, The
    (Aganbegyan), 237n, 239n, 240n
"Economic Development in the German
    Democratic Republic" (Cornelsen),
    238n
Economic History of the USSR, An (Nove),
    238n
*Economics of Eastern Europe and Their
    Foreign Economic Relations, The*
    (Joseph), 238n
economies of scale, 33
economy:
  of China, 56, 59–63, 89, 95, 114, 115, 125,
    210, 233
  of German Democratic Republic, 56–58,
    62
  of Hungary, 56, 58–59, 210
  of Third World countries, 48
economy, Soviet, 45–52
  Abalkin and, 208–14, 217–20, 230
  Aganbegyan and, 86–90, 96–98, 207–8,
    213, 216, 219
  Andropov and, 64
  budget deficits and, 129–37, 144, 146, 212,
    217, 219
  collapse of, 18–19, 26, 28–30, 47–52,
    128–39
  cult of personality and, 43, 45–47
  depression and, 28, 35, 120, 154–55, 229
  ethnic unrest and, 153–54
  inflation and, 28, 29, 47, 68, 97, 128,
    136–38, 142, 215–16, 228, 229
  Khrushchev and, 36–38, 54–55
  Kryuchkov's views on, 195–97
  Shatalin plan and, 97, 139, 143, 216–21,
    232
  sovnarkhozy and, 54–55
  Stalin and, 32–35, 49
  Western advice about, 209–11
  Western decision-making techniques and,
    55–56
  worker unrest and, 149–52
  see also GNP, Soviet; reforms, Gorbachev;
    reforms, pre-Gorbachev era; trade,
    Soviet
Economy of the USSR, The, 246n
Edinstvo (Unity), 185
education, Soviet, 48
  of Gorbachev, 71–72, 73
EKO, 86
elections, 189, 190
  Gorbachev's call for, 103
  of managers, 120

elections (*continued*)
  of 1989, 44
  of 1990, 22–23, 44
Electrical Engineering Ministry, Soviet,
  Research Institute of, 179
emigration policies, 65, 189
"*Emigré Reports, An*" (Mithta), 239*n*
engineers, Soviet, 76, 194
Enterprise Law, 118–20, 139–42, 204
Entov, Revold, 242*n*
Ericson, Richard E., 241*n*
Estonia, 124, 148, 149
ethnic unrest, 18, 28, 29, 149
  in Baltic states, 121–24, 224–25, 232
  economic effects of, 153–54
  repression of, 43, 44
European Economic Community (EEC;
  Common Market), 26, 57, 228
exchange rates, 47, 196
exports, Soviet, 92, 156–57
  grain, 35, 79
  military equipment, 113–14
  oil, 49–50, 131, 133, 134, 160–61, 195

factories, Soviet, 86–87
  anti-reform efforts and, 192–93
  closing down of, 28
  Gospriemka inspectors in, 177
  raw materials wasted by, 49
fascism, *Pamyat* and, 112, 188–89
Federalist Papers, The, 102–3, 240*n*
Federation Council, 204–5, 217
Finance Ministry, Soviet, 131, 135, 144–45, 157
Five Hundred Day Plan (Shatalin plan), 97,
  139, 143, 216–21, 232
five-year plans, 129, 152, 213
  Stalin and, 33, 34, 35
flower selling, 114
food:
  breakdown of distribution of, 153, 154
  price controls for, 212, 218
  price increase for, 19, 37, 144, 219
  see also grain
Food Program, 78, 80, 83, 85
Foreign Economic Relations Ministry, Soviet,
  157
foreign policy, Soviet:
  Afghanistan and, 108, 197, 198
  Arbatov's views on, 16–17
  Flight KAL 007 and, 66
  Geneva talks and, 51, 66, 67, 84, 92–93
  Middle East and, 110, 199
  superpower aspirations and, 43
Foreign Trade Ministry, Soviet, 156–59, 164
foreign trade organizations (FTOs), 158
France, 75, 114, 159
Frankland, Mark, 238*n*
Frunze Scientific Production-Combine, 92
full employment, 68

Gaida, E., 242*n*
Geneva, arms control talks in, 51, 66, 67, 84,
  92–93
Geneva summit (1985), 75, 92–93

Georgia, Georgians, 113*n*, 117, 225
German Democratic Republic (GDR; East
  Germany), 45, 197–98
  Berlin Wall and, 16
  economic reforms in, 56–58, 62, 89
Germany, Federal Republic of (West
  Germany), 51, 57, 66, 75, 159, 197
Germany, Nazi, 34, 56, 62, 71, 121, 123
Germany, reunification of, 18, 57, 197–98
Gerschenkron, Alexander, 31, 237*n*, 238*n*
Gerschenkron effect, 46
Gibbins, Colin, 196
gigantimania, 209
glasnost (openness), 82–84, 88–89, 96,
  100–106, 122
  failure of, 203
  perestroika and, 102–3, 124–27
  press and, 101–2
  reaction to, 174, 221
  restraints on, 100–102
  use of term, 100
"Glasnost's Ghosts" (Laquer), 244*n*
"Glubokaia reforma ili pevanshbiurokratri?"
  (Seliunin), 240*n*
GNP, Soviet, 135, 229
  Belkin's views on, 46–47
  education and research in, 48
  Gerschenkron effect and, 46
  military expenditures and, 43, 51, 84,
    107–8, 130
  1990 fall in, 47
GNP, U.S., 46
Goldman, Marshall I., 237*n*, 238*n*, 240*n*
Gorbachev, Irina, 72
Gorbachev, Mikhail Sergeevich, 15–30,
  65–152, 169–92, 197–236
  advisors sought and selected by, 85–88,
    207–20
  Andropov compared with, 65–67, 81, 84,
    85
  anti-alcohol campaign, 176
  background of, 29, 68–71, 83
  Chinese reformers inspired by, 62
  Churchill compared with, 15, 18
  confidence of, 106
  decline in domestic popularity of, 17–19,
    25, 146–52, 199, 202, 230
  domestic travels of, 94–95, 97–99, 101,
    122, 174
  education of, 71–72, 73
  ethnic problems and, 44, 121–24, 149,
    224–25, 232
  flexibility of, 27, 75, 108, 109
  foreign trade and, 160, 161
  foreign travels of, 75, 122, 181
  Geneva summit and, 75, 92–93
  international diplomacy successes of,
    92–93, 106–10, 197–98
  labor unrest and, 148–52
  mentors of, 65, 72–74, 77, 78, 80, 100, 106
  as Mineral Water Secretary, 176
  Nobel Prize of, 66, 198
  political rivals purged by, 96, 100, 101,
    111, 112, 172–75

in polls, 17–18, 40
reform efforts of, *see* glasnost; perestroika;
    reforms, Gorbachev
rise of, 29, 69–83
Shevardnadze's beach walk with, 83, 84
speeches of, 81, 82, 84, 88, 89, 98, 104–5,
    136
tensions between military and, 200
Washington summit and, 17, 19–20, 22
worldwide popularity of, 15–17, 198, 224
Gorbachev, Raisa, 19, 72, 75, 85, 126–27
Gorbachev (Doder and Branson), 238*n*, 239*n*,
    241*n*, 243*n*, 244*n*
Gorbachev (Medvedev), 238*n*, 239*n*
Gorbachev's Challenge (Goldman), 237*n*,
    240*n*
Gorbachev's Economic Plans (Joint Economic
    Committee of the Congress), 240*n*
Gorbachev's Struggle for Economic Reform
    (Aslund), 241*n*, 242*n*, 245*n*
Gordievsky, Oleg, 238*n*
Gosagroprom, 73, 89–90, 170, 192, 204
Gosbank, 92
Gosplan, 119, 129, 152, 153, 155, 192–93,
    228, 229
Gospriemka (State Quality Acceptance
    Committee), 90, 94, 170, 175, 204
    inspectors from, 177
Gossnab, 152, 153, 154, 193
Gosteev, Boris, 129–30, 135
goszakazy (state orders), 119, 139–41
grain, 73, 154
    incentives to increase harvest of, 145–46
    Soviet exports of, 35, 79
    Soviet imports of, 50, 78, 79, 133, 159,
        195–96
Great Britain:
    Soviet spies expelled from, 106
    steel production of, 34
Grishin, Viktor, 67, 96
Gromyko, Andrei, 67, 81–82, 92, 96

Hanson, Philip, 242*n*
Hardt, John, 237*n*
Havel, Václav, 173
Hawthorne effect, 75
health care system, 50, 54
Helsinki Watch, 65
Hewett, Ed, 238*n*
Hitler, Adolf, 49, 181
Holzman, Franklyn, 241*n*
Honecker, Erich, 45, 198
Honeywell, 163
Humanité, L', 100
Hungary, 199
    reforms in, 56, 58–59, 210

"I Cannot Renounce Principles"
    (Andreyeva), 180–85
Implementation of the Helsinki Accords,
    241*n*
imports, Soviet, 156–57
    consumer goods, 133, 134, 135, 138, 150
    grain, 50, 78, 79, 133, 159, 195–96

illegal, 117–18
machinery, 50, 131, 134, 157
incentive system, 55–56, 153
India, 47
industrialization, in China, 59–60
industrialization, industry, Soviet:
    Gorbachev reforms and, 86–91, 203–4
    Gorbachev's lack of experience in, 75–76
    nationalization and, 33–34, 35
    production figures for, 90, 91
    Stalin and, 32–35, 46
    see also factories, Soviet
Industrial Revolution, 34–35
inflation:
    in China, 60–61
    GNP decline and, 47
    in Hungary, 58
    in Soviet Union, 28, 29, 47, 68, 97, 128,
        136–38, 142, 215–16, 228, 229
information:
    need for, 104
    restriction of, 97–98
Inside Perestroika (Aganbegyan), 238*n*, 239*n*,
    245*n*
intensifikatsiia (intensification), 82, 88, 94,
    96, 170, 177, 204
"Interests and Self-Interest" (Nove), 239*n*
Interregional Group of Deputies, 200–201,
    202, 231
investment, 37–38, 46, 86–87
    nationalization and, 33–34
Iraq, 199
    Kuwait invaded by, 110, 161
iron mines, 54
"Istoki" (Seliunin), 237*n*
Italy, 75, 159
Ivanov, Ivan, 243*n*
Izvestiia, 216

Japan, 159
jeans, prices of, 114
Jews,
    Soviet emigration of, 65, 112, 187–89
    see also anti-Semitism
joint ventures, 117–18, 161–70, 211
    McDonald's and, 165–68
jokes and anecdotes, 38, 116, 126–27, 138–39,
    140, 176, 220, 235–36
Joseph, Philip, 238*n*

Kaganovich, Lazar, 187–88
Kazakhstan, 122, 225
KGB, 16, 21, 45, 51, 106, 107, 189, 205, 217,
    225
    Andropov in, 64, 65
    anti-reform efforts and, 194–97, 201
KGB—The Inside Story, The (Gordievsky
    and Andrew), 238*n*
Khabarovsk, 101, 102
Khanin, Gregory, 47
Khrushchev, Nikita, 40, 42, 73, 85, 126, 175,
    232
    reforms of, 36–38, 54–55, 178, 233
    sovnarkhozy and, 54–55

Kirov, Sergei M., 181
Kiser, John W., III, 238*n*
Kislovodsk, 77
Kisolev, Anatoly, 245*n*
Klose, Kevin, 242*n*, 244*n*
Klushin, Vladimir, 180
kolkhozy, see collectivization, collective farms
Kombinate, 57, 89
Komsomol, 53, 72–73
Komsomolsk, 98
Korean Airlines Flight 007, 66
Kornai, Janos, 233, 246*n*
Kostandov, Leonid, 157
Kosygin, Aleksei, 56, 74*n*
Krasnodar, 103
Kryuchkov, Vladimir, 194–97, 201, 241*n*
Kulakov, Fyodor, 69, 72–74
    death of, 74*n*, 77
kulaks, 38, 116
Kuwait, 160
    Iraq's invasion of, 110, 161
Kuzbass region, 151–52

labor unrest:
    in China, 60–61
    in Soviet Union, 26, 28, 148–53, 185
Laquer, Walter, 244*n*
Latvia, 117, 123, 124, 148, 174
law, lawyers, 41
    Gorbachev's study of, 71–72
leaders, leadership:
    checks and balances and, 40–42
    democratic, 40
    route to, 44, 52–53
    see also specific people
Leggett, Robert E., 239*n*–40*n*
legislative institutions:
    Gorbachev's inconsistency in dealing with,
        205–7
    see also Congress of People's Deputies;
        Supreme Soviet
Lenin, V. I., 43, 49, 126, 173, 187
Leningrad, 26–27, 147–48
Levikov, Alexander, 244*n*
Liberman, Yevsei, 55–56
Ligachev, Yegor, 81, 111, 112, 116, 170, 174,
        178–79, 185–86, 189
    Andreyeva letter and, 180–84, 244*n*
    Peasant Union and, 191–92
Lipton, David, 246*n*
Lithuania, 124, 224–25, 232
Lukyanov, Anatoly, 210
Luxembourg, Abalkin in, 209–10

McDonald's, 165–68
machine-tool industry, 29, 36, 46
    budget deficit and, 131, 133, 135
    Gorbachev reforms and, 86–89, 96, 97,
        124–25, 131, 133, 135, 177, 204
macroeconomics, 128, 136, 155
mafia, Soviet, 63, 113, 115, 155
Magna Carta, 40
Malenkov, Georgi M., 40
managers, Soviet, 76, 103, 119–20, 139–42, 153

anti-reform efforts and, 191–94
Enterprise Law and, 119–20, 139–42
foreign trade and, 157–59
"Man Who Changed the World, The"
    (Sheehy), 239*n*
Mao Zedong, 42, 50
"Market and Non-Market Systems" (Berlin),
    238*n*
market-oriented system, 76–77, 111, 143–46
    Abalkin and, 208–14
    attractions of, 152–53
    regulated, 95, 214
    Shatalin plan and, 217–18
Marx, Karl, 187
Masons, 187, 188
Mazowiecki, Tadeusz, 162
meat, 147, 154, 165–68
Medvedev, Roy, 183, 244*n*
Medvedev, Zhores A., 80, 238*n*, 239*n*
Melinkov, Alexander, 18
Memoirs (Sakharov), 241*n*
Mesyats, Valentin K., 78
microeconomics, 128
microprocessors, 87
Middle East, 110, 160, 161
"Mighty Monopolies" (Skopolsky), 242*n*
Mikhailin, A., 216
military, Soviet, 50–51, 66
    anti-reform efforts and, 197–202
    expenditures for, 43, 50, 51, 84, 92–93,
        107–10, 130, 211, 217, 221, 234
    pricing and, 130
    see also Army, Soviet
military parity, 51, 66, 84
military superiority, 51, 66, 84
miniaturization, 48
missiles, 51, 66, 67, 84, 108
Mithta, Andrew, 239*n*
Mitterrand, François, 220
"Monopolizm v ekonomike SSSR i Faktory
    ego o buslovlivaiushchie" (Yakovlev),
    242*n*
monopoly, 147, 154
Moscow:
    in anecdotes, 138–39, 140
    author's presentation in, 210–11
    food problems in, 154, 165
    Gorbachev's return to, 77–78
    McDonald's in, 165–68
    retail sales and shopping in, 138–39,
        146–47, 148
    subway system of, 187–88
Moscow News, 161, 169, 181, 182
Moscow State University (MGU), 71–72
municipal protectionism, 146–48
Murakhovsky, Vsevolod, 72–73, 89

Nagorno-Karabakh, 149, 208
Nakhodka, 169
"Na novom etape ekonomicheskogo
    stroitel'stva" (Aganbegyan), 240*n*
narodnik effort, 190–91
National Center for Sociopolitical Studies in
    the Soviet Union, 17–18

National Democratic Institute for
International Affairs, 207*n*
nationalism:
in Baltic states, 121–24
nineteenth-century, 201
repression of, 44
Russian, 112
nationalization, 33–34, 35
National Rifle Association, 176
natural resources, 49, 218
see also oil
Nazi Germany, 34, 56, 62, 71
Soviet pact with (1939), 121, 123
Neuberger, Egon, 246*n*
Neues Deutschland, 181
New Economic Mechanism (NEM), 58
"New Enterprise Law, The" (Ericson),
241*n*
New Russians, The (Smith), 243*n*, 244*n*
New Zealand, 159
Nikonov, Viktor, 244*n*
19th All Union Communist Party
Conference, 178–79, 204, 208
Nixon, Richard M., 235
Nizhnevartousk, 98
nomenklatura, 120
as Gorbachev obstacle, 99–100
privileges of, 53, 98–99
Nove, Alec, 238*n*, 239*n*
Novgorod, 147–48, 169

oblast, 53, 100, 173, 174, 193, 198
Odessa, 26–27
Ogonyek, 181
oil, 90, 98, 118, 199
1973 embargo of, 58
Soviet exports of, 49–50, 131, 133, 134,
160–61, 195
Old Regime and the French Revolution, The
(Tocqueville), 241*n*
openness, *see* glasnost
Orlov, Andrei, 242*n*
Orlov, Vladimir, 136
Orlov, Yuri, 39–40, 106

Pamyat, 112, 187–89
Pavlov, Valentin, 135, 196–97, 213, 221*n*
peasants:
Chinese, 59, 62, 114
in Czarist Russia, 32, 34, 70
Hungarian, 58
peasants, Soviet:
anti-reform efforts and, 191–92
Gorbachev and, 62, 80, 115–17, 145
hard currency and, 145
Khrushchev and, 37–38
as kulaks, 38, 116
private gardens and farms of, 78, 80, 111,
112, 115–17, 217, 221, 234
Stalin and, 33, 34, 35, 62, 116
supply-side disruptions and, 154
World War II and, 62
perestroika (reconstruction):
collapse of, 128–71

glasnost and, 102–3, 124–27
mid-course correction of, 94–127
origins of, 82–84
reaction to, 172–202, 221; *see also*
anti-reform reaction
see also reforms, Gorbachev; *specific topics*
Pershing II missiles, 51, 66, 67, 84, 108
personality, cult of, 41–47, 104
economic legacy of, 43, 45–47
political legacy of, 43–45
Peter the Great, Czar of Russia, 32–34, 182
Petrakov, Nikolai, 192, 213, 214
Petrushenko, Nikolai, 200, 202
planning, *see* central planning; five-year plans
pluralism, 18, 21, 40, 42
pokazuka (Potemkin villages), 98
Poland, 143, 162, 167, 211, 233
"Poland's Economic Reforms" (Sachs and
Lipton), 246*n*
Politburo, 22, 52–53, 67–68, 77, 108
Andreyeva letter and, 183, 184
diminution in function of, 204
Gorbachev's joining of, 78
information denied to members of, 97–98
Kulakov in, 74
purges of, 96, 112, 173
political independence, drive toward, 23–27,
29, 121–24, 227–28
political prisoners, Soviet, release of, 16, 45,
65, 107
politics, Soviet:
cult of personality and, 41–47, 104
purges and, 96, 100, 101, 111, 112,
172–75
see also elections; *specific groups and
branches of government*
"Politics and Guesswork" (Holzman), 241*n*
Polizhkov, Ivan, 25
Popov, Gavril, 201–2
power:
formal vs. effective, 205
of republics, in Shatalin plan, 218–19,
221
separation of, 40–42
Pozner, Vladimir, 16, 17
Pravda, 55, 183, 184
pre-Gorbachev era, 31–51, 169
foreign trade in, 156
reforms in, *see* reforms, pre-Gorbachev era
Presidential Council, 112, 191, 204, 217, 220
press:
glasnost and, 101–2
see also specific newspapers and magazines
price increases, 19, 26, 28, 113, 114, 137–39,
144, 148, 211, 214–16, 223
food, 19, 37, 144, 219
Khrushchev and, 37
oil, 58, 131
prices, 114, 211–19, 221
bread, 19, 144, 212, 214
military equipment, 130
oil, 58, 131, 195, 218
"Principles of Perestroika" (Yakovlev),
183–84

private property, 89, 115, 143, 172, 190, 212
privatization, 211, 212, 217, 218, 219, 234
Privolnoe, 69–71
Project on Strengthening Democratic
  Institutions of Harvard University,
  207n
property:
  Abalkin reforms and, 212
  private, 89, 115, 143, 172, 190, 212
  state, sale of, 217
protectionism, municipal, 146–48
Protocols of the Elders of Zion, 187
public opinion polls, Soviet, 17–18, 40
purges, 96, 100, 101, 111, 112, 172–75
Rahr, Alexander, 238n, 239n
Rasputin, Valentin, 69, 112, 170
Rayatskas, Ray, 240n
Reagan, Ronald, 16, 66, 67, 84, 108–9, 225
  Geneva summit and, 75, 92–93
reconstruction, *see* perestroika
reforms, Gorbachev, 15–17, 20–23, 43, 68,
    81–236
  Abalkin and, 208–14, 217–20, 230
  Aganbegyan's influence on, 86–90, 96–97,
    207–8
  back and forth patterns of, 74–75, 111–12,
    143, 203–216, 219–20
  budget deficit and, 129–37
  discipline and, 81, 96, 98, 103, 105,
    124–25, 204
  Enterprise Law and, 118–20, 139–42, 204
  industrial strategy and, 86–91, 203–4
  intensification and, 82, 88, 94, 96, 170,
    177, 204
  joint ventures and, 117–18, 161–70, 211
  limits of Gorbachev's background and,
    75–76
  machine-tool industry and, 86–89, 96, 97,
    124–25, 131, 133, 135, 177, 204
  mid-course correction of, 94–127
  in 1987, 110–118
  nomenklatura as obstacle to, 99–100
  origins of, 82–83
  reaction to, *see* anti-reform reaction
  Shatalin plan and, 97, 139, 143, 216–20
  spontaneous, 155, 234
  superministries and, 89–91, 94, 96, 124–25,
    142, 204
  uskoreniie and, 82, 88, 94, 96, 169, 204
reforms, pre-Gorbachev era, 22, 29, 31–42,
    54–68
  of Andropov, 64–67, 172
  Chinese influence on, 56, 58–63
  East German influence on, 56–58
  focus of, 54
  Hungarian influence on, 56, 58–59
  incentive system and, 55–56
  of Khrushchev, 36–38, 54–55, 178, 233
  of Peter the Great, 32, 34
  of Stalin, 32–35, 62, 226
  of Stolypin, 35, 116
regional economic councils, *see* sovnarkhozy
Road to a Free Economy, The (Kornai), 233,
    246n

Romania, 45, 123
Romanov, Grigori, 67, 96
Roosevelt, Franklin D., 96
rubles, 98, 129, 133, 135, 145, 222
  collapse of, 153, 154
  currency reform and, 196–97, 211, 213,
    217, 218
  exchange rate for, 47, 196
  foreign debt in, 159–60
  printing of, 136, 137, 211
  smuggling out of, 195
Rumer, Boris, 245n
Russia, czarist, 173
  intellectuals in, 53
  modernization efforts in, 22, 31–32, 34–35
  peasants in, 32, 34, 70
Russia and the Russians (Klose), 242n, 244n
Russian Republic, 22–27, 117, 135–36
  Communist Party of, 24–25
  economy of, 23, 24
  Supreme Soviet of, 17–18, 22–24, 220
Russian Revolution (1917), 42
Rust, Mathias, 197
Ryzhkov, Nikolai, 19, 76, 114, 150, 196
  Gorbachev's fear of resignation of, 220,
    221n
Ryzhkov-Abalkin plan, 213–14, 218–20

Sachs, Jeffrey, 233, 246n
St. Petersburg, 32
Sakharov, Andrei, 106–7, 241n
Saransk semiconductor factory, 92
Saudi Arabia, 160
Schultz, George, 92
Secretariat, 52–53, 204
Secret Incomes of the Soviet State Budget
    (Birman), 242n
Security Council, 205
Seliunin, Vasili, 19, 137, 237n, 240n
Shatalin, Stanislav, 97, 112, 143, 216–21
Shatalin plan, *see* Five Hundred Day Plan
Shcherbitski, Vladimir, 45, 67, 101
Shchit (Shield), 200–201
Sheehy, Gail, 239n
Shelton, Judy, 129, 242n
Shevardnadze, Eduard, 96, 103, 122, 197,
    199–201, 221, 225, 227, 232, 241n
  Gorbachev's beach walk with, 83, 84
  resignation of, 185, 186–87
Shevchenko, Arkady N., 63–64, 238n
Shiryaev, Yuri, 238n
Shmelev, Nikolai, 61
shortages, 137–38, 147–49, 154–55 *see also*
    inflation
shock-therapy strategy, 211, 215
Siberia, 98, 150, 151–52, 198
Singapore, 231
*Sixth Continent—Mikhail Gorbachev in the
    Soviet Union, The* (Frankland), 238n
Skopolsky, Stanislav, 242n
Smirnov, Pavel S., 241n
Smirnov-Ostashvili, Konstantin, 189
Smith, Hedrick, 243n, 244n
Sobchak, Anatoly, 25–26

social contract, Soviet, 68
socialism, Soviet, 18, 42–43, 111, 112, 210
Soiuz (Union), 185, 200
Solomentsev, Mikhail, 81
Solzhenitsyn, Alexander, 188
South Korea, 35, 231
Sovetskaia Rossiia, 180, 182, 183, 184
Soviet Economic Statistics (Treml and Hardt,
  eds.), 237*n*
"Soviet Investment Policy" (Leggett),
  239*n*–40*n*
"Soviet perceptions of Chinese economic
  reforms" (Goldman), 238*n*
Soviet system, benefits of, 53–54
Soviet Union:
  China compared with, 41–42, 50, 61, 114,
    115, 125, 159, 224–25
  Gorbachev's selling out of, 18
  name change suggested for, 27
  Nazi invasion of, 34, 62, 71
  as superpower, 43, 51, 66
  see also specific topics
sovkhozy, see state farms
sovnarkhozy, 54–55, 169
spas, 77
special economic zones, 169
spontaneous reform, 155, 234
Sputnik, 36
Stalin, Joseph, 24, 42, 87, 128, 226
  Andreyeva's defense of, 181–82, 183
  Gorbachev compared with, 75
  modernization efforts of, 32–35, 62
  Pamyat and, 187, 188
  repression under, 43–44, 49, 116, 126
Stankevich, Sergei, 201–2
Starkov, Vladislav A., 40
Starodubtsev, Vasily, 191
State Committee of Foreign Economic
  Relations, 157
state farms *(sovkhozy),* 34, 50, 112, 116,
  204
  anti-reform efforts and, 191–92
  breaking up of, 211, 212, 217, 221, 234
State Foreign Economic Commission, 157,
  160
State Quality Acceptance Committee, *see*
  Gospriemka
statistics, inaccurate, 46–47, 129
Stavropol, 72–75, 77
Stavropol Agricultural Institute, 73
Stavropol City Communist Party, 74
steel production, 34, 54, 63
stock market, 155
Stolypin, Pyotr, 35, 116
Strategic Defense Initiative (SDI; "Star
  Wars"), 51, 66, 67, 84, 108
"Strategiya uskoreniia sotsial'no
  ekonomecheskogo rezvitiia"
  (Aganbegyan), 240*n*
strikes, 26, 60, 149–52, 177
subway, 53, 187–88
sugar shortage, 137–38
Sumy, Frunze Scientific Production-Combine
  in, 92

superministries, 89–91, 94, 96, 124–25, 142,
  204
Supreme Soviet, 17, 44, 185, 190, 206, 208,
  213, 222
Supreme Soviet, Belorussian, 24
Supreme Soviet, Russian, 17–18, 22–24,
  220
Supreme Soviet, Ukrainian, 24
Sushkov, Vladimir, 117–18
Suslov, Mikhail, 69, 74*n*, 77, 80
Sverdlovsk, 153, 193
Switzerland, 195

Taiwan, 35, 231
tariffs, 17, 148
Tass News Agency, 181
taxes, 128, 135, 136, 144, 207, 218
  Abalkin plan and, 212, 213
technology, 43
  Soviet advances in, 36, 48
  Soviet falling behind in, 35, 118
  Soviet weaknesses in, 48
Telen, Lyudmila, 169
television, 151, 188
Teller, Edward, 108
Thatcher, Margaret, 106
Third World, 43, 48
Tiananmen Square, protests in, 41, 60–61, 62,
  123, 224–25
Tikhonov, Nikolai, 96
Tocqueville, Alexis de, 121, 241*n*
Togliatti, Volga auto plant in, 92
tractors, 153–54, 166, 229
trade, Soviet, 204
  domestic, 89, 111–17, 143, 155
  foreign, 17, 131, 156–61
  see also exports, Soviet; imports, Soviet
Trade Union Congress, Gorbachev's speech
  to, 104–5
trade union movement, Soviet, 185, 189–91
traffic authorities story, 140
train story, 126–27
Treml, Vladimir G., 237*n*
Trotsky, Leon, 181, 187
"Trudnyi vybor" (Gaidar), 242*n*
tulip craze, 42
22nd Communist Party Congress, 73
27th Communist Party Congress, 100, 204
28th Communist Party Congress, 20, 23–24,
  27, 112, 184
Tyumen oil fields, 90

Ukraine, 24, 62, 115, 117, 150, 154
Union Carbide, 159
Union of Soviet Socialist Republics (USSR),
  see Soviet Union
United Russian Workers Front, 112, 190–91
United States:
  Abalkin's visits to, 209
  Daniloff arrest and, 106
  Khrushchev and, 36
  lawyers in, 41
  Soviet arms talks with, 51, 66, 67, 84,
    108–10, 197

United States (*continued*)
Soviet critique by, 16
Soviet policy of, 17
Soviet support for, 199
Soviet Union feared by, 51
Uralmash, 193
uskoreniie (acceleration), 82, 88, 94, 96, 169, 204
USSR in Crisis (Goldman), 238*n*
USSR Peasant Union, 191–92
"USSR State Enterprises and Amalgamations" (Smirnov), 241*n*
Uzbekistan, 63, 113*n*

valuta (convertible currencies), 145, 155–58, 160
Vanous, Jan, 238*n*
Vasiliyev, Dmitri, 187–88
Vilnius incident, 224–25
Vladimir, tractor factory in, 153–54, 229
vodka:
crackdown on sales of, 135, 137–38, 175, 176–77
Estonian price increase for, 148
Volga automobile plant, 92
VOOPIK (All Russian Society for the Preservation of Historical and Cultural Monuments), 187
Vorotnikov, Vitali, 67

wages, 142, 150, 177, 178, 212, 215
Shatalin plan and, 217–18
Washington Post, 64

Washington summit (June 1990), 17, 19–20, 22
wholesale, 155, 234
World War II, 34, 49, 56, 63, 181–82
Gorbachev in, 70–71
monuments to Soviet victory in, 188, 198
Writers' Club, Soviet, 188–89

Xerox, 161

Yakovlev, Alexander, 85, 121, 123, 124*n*, 232, 242*n*
anti-reform efforts and, 180, 183, 185, 201
Yakutia, political sovereignty in, 26
Yanayev, Gennady, 175–76, 185
Yarin, Veniamin, 112, 170, 190–91
Yavlinsky, Gregory, 216, 222
Yeltsin, Boris, 22–27, 184, 189, 206, 216, 217, 220
elections of 1990 and, 22–23
as Gorbachev critic, 20, 22–23
popularity of, 17–18
press conference of, 23
resignation of, 20
Yeltsin plan, 221
Yugoslavia, 120

Zadornov, M., 216
Zakharov, Gennady, 106
Zaslavskaia, Tatiana, 64, 85, 104, 239*n*
zastoi (stagnation), 19, 149
Zhivkov, Todor, 45